GW01339616

IMPERIAL MAPPINGS
In Savage Spaces: Baluchistan and British India

IMPERIAL MAPPINGS
In Savage Spaces: Baluchistan and British India

Simanti Dutta

B. R. Publishing Corporation
[A Division of BRPC (India) Ltd.]
Delhi - 110035

Distributed by :
BRPC (India) Ltd.
4222/1, Ansari Road,
Darya Ganj, New Delhi-110 002
Phones : 3259196 3259648
Fax : 3201571
E.Mail : *brpcltd@vsnl.net.in*

© 2002 Simanti Dutta (b. 1950 —)
ISBN 81–7646–236–5

All rights, including the right to translate or to reproduce this book or parts thereof except for brief quotations, are reserved.

Published by :
B.R. Publishing Corporation
[A Division of BRPC (India) Ltd.]
3779, Ist Floor
Kanhaiya Nagar, Tri Nagar
Delhi–110 035
E.Mail : *brpcltd@vsnl.net.in*

Lasertypeset by :
Jain Media Graphics
Delhi-110035

Printed by :
Chawla Offset Printers
Delhi-110052

PRINTED IN INDIA

To my husband, Susanta

Acknowledgements

The inception of this book started with a suggestion from David Dilks, Vice-Chancellor, University of Hull, and Professor Malcolm Yapp, of the University of London, that I should publish my research findings on imperialism and the Indian frontier.

Taking up the idea, I re-presented the data in book form, to enable the subject matter to reach a wider audience. With regard to compiling and writing the text, I would particularly like to thank Professor Ashis Nandy, of the Centre for the Study of Developing Societies, New Delhi, for reading, and commenting encouragingly on the manuscript. I also wish to acknowledge the involvement of David Page, of the BBC, and Gowher Rizvy, formerly of Nuffield College, Oxford, in reading the initial draft versions. I am grateful to Steve Heath of Motorola, for his continuing support of the project. And I would like to thank, Dipali Ghosh of the British Library for useful advice, and also Mr. Dogra of SOAS Library. I would also like to acknowledge use of the archival facilities, made available at the Bodleian Library, Oxford, SOAS Library, London, and the British Library, London, that made this book possible. And most of all, I would like to express gratitude to my husband, Susanta, whose optimism, sustained the writing, and ensured its completion.

Dr. Z.H. Zaidi, of the University of London, also encouraged and supported the project, for which I am grateful.

Simanti Dutta

CONTENTS

Acknowledgements	vii
List of Plates and Maps	xi
Introduction: The Space of the Savage and the Idea of an Imperial Boundary	1
1. Text and Context: Inscribing an Imperial Margin in Tribal Baluchistan, 1876	13
2. Form and Transformation: The Genesis of British Baluchistan, and the Semantics of Boundary Making, 1876-1905	36
3. Image and Identity: Constructions and Misconstructions of Tribalism in Imperial Eyes	59
4. The Coercion of Power: The Discourse of Discipline in Resignifying the Tribal Margin	78
5. In the Mirror of Meaning: Imperial Translations in Tribal Space, as Point and Margin, Time and Text, Place and Power, 1876-1905	98
Bibliography	115
Index	125
Plates	

List of Plates and Maps

PLATES

1. **The Quetta Fort (miri) 1875-1880.**
   It captures the exoticism of place and culture, i.e., the threat of the desert, and the imprint of war in the sign of the fort, symbolizing the savage gestural language of tribal existence.

2. **View of a Camel Caravan in Quetta, 1889.**
   It images the proximity of opposites. Camels juxtaposed against snowcapped mountains, suggest the presence of sand and snow to confer dimensions of strangeness on a space, alien to the norms of visual expectation. There is also the temporal perspective conveyed in foregrounding of the Victorian lampost in an oriental bazaar scene, to mirror the moment of translation of one time by another i.e., English imperialism rearranging an Eastern view.

3. **The Quetta Residency, 1890's.**
   This typifies colonial architecture and its inner text. The graceful Residency, its ornamental gardens and statuary, signified the aesthetics of a Western imaginary, imprinting culture in a wild place. As a structural icon of Western aestheticism, the Residency was a metaphor for the central text of empire, i.e., the civilizing mission, to landscape the desert in the nostalgic green of England, offering an idealization of place as the desired point of migration for the colonized, to acquire the redemptive touch of a higher cultural norm.

4. **Quetta Decorations for the Duke and Duchess of Connaught.**
   This picture allegorizes the theme of empire as a celebration of the rule of right, the promise of Pax Britannica, the consent of the governed, to signify the utopic place of hope, harmony, certainty.

5. **View near Bolan Pass.**
   Mapping the geography and history of the region, the Bolan Pass with its wild rocky terrain, virtually anticipates the image of the wild man, the savage tribe, as its only possible human inhabitant, confirming the conspiracy of geography to create the savage in history. As the breach in the mountain barrier, the Bolan Pass was also the medial space for other histories to enter the space of savage inscriptions. Within this angle of meaning, the Bolan Pass was conscripted as the playing field of the Great Game for empire between England and Russia, that would force the wilderness to enter the fencings of power and property, the savage to submit to the history of the civilized.

6. **Bolan Pass; horse shore curve.**
This offers a scenic and dramatic view of the Bolan, heightening the meaning and menace of the place.

7. **Chappar Rift : Sind-Pishin Railway**
This dramatizes the challenge of the landscape in constructing the railway, and the struggle of its human engineers. It narrates the story of the imperial railway on the Indian frontier, calculated to create a 'space in motion' of moving columns, guns and ammunition, to suggest a theatrics of power that would intimidate the enemies of empire, internal and external. On a more symbolic level, the picture also suggests the heroism of taming an impossible landscape by rail power, and the historical urge to 'master nature' in the Western mind.

8. **The East Khwajak Valley.**
This panoramic view of the snow covered Khwajak valley, bears a strategic and savage content, in serving as a passage for trade between Sind and Qandahar, while constituting the home ground of the fierce Achakzai Pathans, to register in imperial perceptions as the place of desire and dread, where possession would mean dispossession of the threat, to shape and own the point and plane of tribal terrain.

9. **Chaman Frontier Post : West Khwajak Valley, at the Qandahar Border.**
This mirrors the desolation of the space of power in Baluchistan. As a typical frontier post in remote desert surroundings, manned by local tribal levies, it is a record of the surveillance of the empty quarter, to quarantine all spatial surfaces from expected danger, in particular to bring the edge of power within the certainty of imperial mappings, measurements, and markings.

10. **Group at the Agency. Robert Sandeman and Khan of Kalat, 1889.**
This is a picture of imperial officials. Robert Sandeman is second from the right. it captures in expression and bearing the formal, rigid, public pose of English officials, to sustain the premises of self and authorial identity in colonial space. The presence of Baluch chiefs in the scene as well, makes the photo iconic of the imperial collaborative ideal, enforced by the British and native elites.

11. **Baluch Chiefs in Ceremonial Dress.**
This picture highlights the extravagance of chiefly demeanours in a society of scarce resources. It confirms the idea of a 'tribal aristocracy', originating within the space of the tribe, and maturing in the imperial context, on the ground of imperial patronage and collboration.

MAPS

1. British Baluchistan Areas 1876-1905 (In Red).
2. Baluchistan showing Racial Distribution.

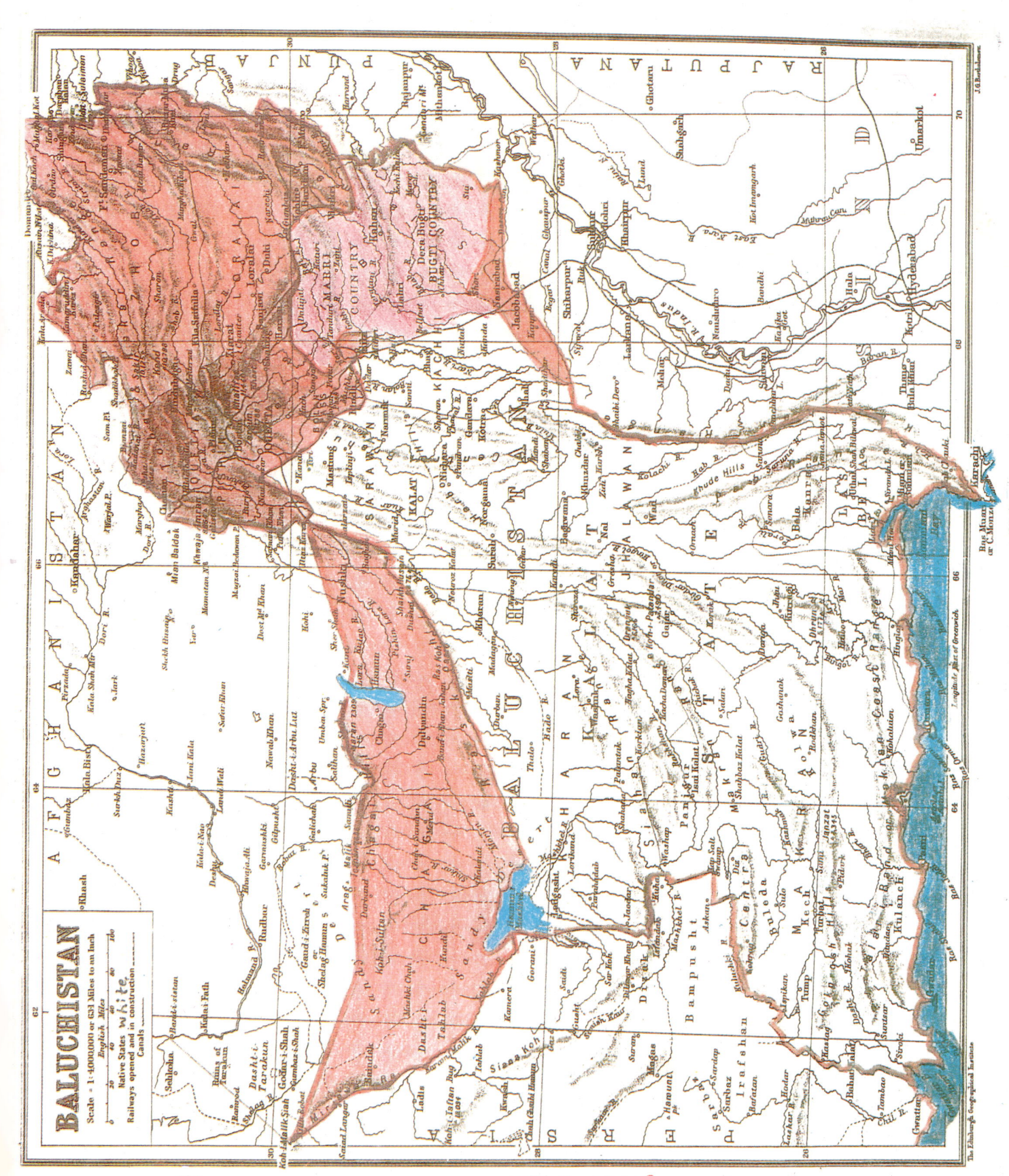

Map 1: British Baluchistan Areas 1876-1905 (In Red).

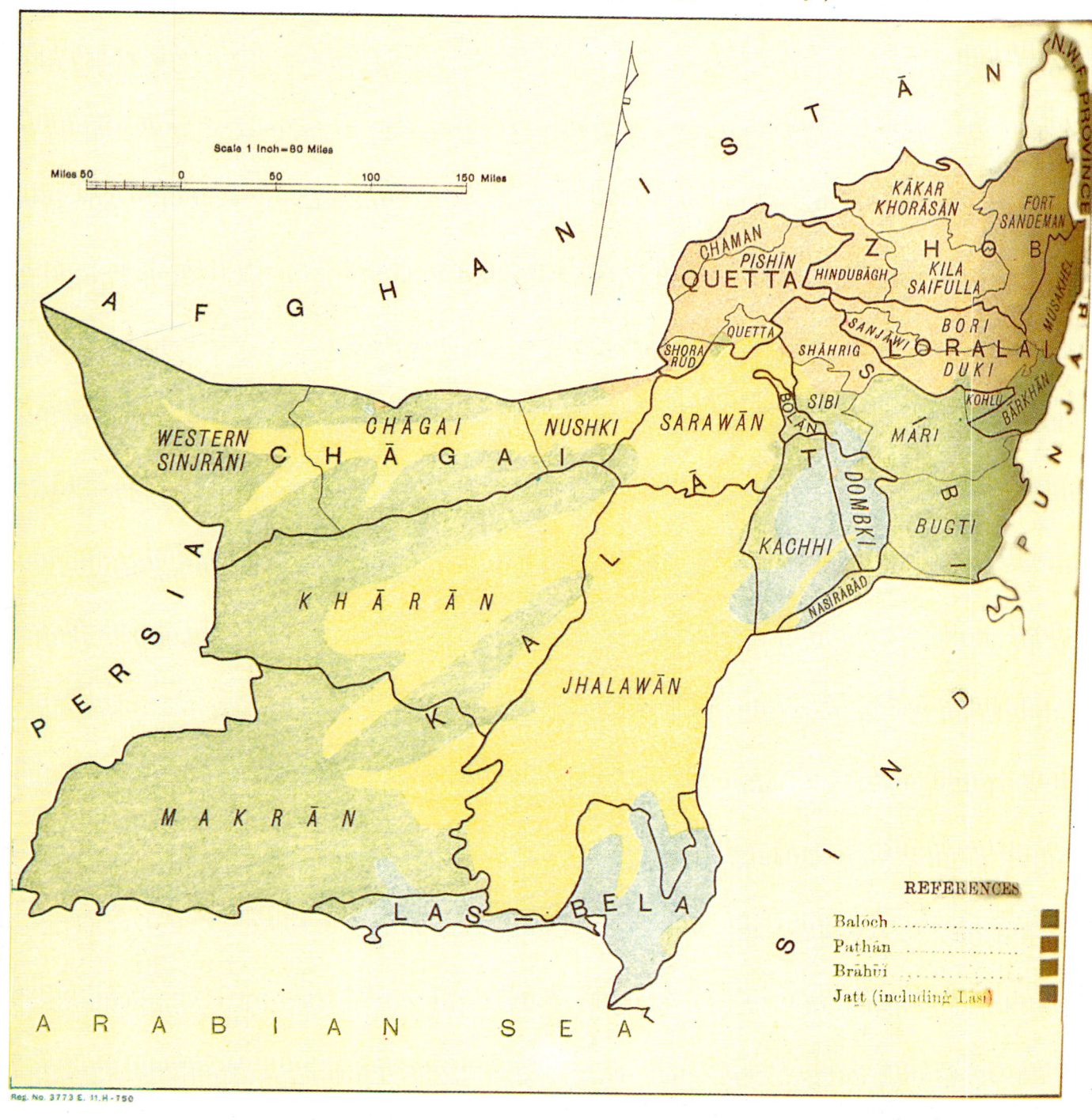

Map 2: Baluchistan showing Racial Distribution.

Introduction:
The Space of the Savage and
the Idea of an Imperial Boundary

The cartography that became the reality of empire was drawn from a discursive engagement with space, that sought to construct and deconstruct boundaries, margins and limits, in order to construct a narrative of power, that would appear as the history of the self written across the body of the other. Language as 'reflection' promoted the idea of colonial space as the intersection of Europe and the Orient, the place for European selfhood to realize its positive mission. The verbal grammar for this representation was premised on the 'logic of visualisation', which promoted the primacy of the intellectual and ideological gaze, in discerning colonial space as the darkness lurking beyond the horizon of European reason, the sensory realm of instinct, from where the enigma of the other, haunted the imperial imaginary, creating fables of self and alterity. This perceptual code forged its own appropriated space, in the narcissistic structures of demand and desire, that sought to inscribe sovereignty and the self in the order of otherness. This figural space was the negative void, waiting to be colonized by the higher reality belonging to the consciousness of the West, and its Enlightenment heritage of reason, race, and authority.

The making and remaking of British India's imperial frontier in tribal Baluchistan in the late nineteenth century, mirrored the symmetries and orientations that designed the representational reality of colonial space in the dialectics of self-fortification and self-confirmation, based on a repetitive differentiation of itself from what it believed to be not itself. Through structure, sign and symbol, the frontier was imaged as the in-between space, signifying presence and absence, desire and dread, to imbricate its representational reality in the ambivalent, the agonistic, and the alien. The mapping of this space as wall and enclosure, in the imaginary of imperial design, to include/exclude the appropriate/ inappropriate, mirrored the European process of representation, to reinforce the familiar at the expense of the strange. This represented place was subjected to the logic of displacement and differentiation, to create the closures of self and object, within which strategic acts of avowal and disavowal could be staged as text and spectacle.

The reduction of the Baluch border to a corner of imperial space, allowed for its mystification in forms and fantasies, through which imperial culture sought to represent reality. Tropes of savagery and sensuality, animality and anarchy, entered language to exoticize the sign of tribal man on the frontier as predatory, primitive and alien. Fixed at the boundary between the animal and the human, exposed to the rigours of wild mountains and deserts that circled India to the north west, tribal space became a site for the phenomenological affirmation of self and other, the symbolic divide between reason and its absence. The visibility of the other was at once a point of identity and a problem. As a permanent sign of negative difference, the tribal 'other' was inscribed in the symbolic register of resemblance and analogy as mute, meaningless, and decaying. His dark gestures of primitive being signified the demonic in human ontology, that had to be sublated and crypted in the ground of horror and disavowal. He was the alienated other of the self, that disturbed and disconcerted the psyche of imperial consciousness with what it was not, signifying the threat of the unknown and the emptying of culture. The phobic image of tribalism provided the masks of conquest, and the alibi to rule the body of the other as the space of the savage, the sensory and the sensual. This presumption to rule, signified as Foucault suggests, "the exalted sovereignty that denounces the others' false sovereignty dispossesses them".[1]

Through erasure and imprint tribal space was mapped on the atlas of empire, providing the Baluchistan frontier with a historical silhouette, originating within the metaphor of vision, complicit with a Western metaphysic of Man. The design for transforming tribal space into a place with a history, belonged to the text of Eurocentric legitimations, for reducing and appropriating the body of the 'other' in the universalizing, and self-validating totality of the imperialism of the same. This overwriting and attempted erasure of alterity, to privilege the self in relation to history and power, carried the fear of negation of its primacy, and the dark dystopia of the return of the repressed and irrational, to threaten the boundaries of self and meaning. The misgivings of this imaginary, traced and retraced the inner and outer boundaries of imperial power in India, along the fractured planes of anxiety and aggression, to affirm and deny the precariousness of power. The tension of presence and absence, created a rhetoricized mentality, that sought to possess through dispossession. As mirror and ally of the binary disempowering of colonial rule, imperial rhetoric was full of its own haunting, of the sublation of the real in the unreal, and the illegitimacy of dominion masquerading as the rational norm of history and evolution. This "splitting"[2] of the space of colonial consciousness, as Homi Bhabha has suggested, was the site of ambivalence and ambiguity, where the self chased its own shadow, and feared the malefic other of its own creation.

This subterranean vein of fear that disturbed the imperial imaginary, acquired surface visibility in the imaged horror of the Mutiny of 1857, when the language of native resistance was read as the sign of human degradation to the frenzied nadir of animality. The dread of the inner enemy was magnified by the perception of a threat from across the frontier, at once sinister and subversive of English presence and permanence in imperial India. The locus of this threat was Tsarist Russia, whose engagement in mapping an Asiatic empire was the object of censure and scrutiny, to measure distances and dimensions of predatory intent, to overwhelm the space of British India with the menace of internal subversion and external aggression. The two obsessions of the dread of unreason lapsing into violence, and morbid fixation on the spectacle of Russia continually reinventing the text of its imperial purpose on the violation of Asian ground, leaned on and reinforced each other, to structure the interventionist logic of British imperial discourse, seeking to construct a counter reality based on image, identity and influence.

Baluchistan entered the space of British India, at this interstitial juncture, where the optics of playing the 'Great Game' with Russia, exaggerated the matrix of meanings associated with frontiers, boundaries and margins. Arid deserts and impossible mountains moved across conceptual space from emptiness to strategic empowerment, as forbidding icons of imperial boundary architecture. The desolate became the desirable, to establish both distance and dialogue, with the rival other caught in the same aporia of playing the game for power and possession. The players were opposed but alike, chasing the same mirage like truths, confusing the symmetries of imitative desire, with the antagonisms of implacable opposition. Pressed against the surface of this mimetic rivalry, the spatial history of Baluchistan was annexed to the meta-narrative of empire, to address the anxiety of being caught in the game, of being implicated in its twists of desire and deceit, to capture the text of the other, perceived as a threat to the presence/freedom of the self. The translation of Baluchistan as desirable, possessable territory occurred in the medium of borrowed language, a reply coined in the sign of the other, to reclaim image and identity from the anxiety of regression and retreat. The aggression of this rewriting in tribal space, belonged to the place of the imaginary, where as Jacques Lacan states: "Desire begins to take shape in the margin in which demand becomes separated from need; this margin being that which is opened up by demand, the appeal of which can be unconditional only in regard to the Other, under the form of the possible defect which need may introduce into it, of having no universal satisfaction (what is called anxiety)".[3]

The imagining of tribal/colonial space in the language of demand and desire, employed a system of representations, a regime of meanings that sought not to interpret tribalism, but to legitimate its reflection in signs and symbols, that reaffirmed the self-reinforcing illusions of imperial rule. Distance from Europe and the Darwinian paradigm of superior-inferior races in the design of civilization, entered the space of representational reality, to establish degrees of difference, primitivity and inferiority on the identities of those forced to live under the sign of Western surveillance. Translations of difference remained anchored to the dichotomization of 'self' and 'other' in the Nietzschean sense of the self as central and moral, and the other as marginalized, eccentric and amoral. The optics of this Eurocentric sense of history, viewed the imprints of tribalism as pathways leading back to the time of space in its original wilderness, the world of the savage and the animal, signifying fury and frenzy. In this simulation of an imaged past, the pictorial became the problematic, allowing imperial rhetoric to engage with tribalism as an error of arrested evolution that needed the corrective culture of a higher rational order. This was rhetoric's mythic imagining of imperialism's "soul making" mission,[4] as Gayatri Chakravorty Spivak puts it, claiming the authority of reason and redemption, while suppressing its silent borrowing of representational devices to frame the 'other' as a category in need of such apostolic conversion.

Representation of the tribal/colonized as a fixed reality, which was at once an other, and yet entirely knowable and visible, was part of the iconography of colonial control, as the derealization of the subject body, allowed its incorporation in the appropriative, and reductive idiom of imperial rule. Orphaned from its contextual meanings, tribalism was reduced to signifying the silence of the ruled, and to accept its own objectification as mere "container" to hold the "contents"[5] of foreign mastery. The erasure of tribalism's savage imprints, and its refiguration in the sign of servility and docility, signified the colonial vocabulary of 'command and demand', that textured the landscape of subjection. Disempowering would occur in the Foucauldian sense, causing the tribe to be "subjected, used, transformed and improved".[6] This remaking of tribal frontier space, in the imaged sign of reason, reform and discipline, indicated the sublation of the real in the unreal, mirroring the megalomania of the imperial self seeking recognition in history as the creator of order and meaning from the depths of chaos.

In looking at the imperial diagram on the frontier, as imaged and perceptual reality, I have been primarily concerned with the way in which imperialism imagined its space, centred the self in a narrative of power and possession, created boundaries of inclusion and exclusion in the place of otherness, and mapped alterities to legitimize their erasure and overwriting in the 'foundation myths' of history, reason, progress. The figure of the tribe entered the space of language as absence, to reassure the imperialist of what he was not. Interpretation as implication, established a threshold of pertinence, where the dilemmas of identity and interest were symbolically resolved in the negative 'difference' of the tribe, and literally redressed by subjecting the tribe to the taboo of imperial order. Ideas of 'imperial' and 'tribal' served as fable and foil to produce the imperialisation of space, mirroring the iconic inscription of a ruling culture seeking its own narcissistic reflection on the surface of the other.

The categories, concepts, and conventions within which this text is situated, have been drawn from the premises of Post-colonial theory, psychoanalytic framings, the semiotics of spatial history, and the tropic significations of Orientalist perceptions. Edward Said's synchronic essentialist vision of European reconstructions of the Orient, marked a beginning for siting the tropic divide of self and other, as a way of reading colonial histories. But the Saidian construct, signifying from a panoptic view of dominion, suggested the idea of a primarily passive Orient, consenting to its appropriation in forms of Western discursive representation. Said's reluctance to engage with the inner dissensions of 'orientalism' as a genre of imperialist historicism, and the assumed regularity of representation and object, within the symmetries of power and powerlessness, repressed the site of ambivalence in the discourse, that could serve as the space of interrogation and resistance. As Homi Bhabha has put it: "There is always in Said, the suggestion that colonial power is possessed entirely by the colonizer, which is a historical and theoretical simplification".[7] Bhabha's reading of 'ambivalence' in colonial discourse as the site of anxiety and hesitancies, suggests a notion of the precariousness of power, that could be exploited to interrogate or interrupt strategies of dominion and hegemony. Arguing that the "colonial stereotype is a complex, ambivalent, contradictory mode of representation, as anxious as it is assertive..."[8], Bhabha defines colonial discourse as a form of mastery, always threatened with the loss of its own controlling gestures of authority and language. This original ambivalence then connects with fantasies of menace, and the sinister 'hybrid' or the native imaged in the likeness of the colonizer, but still different – 'not quite, not white'– to perceive the return of the suppressed as a contesting question from the space of otherness, engaged in "strategies of subversion that turn the gaze of the discriminated back upon the eye of power".[9] Bhabha's engagement with the psycho-pathology of the colonial relation, to shift the focus of 'cultural racism' from the politics of nationalism to the 'politics of narcissism', both disorients and disrupts forms of Western rationality and historicist narrative, that intervene in the construction of colonial form and content. In suggesting the limits of colonial discourse, and its interruption from the space of otherness, Bhabha recovers the uncertain, shifting terrain of colonial power and perception, to allow for subversive gestures from within. However as Robert Young has observed, perhaps some of Bhabha's ambivalence spills over into the terms of his own text, so that the reader is left to wonder whether his models work by suggestion and proposition, or do they relate to empirical historical phenomenon.[10] Despite this ambiguity, Bhabha's psychological reading of self and identity, points to new depths of meaning in which structures of representation may be sited, as ways of extending the lines and limits of interpretation and comprehension.

Mapping the territory of colonial identities from a deconstructivist, Marxist position, Gayatri Spivak, suggests the usefulness of 'subject-positions' and 'subject effects' to retrieve the sign of the native as object and instrument in the exercise of imperial power, as well as a form of 'lost consciousness' obliterated in the constructs of the imperial narrative. Envisaging history as a process of 'epistemic violence', an interested construction of a particular representation of an object, Spivak constructs the position of the native, as a historically muted subject. She speaks of the English Agents's intrusion into the space of the other, obliging the native to "domesticate the alien as Master",[11] as the instance of the native being forced to collude in his own subject formation as mute and voiceless. The idea that the subaltern (i.e. subject-native) cannot speak, exposes Spivak to the criticism of arbitrarily dismissing the entire body of native language and political resistance that existed in defiance of the empire. But in proposing the specificity of the subject-position on the bases of race, class, gender, she introduces a heterogeneity that problematises the notion of an undifferentiated colonial subject, thereby proposing a new hermeneutics for studying the field of history and colonialism.

In my own engagement with the problems of representation, as the imaged and the real, in the constructions and contortions of power and its denial, I have preferred to illuminate the text through a series of conceptual categories, that probe the "internalized grammar" of the mind[12], that computes form and meaning, and determines their purpose and performance in the matrices of abstraction, action and assimilation. Proceeding from Foucault's contention that knowledge is constructed according to a discursive field, which creates a representation of the object of knowledge, I have treated the official and non-official literature of British India, as a form of 'colonial discourse', that described and inscribed form and content, within subject-object interpolations imparting the dynamic, that allows a Hegelian reading of the latter as an "emergence, as a generation out of each other".[13] If, as Aristotle suggests that the function of 'discourse' is to let something be seen in terms of relationship, judgement, I have tried to capture some of this visibility through interpretation of the word, understanding of perception, and mapping of the spatial sign, to suggest a geometry of the imperial apparatus that implied a circularity of meaning, a system of significations arbitrarily related to reality, and in fact only related to itself.

To recover the textual truths of colonial discourse, I have found it necessary to look at the literal meaning of the statement, as well as the suggested meaning, that requires a historical-situational context as referent, and the mediating interest, bias, wish of the enunciator. The relationship of the manifest to the latent meaning is as Tzetvan Todorov puts its: "The literal meaning is an envelope; the spiritual meaning is the thing itself".[14] The text existing within this hierarchy of meanings, acquires significance in the relationship between that meaning or meanings and a person, conception or a situation. This introduction of external norms in the morphology of interpretive forms, allows for the distinction between different types of understanding, value-judgement and conclusions. From these premises, it is possible to discern the function of language as translation, as resemblance and association, and as evocation, in the texts of colonial discourse, attempting to reflect the ground of subject-predicate relationships, and at the same time remaking it, within the intentionality and temporality of its own representative structures. Through metaphoric similarity, metonymic displacement, and symbolic evocation, imperial rhetoric sought to map the strangeness of the human terrain witnessed in the colonial field. The adequacy of this representation to the object, belonged not so much to the external reality of the latter, but to the subjective truth of the observer. Enunciation may be perceived here as "action ...and the implication concerns the speaker, the subject and not the object".[15] Translations of the object of scrutiny occurred in the locus of the collective consciousness of association and meaning, that led imperial vision to affirm a language of representation drawn out of its world to verbalise the boundaries of another, in hegemonic, naturalistic and representational conventions. The central polemic of savagery in imperial discursive illustrations of the 'tribal', corresponds to what Gilles Deleuze has suggested, was the observation of no longer "recognizable objects, but things which do violence, encountered signs", that lead to the constitution of essences that "dwell in the dark regions, not in the temperate zones of the clear and distinct".[16] The syntagm or proposition of the primitive, barbaric tribe trapped in the gap between nature and culture, was culturally coded in the sacral terror of man's dark, and disturbing origins. The sign of the tribe functioned as the limit of this sensibility, its extreme exercise; it suggested the reading back to an "ancient chaos of ... nature on the point of overwhelming consciousness".[17] The construction of this historical trope in language, the intentionalization of the concept in its verbal form, implied the translation of tribalism as censorship, as the twisted fragment from the past, the natural adversary of civilization itself.

The metonymic displacement of the tribe in associations and assumptions of the negative and discordant, proceeded from a perspectivism engaged in presenting and representing 'difference', in the subject-object situation to suggest lines of image and identity, signifying degrees of distance in the mental and moral mapping of imperial self-consciousness and tribal otherness. On the level of discursive reality, 'self' and 'other' may be viewed as affirmations and disaffirmations of subjective consciousness and objective definition, seeking validity in the Lacanian sense of the "Symbolic, the Imaginary and the Real".[18] The 'presentation' of experience outside discourse as such, (perception and fantasy), – but necessarily mediated by it – constituted the category of the referent of the signified. This 'thing presentation', (to avoid any implication that the referent is real), could refer to the subjective content of the personal fantasy, or the objective definition of visual perception, or a word proposition. From these premises it is possible to see the category of tribal otherness in imperial discourse, as constituted by the subjective intention of the self, at once recognizing and repudiating the instinctual and sensual represented in the sign of the tribe, as the margin of the taboo and forbidden, in the topography of the Western imaginary seeking to suppress the bestial in man, the horror of the primitive. The symbolic reading of tribalism as the dark interiority of the savage mind, was a symptom of the recording self, rearranging the order of reality, through symbolic transference, where the correspondence of the subject's language to reality slips and returns as verbalisations of binary semantic oppositions, in which the opposition is valued over the content. This displacement of the image of otherness in a category of difference as the unwanted and unacceptable, was tied to the subjectivity of the self, seeking to affirm its own ground through the assumed negativity of the object. The sense of the negative, acquired from the Hegelian idea of the divisive abstractive power of understanding, developed further in Freud's concept of disavowal by the subject, and reiterated by Lacan as repudiation, functioned as a defensive reflex and a condemning judgement. The negation "was a means of defence", as Freud wrote in 1894, against "incompatible ideas".[19] The tribal text signifying an older vocabulary of nature, preserving in the darkness of its temporal structure the earlier chaos of instinctual force, incohate, pre-individualistic, became the object of symbolic abolition, whose truth was suppressed to create the myth of the monster, that the sovereign imperial self had to overcome by repudiation and negative judgement, to defend that fragment of identity, which paradoxically needed and negated the difference of the other to define its own subjective contours. The narcissistic aggression of this self-identity, was the locus of the desire to inscribe the master-slave relationship between self and other, to sustain the opposition of 'noble consciousness' and 'base consciousness', demanding absolute recognition of its subjectivity by seeking to possess, and denying autonomy to the other of the self. 'Otherness' in imperial discourse, may be therefore read as a disguised expression, and as an alienation of reality, and an accommodation with it.

Introduction : The Space of the Savage and the Idea of an Imperial Boundary

The verbal, visual and perceptual codings of self and otherness, acquired specificity and historical anchorage, through the temporal and spatial structures of the imperial narrative apparatus, that intentionalized representation as a way of engaging with the real that must always transcend it. The situational and historicizing logic of the narrative, imparted a structure of the image not fixed in perpetuity, but as a specific phenomenon mirroring its own peculiarities, which as Fredric Jameson puts it, "identifies itself as a process of symbolizing, which is conscious of itself as 'irrealizing the world'".[20] Significations of otherness as a category and judgement, developed in close proximity to the periodization of time that belonged to the 'age of empire', with its icons of character and differential identity, its tropic fixation on the fetish of the uncivilized, that served as intrinsic and extrinsic boundaries of the privileges of race and dominion, that constituted the self-conscious text of historical record and representation. It mapped the language of a period preoccupied with distance and definition in the subject-object axis, locating otherness within the margin of the colonized as a form of damaged existence, and offering this reading as the ground for interventionist remaking of the lowly within the visuality of the higher imperial self. Imperial investments of the tribal borderland in Baluchistan, between 1876-1905, were tied to abstractions and conceptualizations working within a temporal sequence of events, to configure perceptions of the self and the strange, as 'moments, figures, tropes, paradigms', of the subjects's relationship to the real itself, on lines of time implicated in the verbalisation of the sign and the corresponding type of truth.

Conceptual and temporal structures within which imperial form and content matured, occurred within a certain mapping of geographical space as text, the place where the object entered the history of the self, through acts of assimilation, appropriation and absorption. The space of the 'other' metamorphosized into the site of desire and destiny, as the gift of providence, which was the duty of empire to realize, through spatial rewriting. Space entered discourse as the place where arguments were traded for power and prestige, and political visions conjured to gratify illusions of omnipotence. The imperial psyche working in the gap between consciousness of power and fear of its loss, viewed space as the fragment of reality, on which it could always reinvent itself in the language of dominion and demand, to elicit the submission of the colonized. Space implied a construction of power and its ideological use as a weapon of aggression/coercion to create topographies of dominion. Dominated space became the synonym for the idea of imperial ascendancy, and its lack, the negation of the self in history, as central, as sovereign, as providential. Imperial boundaries in space were therefore never absolute, but always emerging, to mirror dimensions and directions of power, that must be seen as transcending former limits, to protect it from the idea of the moribund and static. The imperial borderland was the vital margin, in which construction and concealment of intent and interest occurred as an 'in-mixing of subjects,' to normalize the act of intervention in historical tropes of need, evolution, progress, to deny the menace of the other by suppressing its form, to signify the place of purpose and presence. Imperial discourse therefore suggested a way of reading space as a text, and a way of constructing it. The empirically given, entering presentational circulation as messages of obstruction, danger, dread, allowed for the remaking of exterior space as the place of self-representation, appropriation, the prohibited. Borderlands in particular, were the symbolic 'beyond' ruled by figures of fantasy and fear, captured in the rhetoric of the 'Great Game' for empire between England and Russia, with tribal space as the mediate margin, providing the textual space for inscriptions of recognition and reputation, demanded by the desiring self. The Great Game mirrored the hauntings of desire, seeking self-definition through new and imagined meanings of the margin, the compulsive journey of the self into the space of the unmapped and uncharted, to enter new horizons of perceptual power. Annexing tribal themes to compose the narrative of the Great Game, signified the repression of the spatial texts and titles of the other, to foreground the representational space of imperial meaning, demonstrating as Henri Lefebvre suggests, how "space serves, and how hegemony makes use of it, in the establishment, on the basis of an underlying logic and with the help of knowledge ...of a system".[21]

I start exploring the time and territory of imperial rewriting on the Baluch frontier, in Chapter 1, titled : *Text and Context: Inscribing an Imperial Margin in Tribal Baluchistan, 1876*. The suggestion here is, that the construction of the margin signified symbolic inscription and political act. Symbolically it was intended to mark the difference between culture and nature. In that difference, in the space it created for verbalising and visualising, imperial history would begin. The textualizing of the strange and savage in tribal space, by the first British explorer was an originating gesture of colonialism itself, making writing an accomplice to the representation of the space of the other, in terms of topoi implying difference, distance, and opposition. Alterity imaged in tropes of savagery and primitivity, emptied the other of human meaning, leaving a nudity of form that needed the cover of imperial rule to bring it out of the wild, into the place of the normal, and readable in social language. This rehumanizing of the tribe was the spiritual symbolism that encoded the margin, bringing the borderland within a cultural mapping, as the imagined place of taming the tribe, of trapping the terrors of nature. The margin as the sign of the symbolic and imaginary, was brought within the sphere of the possible and probable, by the political geography of the Great Game. As the in-between space separating Russia from British India, Baluchistan entered the visuality of the game as the playing field, on which image and power would be contested to affirm or negate dominion in the heartlands of empire. The intervention of perception, to configure reality in notions of power and powerlessness, was the surreal vision of the Great Game, that dictated imperial patterns in tribal space to reflect confrontation, exclusion and appropriation.

Chapter 2, *Form and Transformation: the Genesis of British Baluchistan, and the Semantics of Boundary Making*, 1876-1905, looks at the polemical and political constructs of the imperialisation of tribal space, to signify the place of fence and frontier, in which the temporality of empire could be conceived, within the framings of power, signifying the order of historical dominion, suppressing and transcending opposition, anxiety, vulnerability. The use of tribal space, to text the frontier of imperial history, privileged the political over the natural, as the pioneering act of rolling back the wilderness, to create the space where culture would not evolve or adapt, but endlessly repeat itself in the language of dominance. The symbolic perception of the tribe as some deeper pre-social reality of the physiological itself, and the need to flee the complicity of being in this a primary site of nature, brought the empirical frontier within the imaginary bounds of exorcising the 'spectral' from the place of power, to transform the sinister space of the savage into the relativized, historicized place of imperial narrative. The refiguration of tribal space in the colonial idiom of boundaries, limits, forts, and the dispossessions they signified, were part of the text of conceiving and collapsing the margins of distance and dread, to expel the unknown and unfamiliar, from the precincts of the imperial self and its imagined territory. This conflict of imperial time and tribal time, that mirrored the making of the frontier, was trapped in the ideological territory of the Great Game, that problematised and produced the symbolic and literal mediations of action, within which temporal and spatial elements of a new frontier visuality, and a place of power could be mapped. The semantics of action, dictated by the terror of the tribe and the menace of the beyond, i.e. Russia, transformed the frontier as watch tower and sentinel, the anxious eye of an imperial political unconscious, gazing into the darkness of perceived danger, to affirm the truth of its own spatial narrative.

Chapter 3, *Image and Identity: Constructions and Misconstructions of Tribalism in Imperial Eyes*, explores representations of tribalism in imperial official archives, travel writing, and ethnographic descriptions. The objective in this section is to look at culture as boundary, by which the concepts of what are intrinsic or extrinsic to culture come into play, making the act of representation a mediation of reality through the act of culture description. As the archives of a time, imperial texts were deviations from, exaggerations and negations of tribal reality. The vocabulary for imperial representation of tribal form was drawn from the dictionary of Darwinian evolution, and the exotic grammar of Social Darwinist interpretation. Social Darwinism was a metaphor for the times, legitimating a rhetoric that was culture specific, and overladen with pervasive oppositions, such as primitivism and progress, the West and the non-West, future and past. It was implicated in Europeanizing the concept of culture, of establishing doctrinal walls between self and object, ego and the world, of perceiving its opposite as the exotic and eccentric other, living in exile from reason and liberation. From the parapets of Eurocentrism, the idea of tribal man as a raw unfinished fragment of humanity was too easily visible, and consciously textualized in imperial records, with their select emphasis on passion and primitivity in mapping terrains of tribal history, identity, and behaviour. The primitive tribe matched the untamed monsters of the medieval mind, and the crude ape like creatures that inhabited the dawn of evolutionary time. This representation did not seek to interpret, but to confine tribal identity to the lower reaches of the human-animal boundary. The Victorian view of the Baluch tribes, "as a hornet's nest of barbarous tribes people living in inaccessible valleys amidst the wilderness of rugged mountains", for whom the imperial touch would signify a "new era... dawning on the wild, wide wilderness... of his savage life".[22] mirrored the ape and essence philosophy of perception, in which the Western intellect was conceived as the pure surface of human reason, that would register the darkness outside its reflective plane, in order to transfigure it in the vision of light.

Official reconstructions of the tribal world as lack, as absence signified by the poverty of its material structures, imprisoned tribal identity in a configuration of negatives, typified in the violent language of warfare, murderous feuds, and savage reprisals, which comprised the frenzied code of savage existence. The tribal structure, that dominated this pictorial, confirmed representational logic, by its sign as a warring unit, composed of ranked leaders commanding the allegiance of ordinary tribesmen, herded into sections and ready for armed action, in aggressive or defensive combat for the political interests of the tribe. This image of a permanently militarised social model, existing within the definitions of force, trapped tribal place in the perennial anarchy of the warring zone, that was considered to be part of a genetic code of disorder, rather than a rational political order. The emphasis on biology rather than economics, in interpreting the genealogy of tribal violence, that really mirrored the problems of survival against the hostility of nature, suggested that imperial reconstructions tended to privilege the darker Hobbesian version of the primitive, than the truth of the whole, bypassing the significance of the local cultural codes that made tribal experience articulate. Tribal constructs in imperial writing, therefore tended to be simulations, impressions of the real, to rediscover the primitive in order to make his arrested development, the site for constructing the text of ruling and remaking. The argument in this section, therefore suggests, that imperial image making was implicated in a discursive partiality shaped by the experience of history and power, and the invention of a point of view, that imposed its own mythic frame of reference on the representation of reality.

Chapter 4, *The Coercion of Power: The Discourse of Discipline in Resignifying the Tribal Margin*, explores the iconography of imperial control, signified by the inscription of subject-positions in the interior of tribalism, to establish topographies of dependence on which dominance could be mapped. The erasure of anarchy and chaos, that bound the tribe within the space of the savage, would occur through the medium of the disciplinary vision, that would coerce the social body, in order to regulate its habits, gestures and movements, to architect the place of docility and decorum. Tribalism would be subjected to the rigours of an abstract field of comparison, where the imperial norm would act as referee, determining the closures of permitted/forbidden behaviour. The tribesman trapped in an observatory of panoptic surveillance, would submit to the demands of discipline, and inscribe on his person, the power relationship that required him to function as the object and instrument of his own subjection. Discipline would combat the sign of nomadic flux and chaos, that defined and deformed tribal existence, in order to transfix him in the mute and silent landscape of coercive imperial order. This refiguring, was the critical violation of the tribal interior, "interrupting their continuity, making them play roles in which they no longer recognize themselves, making them betray not only commitments but their own substance".[23] But, as I will discuss, the site of repression became the ground of contention, the place from where the subjugated tribe interrogated the constraints of confinement, through resistance and dissent, to reclaim the lost sign of subjectivity and self, buried in the tropic place of imperial significations of power, possession and ownership. The sign of reversal in tribal consciousness, implying the slippage of control and authority in the imperial model, referred the dominant discourse back to the predicament of power that had from the outset shaped its vision, vocabulary and articulation.

Chapter 5, *In the Mirror of Meaning: Imperial Translations in Tribal Space, as Point and Margin, Time and Text, Place and Power*, concludes by looking at boundaries of perception, that led to the universality of Western reason to renounce the singular, in writing the history of self and other. Discursive depiction was manifested in the style, of a "fragmentary, discrete presentation, constantly seeking an interpretation from above".[24] In this perception, ontology was inscribed in a philosophy of power as egotism, in which the relationship with the other, was accomplished through its assimilation in the self. Politically, this was an argument for the incorporating self to always imagine its space, in a perception-consciousness system that stressed: "Possession is pre-eminently the form in which the other becomes the same, by becoming mine".[25] Within this object consciousness, colonial alterity functioned as the site for perceiving subject matters and subject races, that shaped the vocabulary of imperial dominion over the non-European world. Through the in-mixing of the sovereign and servile, European man asserted his self-authorizing and self-legitimating ground. As Sarte observed: "...the European has only been able to become a man through creating slaves and monsters".[26] 'Difference' translated as dependence and disempowerment, configured colonial space in a Hegelian form of master-slave intimacy. The servility of the subjected, belonged to ideas of discourse that were assertively European. Language determined by the history of the writer, textualized representations of the other in a web of significations, that invested perception itself with the mediating power of placing and displacing cultural difference. The visual enframing and metaphorical transformations, that characterized the imaginary and symbolic reading of the other as dark, discordant and distant, signified negation, the emptying of the space of the other, for imaginative appropriation and the pursuit of desire. This definition of the space of the other largely

Introduction : The Space of the Savage and the Idea of an Imperial Boundary

by what it was not, allowed its remaking through strategies of mastering and mapping, aligning identity and interest, arranging and deepening the scene as the object of desire and redemptive rewriting. It was a text that sought to disguise the act of appropriation, by appropriating the means by which such action was to be understood. In this representation of reality, the narrative of the other was a margin in which the self was made.

NOTES

1. M.Foucault, *Madness and Civilization*, p. 263.
2. H.K. Bhabha, 'Foreword', in F. Fanon, *Black Skins, White Masks*, p. xiv.
3. J.Lacan, *Ecrits*, p. 311.
4. Quoted in B.Parry, 'Current Theories of Colonial Discourse', *The Post-Colonial Studies Reader*, ed. B.Ashcroft *et al.*, p. 39.
5. H.Lefebvre, *The Production of Space*, p. 94.
6. M.Foucault, *Discipline and Punish*, p. 136.
7. Quoted in R.Young, *White Mythologies*, p. 142.
8. *Ibid.*, p. 143.
9. *Ibid.*, p. 148.
10. *Ibid.*, p. 148-156.
11. Quoted in B.Parry, *op.cit.*, p. 38.
12. A.N.Chomsky, *Rules and Representations*, p. 220.
13. F.Jameson, *Marxism and Form*, p.328.
14. T.Todorov, *Symbolism and Interpretation*, p. 130.
15. *Ibid.*, p. 60-61.
16. G.Deleuze, *Proust and Signs*, p. 166; p. 165.
17. F.Jameson, *op.cit.*, p. 61.
18. J.Lacan, *The Language of the Self*, Trans. A.Wilden, p. xiv.
19. *Ibid.*, p. 278.
20. F.Jameson, *op.cit.*, p. 397.
21. H.Lefebvre, *op.cit.*, p. 11.
22. T.H.Holdich, *The Indian Borderland*, pp. 385-386; p. 191.
23. R.Young, *op.cit.*, p. 13.
24. St.Augustine, quoted in G.Gueber and C.Wulf, *Mimesis*, p. 20.
25. *Oxford Literary Review Seminar*, 1979.
26. Quoted in R.Young, *op.cit.*, p. 125.

1

Text and Context:
Inscribing an Imperial Margin
in Tribal Baluchistan, 1876

The act of scripting Baluchistan in the narrative of British India, was situated in a rhetoric of power and paranoia, which sought to legitimate in document and fable, the experience of expansion, and expectation of the exotic and exceptional. Baluchistan was acquired as part of British India's troubled search for a border in the mind and on the map. Across the Indus in areas like Baluchistan, lurked the bestiary of the imagination, typified by fragments of savage disorder, without law and geometry. This was the space of the 'other', signifying for imperial culture the strange and unreadable, that had to be suppressed to reduce the danger of its 'otherness'. The discovery of this alterity, would force reflexive erasure, as part of the imperial project of possession through dispossession. Through this appropriation, the space of the 'other' was transformed into the cultural place of empire, the site for a new text of mapping and measuring distances and directions of power and powerlessness.

Imperial desire for this tribal space as possessable, translatable territory grew out of the predicament of power in the Indian context: its rifts, its instabilities and its flaws. The insecurity of dominion, created the psychological territory for perceiving configurations of danger, which needed to be combated by an armoury of self-reinforcing illusions. Doubt and anxiety created the spectres of internal subversion and external invasion, which would provide the conceptual framework for propagating expansionist texts. Representations of this inner fear of loss and survival in imperial discourse, created an imaginary world of demons and dangers, which provided permanent anchorages for polemic and policy, in shaping the imagined outlines of British India.

Fear, scepticism, desire and the politically concrete, structured the verbal medium, that shaped and produced the representational categories of plot and time, in which the story of empire was charted. The signification of this representational exercise was to read the world of events, in order to capture this world in appropriate symbols, and to construct a narrative context in which to place the events. Language and historical situations in their capacity as mirrors and agents of reality, realized and expressed the narrative of the empire's engagement with political map making, from the interiority of self-attachment and self-obssession. In a sense, the metamorphosis of British India was embedded in a real act, and a way of seeing it. The starting point of this paranoia and dread was Napolean's vertiginous vision of claiming Egypt and Persia as signs and symbols of French power, on the route and rim of British India. In the event, Egypt eluded French control, although Persia emerged as the hub of French intrigue, and the consequent subject of British imperial introspection as the possible road of an invasion of India from the west. The French encampment in Persia was temporal and tenuous, but it provided an early frame for the pathology of an idea, namely anxiety for the precariousness of power in the Indian imperial scene. This ideational complex, evoked the imaginary drawing of empire as fort and cell, encircled by boundaries and barriers of space and structure, to perpetuate a critical distance between the external and the internal, the political and the psychological, to protect the self from the enemy outside. The drive to paralyse Napolean's scheme by concluding an Anglo-Persian Treaty in 1810, the refiguration of the western threat on the site of Russian ambition, in the aftermath of French defeats in Europe, attested to the strength of the perceived reality of danger from the west, that would disturb and damage the imperial self in India. The event horizon in the west, allowed this reading to take root, and branch into the nervous imaginary. Turkey and Persia, politically weak but geographically close to Russia, carried the burden of Tsardom's expansionist ambitions. By 1810, Russia detached Georgia from Persian control, and by 1829 she threatened to enter Constantinople. As Russia dissolved old boundaries of power, the British chose to interpret the significance of the new in sceptical texts, suggestive of the subterranean and sinister, in Russia's intentional remapping of Eurasia.

Polemicists, explorers, and analysts sought to situate the iconography of Russian expansionism, within contextual meanings derived from the specificity of political view points. Officials close to the idea of structuring British interests in Persia, like John Malcolm, (directed to negotiate another defensive Treaty with Persia in 1810), were drawn to interpreting Russian designs by presenting the real in relation to imaginary variations, in language that conveyed a sense of urgency and crisis. Malcolm warned that the Persian court without aid from Britain would drift into dependence on Russia, impairing Britain's imperial standing from the "Araxes to...the Ganges".[1] Led by his own speculative conjectures, Malcolm instructed a junior officer, John Macdonald Kinneir, to enquire into the political inclinations of the countries lying between Russia and British India. In his *Memoir on Central Asia*, Kinneir remarked on the :

> "... eventful changes in Europe, which BY THE AGGRANDIZEMENT OF RUSSIA HAVE ENDANGERED THE SAFETY OF OUR EASTERN POSSESSIONS.
>
> It cannot however be denied that the Persians would seize with avidity any proposal of this nature – (an invasion of British India); the love of plunder, the example of Nadir Shah, and the idea which they have formed of the wealth and weakness of our Eastern possessions, would alike stimulate them to the undertaking".[2]

Kinneir's political reading was displacing the real into a simulated angle of a perceived threat, and representing Persian character in the image of an avaricious, iconoclast, to signify the sign of danger as imminent and inevitable. Agreeing with the verbal reality of impending crises, Malcolm decided to map the political geography of the space across the Indian frontier, stretching through Afghanistan, Baluchistan to Persia, in order to measure the menace of this distant corridor to the empire. He instructed Lieutenant Henry Pottinger, of the East India Company's Bombay Army to undertake a confidential political exploration of Baluchistan in 1810. As Pottinger proceeded to translate this unfamiliar marginal space, in terms of routes, tracks and tribes, he established a dialogue with a recognizable place, allowing the landscape of Baluchistan to enter history. This spatial text originating within the larger context of European imperialism in the east, developed in meaning and making, from the rhetoric of language and the intentional gaze, which came to represent and ritualize overlapping imperial desires and demands, as the 'Great Game' between England and Russia for mastery in Asia.

I

Pottinger initiated an engagement with the road and horizon in Baluchistan, which was continued by later travellers and officials, allowing the world of the observed to be recast in the cultural idiom of the observers, for whom the outline of the alien was usually dark, disturbing and exotic. Exploring Baluchistan, Pottinger confronted an empty wilderness, lost inside the bleak desert and mountain environment of India's desolate northwest frontier. His tortuous experience with the furnace hot desert -scape in the west, imprinted the image of a savage wasteland, beyond the redemptive touch of the human hand. Its only use lay in the function of the desert as a physical barrier for any approach to India from the west, and Pottinger recorded his route in a sketch map, that became the first military map of India's western approaches. The malevolence of this terrain, where Baluchistan touched the great Helmund desert, became for Pottinger and later explorers a defining quality, for registering the measure of physical difference on which the individuation of space, and the distinctive idea of a landscape could be sketched. At a later time, to another traveller this empty quarter of sandhills and sandstorms seemed to signify the "general wilderness" of Baluchistan, as a "houseless, treeless space", where life was probably "not worth living".[3]

Drawing eastwards from the Perso-Baluch borderlands, the stark imprint of the desert merely gave way to "Rugged, barren, sunburnt mountains, rent by huge chasms and gorges".[4] The highest mountain mass, called the Brahuik Range by Pottinger, encircled Quetta, the main town in Baluchistan, rising to about 12,000 feet at Tokatu, to the north of the Quetta district. South of Quetta in the Central Brahui Range, lay the historic Bolan Pass commanding the main passage to India from southwest Afghanistan. This tangled mountain mass which only permitted human habitation in narrow valley strips like Pishin, Sibi, and Zhob, entered imperial description as the space of the barren, bare and disfigured. The bleakness of the mountains seemed to match the emptiness of the desert sands. As Thomas Holdich observed, while mapping the borderland:

> "The hills tower in rough and fantastic forms on either side of the narrow valleys ... All this country is about 6000 feet above sea level, and there is a dry bracing atmosphere which possesses however the faculty of rapid alternation between furnace heat and intense biting cold...There is water in these valleys, but it is frequently salt water, and it leaves a leprous white edge to its trickles in spite of its delusive clearness".[5]

Extremes of temperature combined with low rainfall, of not more than 3-12 inches annually, ensured the barrenness of the dry rocky terrain. Upper valleys had thin coverings of cedar and juniper, while the lower ones had some covering of bushes and shrubs. The absence of large forest trees and the bleak, bare and brown mountain slopes led Lord Dufferin the Indian Viceroy passing through the Baluchistan frontier in 1887, to remark: "It is awful country to pass through – bare and highly mountainous, and empty of everything but desolation".[6] This was the desolation of an original wilderness, deserted, daunting and dark. The absence of life was ensured by the scarcity of water, for rivers draining the region like the Pishin Lora, Zhob, and Nari carried no significant, permanent volumes of water. Autumn rains created flash floods in river beds that for the rest of the year, contained no more than shallow streams that disappeared into the pebbly bottom. Pottinger and Charles Masson (another traveller in the region) frequently mentioned dried up river beds, and empty villages, abandoned due to drought. The irony of this strange landscape, where appearance and reality did not quite fuse to bear out familiar notions of the world of nature, led Denys Bray while compiling a profile of the region to remark that Baluchistan was a "land of rivers without water, of forests without trees".[7] The paradoxes suggested in imperial texts on the wilderness of Baluchistan, however, were not just descriptive, for they occurred within the travellers' state of expectation. Forced to negotiate with images of rivers, mountains and forests which contradicted the normal visual logic of perceptions associated with such natural formations, the imperial imagination sought refuge in rhetorical constructions of an impossible landscape, engaged in a permanently hostile dialogue with its human inhabitants.

The mapping of space was consciously accompanied by an interrogation of the human types who lived on such land. To Pottinger, the Baluch tribes who roamed the western deserts typified the instinctual and bestial, located in the 'other' frontier, symbolic of the immoral and unacceptable. He wrote:

> "Bound by no laws, and restrained by no feelings of humanity, the Nharooe's [tribal group in west Baluchistan] are the most savage and predatory class of Belooches: and while they deem private theft dishonourable ... they contemplate the plunder and devastation of a country with such opposite sentiments that they consider it an exploit deserving of the highest commendation, and steeled by that feeling, they will individually recount the assistance they have rendered on such occasion, the number of men, women, and children they have made captives and carried away or murdered, the villages they have burned and plundered, and the flocks they have slaughtered when unable to drive them off".[8]

Pottinger's text on tribal character expressed a perspective and a preference. In his imaging, the Baluch, orphaned from the moral context of civilization, and the linear progress of history, lived in a natal zone of primitivity, symbolizing the sovereignty of unreason in his animal person, whose dark gestures were a celebration of the freedom of the amoral and anarchic.

The captivity of tribal man in instinct and ignorance, was confirmed not contradicted, by the character reading of the other two major tribal groups in Baluchistan, the Brahuis and the Pathans. Pottinger considered the Brahuis to be hardy mountaineers from Tartary. He judged them to be less rapacious than the Baluch, but quite illiterate and barbaric, like the lower human species. But Charles Masson, travelling in Baluchistan two decades after Pottinger, described the Brahuis as savage, with a passion for 'intestine' wars in which several persons would be slain on either side.[9]

Both Pottinger and Masson found the Baluch and Brahui tribes existing in a tribal system that stated and structured its inner space in the language of force. In structure, the system resembled a political fighting machine, based on a hierarchy of sections and leaders, always ready for combat. At the highest level of tribal segmentation, the section was termed *takkar* in Baluch and Brahui; below this level came the subsection known as *shalwar* in Brahui and *phalli* in Baluch; the minimal lineage group at the lowest level, was called *pira*, in Brahui and *paro* in Baluch. Sectional membership was based on filial ties and land shares, with the *pira/paro* denoting the extended family, and the *shalwar*, comprising the agnatic kin group, occupying a common area based on patriliny and patrilocality. At the level of the tribal section itself, membership was ascribed by a share in the section's landed estate, that was granted to male members only on the basis of their agnatic status as patrilineal descendants. But overriding these structural determinants of family, kinship, and inherited land shares, was the idea of political union based on contract, and ideological commitment to the 'good and ill' of the tribe, on the basis of which new members were admitted, rendering identity both fluid, and implicated in a consciousness bound up in defending the space of the tribe with the sanction of force, if necessary, against an opponent. The operation of force in fact, in sustaining the boundaries of tribalism, was mirrored with power and precision in the concept of the 'blood feud', that turned on violent revenge and retaliation as the desired medium, in which to reverse any sense of loss and damage to the tribal self, from an external agency. As all newcomers had to subscribe to the dictates of the blood feud paradigm, the tribe increasingly appeared on the surface of perception as a savage machine, making and remaking its ground in blood and battle.

In Pottinger's description the process of adding new members to restructure a tribe, usually started when a tribesman guilty of committing a crime likely to draw on himself the displeasure of the group to which he belonged, would seek to escape punishment by absconding to another part of the country, in order to seek asylum in another tribe. Such newcomers were termed *hamsayas*, and in return for accepting the corporate blood feud liability, they would be given membership and a share in the tribal lands. The inclusion of offenders in the tribal scheme, and their freedom from punishment, led Pottinger to conclude in a judgemental vein:

> "... in a society, where every man is by birth, and education a professed robber, where there are no laws to protect either property or person, it is obvious that to partial condign punishment would prove unavailing for suppression of outrage, and if every instance of the latter were visited its concomitant award, the province would soon be depopulated".[10]

In this reading of tribalism as a criminal, manic mode of existence without a moral centre, the writer was establishing a symbolic barrier between the cultured self and the savage 'other', who could be scrutinized and measured, but not accommodated in the observer's code of understanding.

The chief or *sirdar*, who presided over the tribal pyramid of sections and members, exercised what Pottinger described as despotic powers. In association with an elite inner circle of relatives known as the *sirdar khel*, that had privileged access to special shares in land and livestock, as well as rights to ceremonial dues at harvest times, marriages and births, the tribal chief concentrated in his person and status, a degree of domestic power, with which he could intimidate and impress common tribesmen. The overlapping boundaries of authority and tyranny in the status of chieftaincy, appeared to Pottinger as the sign of the arbitrary in the tribal temper, and ignorant surrender to despotic individual direction. He described how everything seemed to depend on the:

> "... caprice and temper of the heads of the various tribes composing the population; but that distinction being hereditary, and the sons being bred up with the prejudices and views of the fathers, they naturally imbibe all their principles and habits ... the measures proposed by the chiefs are more frequently adopted than those of any other advisor; this ... seems to be the result of a belief that they have had better means of judging the subjects under discussion (which are commonly connected with incursions into neighbouring districts) than any other members of the commonwealth. A similar feeling, combined with that awe and respect which the wealth and station of the head of each tribe must superinduce to a certain degree, impels those who reside under his guidance, to look to him as the arbiter of all ... disturbances among themselves".[11]

Pottinger's textualization was situating the tribal narrative in temporal structures of primitivity and error, iconically signified in the abject obedience of a silent majority, unable to exercise reason and judgement, respecting figurations of barbaric leadership, implicated primarily in promoting pure destruction.

Early travellers also recorded another dimension in the tribal apparatus, visible at the superstructural level, where Baluch and Brahuis combined to establish a confederate structure in the manner of a tribal fraternity, to establish common ground where strategic decisions were taken, battles were fought and alliances pledged to protect mutual interests. According to Masson, the Confederacy originated in the seventeenth century, when a Brahui chief named Kamber deposed the local Hindu ruler, exterminated and expelled the remaining Hindu population to establish the ruling house of Kalat. Successive chiefs like Mir Ahmed I (1665-1695) and Mir Abdullah (1750-1730) pursued raiding activities against neighbouring states like Sind to expand Kalat territorially. Later Nasir Khan I (1750-1793) acquired Quetta, and threw open the Confederacy to local Baluch tribal chiefs. This expansion was accompanied by a form of internal restructuring, that confirmed its conceptual and historical signification as an instrument of war, designed to write its evolutionary text in the language of ambition and aggression. The new inner constitution, required every member tribe to provide a quota of armed men to fight for the Confederacy, in return for which status and titles were awarded. From the start, therefore, the Confederacy seemed inclined to appropriate the language of contest and conflict, and Masson wrote that its principal occupation consisted in getting up raids against neighbouring powers.[12] The Khans of Kalat served as figure heads of the Confederacy, occupying a position more ceremonial than real, as the internal government of every member tribe remained completely under the authority of individual tribal chiefs. This effective decentring of the centre, left the Confederacy vulnerable to the caprices of individual tribal temper. As one mid-nineteenth century European traveller reflected on the nature of the Confederacy:

> "There are as many rulers as tribes: the tribal leader is at the same time hereditary administrator; the central government in its relations with the unruly chieftains, who are as prone to violence as were the Barons of England in the days of the Plantagenets, is exceedingly weak and in a great measure dependent upon the favour of the nobles of the country. This appears most conspicuously ...in the army, and in the difficulty of bridling the feudatory tribes".[13]

Structured imbalances implied that union in the Confederacy was usually episodic, expressed against a common external enemy, but likely to lapse in its absence. And the history of the Confederacy mirrored this lack, as lesser Khans after the rule of Nasir Khan I, were unable to manage political intrigues or subdue insurgent tribalism at the margins. By the time of Mehrab Khan in 1838, the Confederacy was contracting territorially, while outlying Baluch tribes like the Marris and Bugtis were virtually repudiating the authority of Kalat, by reverting to individually determined options of raiding and plundering.

The originary violence of its inception, and the subsequent violations of its historical inscriptions, situated the Confederacy on the plane of imperial representation, as a mimetic construct of the savage sensuality that signified the space of the tribe. Denys Bray, while compiling the Census of 1911, located the genesis of the Confederacy in a common fear and greed, which had its reference image in the idea of the tribe permanently at war to defend the boundaries of avarice, aggression, and anarchy. In this perception, the fragility of the Confederacy seemed to derive from its location in the idea of the negative, to protect the space of self-interest from what appeared as external and opposed to it; the absence of any higher mediating principle, ensured the collapse of the collective in fragments of disorder and dysfunction. Masson travelling in Baluchistan in 1843 noted the predominance of the fragmentary and divided, in the political arena; he wrote:

> "... the Baloch tribes have ... very distinct and jealous feelings towards each other. Between many of them blood feuds of old standing prevail, and their discords are encouraged by the Khan and his government for the sake of maintaining ascendancy over them, according to the maxim divide et impera. This policy prevents so cordial a union amongst the tribes as might endanger the Khan's authority, and enables him on the revolt of some to direct against them the resources of the other".[14]

Masson was offering a picture of deceit, discord and despair, that symbolized the fracture, and interruption of political existence, caught up in the momentary and transient, with no perceptual space for the permanence of a commonality of purpose and vision.

The tribal text, associated with the Baluch and Brahui, entered a different descriptive terrain, as it sought to negotiate the sign of Pathan tribal identity, to complete the ethnic mapping of Baluchistan. The Pathan corridor, stretching in a north-easterly arc from Quetta to the Zhob valley, was testament to a tribal history of recognition and resistance, to neighbouring imperial powers, Mughals, Persians, and finally the Afghans in the nineteenth century, to secure the boundaries of political autonomy. This defence and defiance model that shaped the narrative of Pathan experience and memory, created a mental terrain where militancy served as image and object, in the desired state of tribal being and consciousness.

The pursuit of a highly individuated freedom, was mirrored in the segmental Pathan tribal scheme, in which small local autonomous groups claimed primacy at the expense of weak, higher level organizations, so as to empower the body rather than the head of the system. Membership to such groups or *khels* was determined by patrilineal descent and agnatic kinship; co-members shared common rights in water and pastures based on agnatic lineage. These primary segments were structurally and functionally equivalent; they tended to function as economically self-sufficient groups, minimizing the need for collective exchange. Leadership was competitive and open to any contender with political ambition. Every aspiring tribal head or *khan* had to prove his competence as leader by making others follow him; he induced compliance by exerting his prowess as a warrior or spiritual leader, or a bit of both. The absence of hereditary leadership hierarchies as witnessed in the Baluch model, and the compulsion to state political authority in the idiom of aggressive conflict, distanced the Pathan even further than the Baluch and Brahui, from the norms of order and organization in imperial texts. To the imperial imaginary, the Pathan was a stranger to the predictable and readable, the archetypal 'other', which needed labelling in paradox and prejudice. As Richard Temple's Report of 1867, described:

> "Now these tribes are savages, noble savages perhaps, and not without some tincture of virtue and generosity, but still barbarians nevertheless. They have nothing approaching to government ... they are superstitious and priest ridden ... they are fierce and blood thirsty. They are never without weapons: when grazing their cattle ... when tilling the soil, they are still armed. They are perpetually at war with each other ... Reckless of the lives of others, they are not sparing of their own. They consider retaliation and revenge to be the strongest of all obligations".[15]

The ambiguity of the Pathan, thus fascinated and repelled the imperial voyeur, burdening his imagination with a sense of the savage and noble, that was impossible to reconcile.

The dramatic content of the tribal narrative was played out on the canvas of an unforgiving landscape, where the material structures of life represented permanent scarcity, that appeared to negate the scale of the human in favour of a wild, natural primitivity, eking an existence from minimal resources. Imperial gazetteers and census reports described the tribes as mainly nomadic flock owners and subsistence cultivators, scratching a living from the scattering of pasture and water resources in the land. Their few material possessions included felts for bedding, skins for holding grain and water, and wooden bowls. Purely nomadic tribes lived in mat tents made from goats' hair that could be easily transported. Permanent villages usually had less than five hundred inhabitants, who lived in squalid mud huts, where humans and livestock grouped together for shelter. The fragility of the human presence was mirrored in the low population density, varying from a mere 22 persons per square mile in Quetta to 2 persons per square mile in Chagai.[16] This imbalance of the human and inhuman in the tribalscape, that made it a tropic space of savage wilderness, reducing life to the endless sign of war and siege, acquired iconic imprint in the chieftain's armed forts. G.N.Curzon, compared the Baluch fort to a medieval European keep, "having lower walled courts and a lofty central tower with a watch tower above all".[17] The sentinel fort seemed to mirror a society permanently under siege from nature, man, culture.

The textualization of tribes and territories by Western observers was a preamble for possession, capturing views of otherness in language that implied the angle of the abnormal, the danger of distance, that had to be brought within framings of the familiar, to make the extraordinary articulate within perceptions of ideological mapping, that translated the exoticism of the unexpected in signs and symbols, that belonged to the consciousness of the knowing self. The neglected landscape, the primitivity of the tribal body, signified an emptiness, that needed imperial rewriting to restore it to history and meaning. The significance of this perception in the economy of the colonial situation, was to bring the desire for spatial appropriation, within the idea of a need, situated in the 'other', of the tribe being unable to escape primitivity, except through the mediations of imperial presence. Space extracted from the primitive, would be endowed with new purpose. As a polemicist of the time put it:

> "The subjugations of nations who are inferior in the scale of social life, is happily not always an unmixed evil – in as much as improvements are in such instances introduced in the train of the victorious army, which may go far to redeem the violation of a general right".[18]

The tribes entered this vision as subject and space of a new territorialism, imbricated in a philosophy of conquest, articulating within the symbolism of progress and purpose.

II

As the new imagined locus of imperial refiguration, the tribal space, suspended on the rim of power, overlooking the tracts of Central Asia, became the discursive site for staking out the symbolic and spatial limits of ambition and aggression. The historical context for this engagement with the tribal frontier as structure and limit, was dictated by the perceived slippages in interest and influence on the distant map of Eurasia, apprehended in the imperial mind, as the dangerous crucible, from where the spectre of an external threat to India would materialize. By the 1830s, the political geo-graphisms of eastern Europe and west Asia carried the marks of Russia's expansive text, that were decoded in British imperial readings as undesirable signs of the Tsarist dreams for oriental empire, that troubled the space of the psyche with the nightmare of loss. Doubt, suspicion, illusion and the empirically given, touched against the banks of discourse, to structure a conceptual space of hallucinatory fears and fantasies, where the enigma of Russia could be symbolically translated to mystify and mirror the predicament of power in India. The dismantling of Persian independence in particular, by the logic of Russia's south-easterly advances, provoked a rhetoric of the exterior impinging on the interior, that resignified the space of the frontier as the critical margin of history, that would empower or disempower the temporal narratives of empire making. John Macneill, British Minister in Teheran, in 1836, emphasized that the British conquest of India carried the 'sacred duty' of her defence from external attack. "For one hundred and sixty years", he claimed, "Russia has steadily kept in view the objects of ambition in the East first contemplated by Peter I, and bequeathed by him to his successors. These were to raise Russia on the ruins of Turkey ... to extend her dominions beyond the Caucasus – to domineer in Persia with a view to open the road to India"[19] and he warned, "The independence of Persia is the only apparent obstacle to the occupation of a position by Russia which would enable her to destroy in Asia, the power of the Sultan ... to threaten [India] with invasion in war – and to oppose to our maritime and commercial superiority her power to shake our empire in the East".[20] This manic image of Russia as the dreaded force of dispossession and displacement in Asia, concealed an inner meaning linked to the anxiety of loss, the eclipse of privilege and position, that Macneill wished to negate, through the rhetorical reconstruction of the Russian problem, in order to draw the British imperial boundary on Persian ground. But polemical verbalisation was unable to surmount the pessimism, that framed the reality of the Persian political view, that it was too deeply implicated in the inscriptions of Russian power, to serve the spatial remapping of the Indian empire. In India and England, the official consensus was to subtract the Persian option from the equation of imperial defence; but the phobic image of Russia was trapped in discourse, to invent the spatial and conceptual co-ordinates within which the renegotiation of imperial history could occur.

To mask the political and psychological retreat from Persia in the west, the imperial imaginary sought to invest the eastern borderlands of Afghanistan and Baluchistan with new significance, for remantling the idea of empire in configurations of permanence and power, that would reverse the signs of damage and despair, chalked in the iconography of the Russianization of west Asia. A dialogue with roads and routes entered the interiority of discourse, to map directions and dimensions of exterior space that could be manipulated, represented, remodelled, and made the object of play, possession and mastery. This active engagement with the road to conquer the pathology of 'Russophobia', brought imperial attention to the threshold of unknown space in the margins of Central Asia, Afghanistan and Baluchistan, that were now discursively represented as essential sites for linking political interests, geographical knowledge and military power. Dimensions of danger and distance met in discourse to signify the far frontier across the Indian border, as the natural place in which to defend the right to empire. As George De Lacy Evans elucidated in his book:

> "Finally, as the precariousness of our tenure of India tends unavoidably to lessen its unequalled value as a possession, so – that very insecurity and sole source of depreciation are the strongest possible reasons for vigilance in regard to its protection. And in all such cases there is a maxim, which can never of course be lost sight of with impunity; – namely, that the defence of dependencies, held by the sword rather than by the affection of the inhabitants, can only be advantageously made, in advance of their frontiers".[21]

Influenced by Evans's diagnostic writing on the perils of possession, Lord Ellenborough appointed as President to the Board of Control in India in 1827, immediately busied himself with mapping the political geography of the unexplored lands between the Caucasus and the Khyber, identified by Evans as Russia's potential military road to India. Accordingly, Arthur Connolly of the Indian Political Service was entrusted with a secret mission to map the external spaces of danger in the west and north, to make their surface texts visible and accessible to the imperial reader. In Connolly's representation the northerly route through Khiva and the Khyber Pass appeared as the space of extraordinary danger and dread, a place to be avoided rather than acquired. As a substitute route for carrying the inventory of imperial needs, he proposed the exploitation of the southerly route through Herat, Qandahar and Quetta into India. As the idea of a frontier somewhere in the mountain and desert terrains of Afghanistan and Baluchistan started to root in the imperial mind, another mission was despatched under Alexander Burnes in 1832, to explore Bukhara and Kabul, to assess the viability of invasion across the high Himalayas. Burnes confirmed fears of the Afghan passes being used as convenient inlets to invade and intimidate India, and his solution was to strengthen the Afghan kingdom under Dost Mohammad, as a political and military buffer against an external enemy. These perceptual recodings of the Indo-Afghan borderlands in terms of imperial boundaries and buffers, signified a new narrative of writing history in the space of the other. This angle of 'otherness' brought power into the interpretive, and the problematics of its architecture and articulation. As one imperial advocate, Armenius Vambery pointed out the empire would now enter the space of the barbarian and engage with such "savage and warlike elements as Beluchis, Afghans ... and others".[22] The question now, was one of model and limit; whether the desire to possess power would overpower the 'other', or tolerate a margin of distance between tribal autonomy and imperial ascendancy. S.S. Thorburn of the Bengal Civil Service, had no doubt that the "ambushing, murdering ... plundering" tribesmen could only be controlled by convincing them that the British were "their masters, and this would only be possible by the employment of large forces and constant vigilance".[23] Lord Auckland, the newly appointed Governor-General, in 1837, also led by the sign of mastery, preferred to contest the ground of the savage rather than negotiate an imperial presence. The search for a road was leading to the logic of capture and control; the anxious scan to deny Russia a route to India was metamorphosizing into a predatory blue-print to establish the imperial boundary in the Afghan-Baluch borderlands.

Persuaded by ambitious subordinates like Claude Martin Wade, Political Agent on the Sutlej, and William Hay Macnaghten his Personal Secretary, Auckland adopted a plan for deposing Dost Mohammad Khan in favour of installing the British protégé and pensionary Shah Shuja on the throne of Kabul, who would act as the stooge of British interests, allowing Afghanistan to be used as a card in the 'Great Game' with Russia. In 1839 Auckland ordered the army of the Indus to march against Afghanistan, through a southerly route across Sind, in order to implement a supplementary plan for invading and constituting Baluchistan as a bridge-head, to secure the strategic heights of dominion in Afghanistan. As the troops moved up the Indus into Baluchistan territory, the British found themselves victims of a tribal terror, expected but not experienced. Raiding bands of Marri and Bugti tribesmen attacked moving columns of men, looted supplies and destroyed lives, confirming the barbaric image of the tribesman, and the need to suppress the fear of this figure in the violence of force. The tribes now entered the descriptive terrain of imperial representation as inhuman creatures 'perpetually at war', as 'robbers' by instinct and inclination, who could be legitimately hunted, trapped and caged by imperial arms. A regiment was despatched under Major Billamore of the Bombay Army to coerce and capture the rogue tribes, and in the course of a three month campaign he was reported to have tracked and captured the Bugti Chief, and inflicted severe losses on the Marri and Bugti tribes. A.W.Hughes of the Bombay Civil Service, describing the campaign, praised the heroism of the commanding officer Captain Brown who held his forces against the 'murderous' Marris who outnumbered him for five months,[24] thereby investing the idea of the heroic in the imperial and the sign of the monster in the tribe.

The idea of the tribe as monstrous, was then linked to the notion of the sinister, to provide an ideological alibi for Auckland and Macnaghten's pre-conceived sub-text, for redrawing the political map of Baluchistan. The savagery of the tribes was now considered to have been unleashed by the treachery of Mehrab Khan, the ruler of Kalat, who had let loose the Marri-Bugti monster to terrorize the British. This charge was a pretext for removing the existing ruler, in order to appoint a British nominee Shah Nawaz as puppet ruler in Kalat. Baluchistan like Afghanistan would be spatially remapped as imperial territory, with dominion not dialogue intended for the tribal person, relegated to the bounds of the inferior and irrational, as a way of stating imperial mastery in political act and cultural inscription.

But history did not quite mirror Auckland's re-writing; the Baluchistan tribes revolted against the deposition of Mehrab Khan, and the confiscations of land that had followed, to finance imperial restructurings in Afghanistan. They appointed a new ruler Nasir Khan II in Kalat, whom the British were forced to accept, as the crisis in Baluchistan coincided with the retreat of the British army across the Indus, the rebellion of the Afghans and the return of Dost Mohammad to his kingdom, that left Auckland's political structure in ruins, with the promise of power reduced to non-meaning and error. A new British envoy, James Outram was despatched to conclude a treaty with Kalat in 1841, that regularized the succession and returned lost lands, but the British gained the right to station troops in the country and control its foreign policy. The text of the treaty signified the language of possession through dispossession, of placing the 'other' in the sign of subordination, barred from writing his own history.

The appropriation of the tribal text in the meta-narrative of empire, continued to occur in the representational space of Russian imperialism seeking always to reinvent image and identity, through new territorial inscriptions. War in the Crimea, in 1853, prolonged the sense of anxiety, in which the British continued to read the Russian problem. England fought against Russia to support Ottoman power, and save the Black Sea route to India, in the hope of shrinking the political and psychological boundaries of Tsarism's imperial reach. But a British victory in the Crimea, was not sufficient to arrest Russia's imperial gaze in the east, that carried the political vision of Russianizing the Central Asian map. Infact, the post-Crimean world emerged as the nervous site of rumours and suspicions of intrigues and covert aggression; in particular, the notion of a fresh Russian advance towards the Dardanelles, Persia and India, imprinted itself problematically on imperial minds in India, always more susceptible to imagining the dark and disturbing in the Russian picture, on account of their proximity to power. Charles Wood, President of the Board of Control, expressed concern that Russian intrigues with Persia, aimed to destabilize the tribal belt along Baluchistan's western borderlands. Proof of this, seemed evident in Persia's preparations to recover control of Herat, commanding the western approaches to India. Wood's solution was to invest imperial resources of men and money in the Khan of Kalat to make him function as an adequate buffer against Persian encroachments from the west. John Jacob, the Military Governor of Sind was entrusted with the task of adding this supplementary text to the existing script of imperial requirements already charted in Baluchistan.

For Jacob, the tribal frontier signified a fallen, meaningless world of "inferior ... vulgar, criminal and disreputable persons"[25] that required erasure and remaking within the sign of empire, drawn consciously across the body of subjection in the diagram of power and purpose, situating the idea of imperial self-hood in the terrain of boundless possession. Jacob's imperial drive manifested itself in the object language of territorial desire; he wrote, "The red line of England on the map", could only be kept, by occupying "posts in advance of it".[26] Jacob's political and predictive reading, made him an advocate for securing Quetta as part of the new treaty negotiations with Kalat, in order to secure possession of the Herat-Qandahar line of approach to India from the west. But London and Calcutta were hesitant to draw the imperial boundary at Quetta, as it would mirror a surplus of power, that might provide ground for the language of opposition from Kalat, in place of the compliance they desired. The Khan received the benefit of the doubt in the treaty of 1854, that assigned him an annual subsidy of Rs.50,000 for the purpose of maintaining an army to quell Persian inroads.

But beneath the meaning of the treaty, a structure was forming that did not resolve the ambiguity of the imperial script in Baluchistan, but determined it. In 1857, the accession of a new ruler in Kalat, Khudadad Khan, marked a reversal of the imperial cause, model and limit conceived in Baluchistan. The new ruler used the British subsidy to raise a mercenary army for deployment against the tribal chiefs, to curtail their hereditary powers and privileges, in order to extend the political base of the monarchy. He ordered the troops to fire on the assembled group of tribal chiefs, who had encircled Kalat to put pressure on the Khan to disband the army. This was the start of a long civil war that fractured the surface of tribal society, and provided the gaps, that allowed the language of external agency to invade the interiority of the tribal self, to structure its dispossession and disempowerment.

Initially the British sought to represent the crisis as the resurgence of barbaric violence, with the gestural language of tribal rebellions signifying the instinctual opposition of the savage to the idea of order and central authority. Seymour Fitzgerald, offering an interpretive of the anarchy in Baluchistan wrote:

> "... a strong government in Khelat, with some element of permanence, is impossible...for many years to come. ...On the one hand there is a population consisting of different tribes, acknowledging only the patriarchal government of their own chiefs, some of them powerful, all restless jealous of their rights and ready to uphold them by force. On the other, a central government, having as a government neither men nor money to control them ... there may be a powerful Khan, but it must always depend on the man making use of the position, and not upon the position itself. ... And ... the approach of civilization has made the Khan's position more difficult, if only by bringing into contact side by side, a strong and settled government and a weak one."[27]

In this reflection, the tribal medium was part of the representational remaking. The tribe as symbolic form and figure of the disorderly fragment, seeking to defend the discordant, deformed its space in the sign of extravagant violence, structuring its gestural language in opposition to Europe's Enlightenment dialectic of order prevailing over chaos. Fitzgerald's critical vocabulary aimed to disfigure tribalism as the pre-logical mind, willing turmoil, that was bound to negate itself in warring anarchy, when confronted by proximity to a civilized power, that threatened to overwrite its barbaric space in the language of a higher, rational political order. Based on this understanding, the British tried initially, to assist the Khan with troops and guns to crush the rebellions, to overwrite chaos in the sign of order, and create a native figure of central authority, who would provide a front for renegotiating tribal space in the political language of imperial discipline, to erase the significations of the barbaric. But the reading was a misreading, for the tribes opted to prolong the story of anarchic agony in the defiant language of violations, that suggested a reality regressing into darkness and despair.

Imperial misgivings mounted as the story of crises on the tribal frontier, was repeated inside British India, in the sign of the Mutiny of 1857, that brought to surface the pessimism and despair of the imperial experience. Rhetoric mirrored the anguish of the imperial mood. Charles Kingsley, the writer, confided to a friend: "I can think of nothing but these Indian massacres. The moral problems they involve make me half wild. Night and day the heaven seems black to me".[28] Charles Dickens wrote that he wished to be commander-in-chief of India, only so that he could impress on the 'oriental' race that he would do his utmost to "exterminate the Race upon whom the stain of the late cruelties rested".[29] The Mutiny was physically crushed but not emotionally erased. For the British in India, distrust, doubt and increasing alienation created a sense of distance with the native, signifying racial exclusion and negative difference. Mistrust and insecurity would chart the course of polemics and policy in the decades after the Mutiny.

The palette of inner fears locked with external anxieties, as the event horizon of the northwest resignalled the dread of Russia resurrecting her vision of hegemony in Asia, at the very time that the Indian frontier was slipping into the chaos of tribal warfare. In Baluchistan, the Khan of Kalat had escalated the conflict, by confiscating the revenue free holdings of the tribal chiefs; this led to renewed violence and the complete paralysis of the Sind-Punjab frontier, and closure of the Bolan Pass to merchant traffic. The language of tribal insurgency now induced a perceptual reversal, forcing imperial observation to retreat from its imagined reality of the Khan serving as the mark and mask of power. A new reading was required to reappropriate the tribal sign in the conceptual ground of imperial meaning and making. The gap between the expected and real, in the figure of the Khan creating the chaos he had been expected to curb, led Lord Mayo, the Viceroy to observe in 1871 that the money poured into Baluchistan had "produced very poor fruit".[30] Others now urged the imperialisation of tribal space, as the only cure for the tribal malady of dysfunction and atrocity. Colonel R.B.Phayre, Political Superintendent of the Upper Sind Frontier, introduced a prophetic note in the picture, by suggesting that the surface anarchy in Baluchistan offered a "natural opening for us to interpose with our good offices".[31] The idea of 'good' concealed the agenda of control, with intervention intended to serve as the political preface for a text of absorption.

In a more practical vein, Robert Sandeman, Deputy Commissioner of Dera Ghazi Khan, was already exploiting the gap created in the breach between the Khan and the rebels, to insert an imperial text in the tribal narrative. Faced with large scale Marri raids on the south Punjab frontier in 1866, Sandeman captured and detained their chief as hostage, until he agreed to take a subsidy in return for providing tribal levies, who would protect, not attack the frontier. This arrangement secured peace on the Punjab frontier, and impressed Lord Mayo sufficiently, for him to transfer complete control of the Marri-Bugti tribes to Sandeman in 1871. A sum of Rs.32,040 was left to Sandeman to distribute among the tribes for levy service, under the name of the Khan of Kalat. The distortions of this restructuring created a web of illusion and reality, with the Khan now merely appearing to rule, while Sandeman was actually grasping the real reins of power. Encouraged by success Sandeman opened an independent dialogue with the rebel chiefs in Baluchistan, to signal support for their schismatic inscriptions, as a way of reconstructing the tribal narrative to carry the imprint of his own medial significance as the arbiter of tribal history. Rumour and innuendo now pointed to Sandeman as an advocate of tribal conflict for the purpose of "ultimately getting charge of the country".[32]

The tribes colluded in Sandeman's purpose of remaking their political ground, by announcing in the aftermath of recent gains south of Quetta, that they would cease their opposition only if there was a British mediated settlement between themselves and the Khan. Through this surrender of the self to imperial dictation, the tribes were writing their own inadequacy and dependency into history, carving their image in the negativity desired and demanded by imperial imaginings. In response, Lord Mayo summoned Sind and Punjab officials to a conference in Jacobabad in 1872, to frame a settlement that would restructure Baluchistan within imperial conceptual margins. The new terms required the Khan to restore all confiscated lands back to the tribal chiefs, in return for which he would receive their allegiance again, and receive one lakh of rupees as compensation from the British. As the Treaty defended the boundaries of chiefly power more than that of the monarch, it signified the marginalization of the Khan in the evolving imperial text, leaving him politically stranded as an obsolete relic of mistaken readings. The Khan sensitive to the abandonment implied in the new imperial script moved into a position of oppositional defiance. He offered his allegiance to the Amir of Afghanistan, and internally started a war of attrition against the British, by reducing the frontier to chaos through savage raids and indiscriminate plundering; the Jacobabad Settlement was virtually buried in this anarchy, the British Agent was withdrawn from Kalat, and by 1874 there were official demands for the Khan's deposition.

As the tribal map splintered in Baluchistan, leaving imperial interests suspended in the space of the unknown and unresolved, the political picture in Central Asia added to the margin of anxiety, by circulating images of Russia engaging with, and acquiring mastery over tribes and terrains stretching from the mouth of the Sir Darya to TransCaspia. By 1876, the steppe country of the Kazakhs as well as the Khanates of Khiva, Bokhara and Khokand were designed into the imperial landscape of Tsarist Russia. As the independence of Central Asia melted into fiction, the British engaged with the spectacle of Russian power, from the ambivalent ground of fear and fascination. The text of Russian imperialism became the symbolic point of destination and departure for the British imaginary. To enter the high ground of oriental empire, the British would have to mimic and menace the Russian model, suppress the interiority of doubt and disbelief, to remake a verbal and visual reality that would represent image and intention in desired structures of dominance and determination.

Disraeli, the newly elected Conservative British Prime Minister in 1874 uncovered a script that adequated ambition to actuality, as it coded image and inscription to restate the empire in an imaginative exteriorisation of power, refiguring its space as the critical medium of self-representation and definition in the sign of history and providence. In this remapping, the in-between space separating Tsarist Russia from British India, metamorphosized into the object of imitative desire. Polemic and policy shaping the political drawing of the Indian frontier and beyond, mirrored the immense rebus of desire, that created the determinate web of aspirations to acquire what the rival possessed, by copying and contesting his object language, to win the same symbols of power in an ambiguous game, that sought to re-invent its ground in illusions of mastery, that separated and united truth and appearance. Language as suspicion and negation, created surfaces of disquiet, that reflected Russia as the oppositional other, oppressing the self and its sense of space and time, by evolving new margins of fear through territorial inscriptions, that threatened displacement, and decentring for British imperialism in the east. Thus, the appearance of the Russians at Khiva in 1873, was read as the annihilation of distance, as the beginning of the undesirable proximity of powers, that would disturb and disfigure the iconography of the imperial landscape, north west of India. Imperial discourse concluded that the Russianization of Khiva, marked the end of the informal understanding, that the River Oxus should be the dividing line between the British and Russian empires; in future the imperial frontiers would be limitrophe, as the "semi-barbarous tribes", in the intervening space were destined "to come more or less under Russian or British control".[33] Reading the psychology of the Russian advance, it was further predicted, that Russia would soon move against Merv, a dependency of Khiva, and then slip into Herat the 'half-way house' to India, thereby confirming the spectral shape of Russophobia, that haunted the interiority of British imperial imaginings. Disraeli proposed to reverse the negative neurosis of Russophobia by proposing the substitute script of the imperialism of the same, with the Indian empire reflecting the mirror image of its Russian counterpart, and sited in an ideology of power that would serve as reply and response to the conquering gestures of the rival. As he put it in Parliament:

> "Whatever may be my confidence in the destiny of England, I know that empires are only maintained by vigilance, by firmness, by courage by understanding the temper of the times, and by watching those significant indications that may be easily observed. Russia knows full well that there is no reason why we should view the natural development of her empire in Asia with jealousy as long as it is clearly made by the Government of this country that we are resolved to maintain and strengthen both materially and morally our Indian empire, and not merely do that, but also uphold our legitimate influence in the East".[34]

Disraeli was clearly pressing for a type of imperial imaging, that would address the issue of primacy from the high summits of power and prestige, relaying back to Russia its own vertiginious vision of empire making. Without this clear signal to Russia of Britain's imperial intent, Disraeli warned that the nation would find itself reduced to "grumbling and growling" without ever taking action, forever vulnerable to the emergence of the Russian apparition in some "dangerous, unprecedented form".[35]

This diary of Russian designs that had been in the making for most of the nineteenth century, provided the context for writing a text of appropriation in the margin, where Central Asia touched India, bringing its tribes and territories within the orbit of desire, for playing the 'Great Game' with Russia on the exotic heights of the high Himalayas and the depths of sandy deserts. The reciprocal character of this game, animated by negative imitation and the desire to be another, implied that the players were opposed but alike, and even interchangeable for they made exactly the same movements. As Russian space moved closer to British India, the game of power and possession was played out in the anguish of envy and obsession that sharpened the edges of desire and despair. Henry Rawlinson, Member of the India Council 1868-1895, voiced the discontent of the imperial mood. Prophesying the inevitability of the contested frontier space being crushed between its 'two colossal neighbours', he urged its immediate annexation to the Indian empire. "It seems impossible", he wrote "that holding India, we should permit Russia to dominate over our entire frontier, or that we should tolerate beyond the Indus a chronic state of anarchy, bloodshed and rapine; I am constrained to believe in the ultimate reannexation of

Afghanistan".[36] Rawlinson's representation of Russia and the frontier in the vocabulary of crisis to legitimate the concept of conquest, signified the fear and fury of desire seeking to possess possession, by excluding the rival other from the space of the self. This idea of exclusion became the central polemic in imperialism's discursive containment of Russia, but the desired space of the self was subject to re-definition. Salisbury, the Secretary of State for India, preferred a more symbolic reading of Russia's new territorial imprints in Central Asia; locating their significance in the field of ideology and image, he suggested that they did not spell any sinister physical danger to India. Instead of drawing the imperial boundary in far away Herat or Afghanistan, that was beyond the reach of the real, Salisbury chose Quetta as the new forward line of the Indian map. In Salisbury's mind, the actual defensible space of the self was not to be sacrificed to the space of illusion and imagination, in which others like Rawlinson wished to invest the imperial idea. As he pointed out, Quetta dominated the approach routes to India from Herat and southern Afghanistan; it was close to India itself for adequate military cover; and it would serve as a metaphor for power, reinvesting the sign of empire in the language of aggression, appropriation and action. For Salisbury, the symbolism of imperialising Quetta was the critical meaning of his text; through this representation of reality, he hoped to verbalise the duel with the rival, conduct a confrontation in pen and paper, to avoid the pain of war and loss. He was playing out the Victorian cold war with Russia as a competitor not a conqueror, in the space of the Asiatic 'other', that could be legitimately written over in the object language of European egos, seeking to reinvent the Orient in the myth and mirror of empire making, to affirm the primacy of the category of the West.

To implement his imperial point of view, Salisbury directed Northbrook, the Indian Viceroy to be as ready for a march to Quetta as the Prussians were for a march to Paris.[37] Northbrook himself did not equate Russia with danger; as he put it: "I feel no alarm so far as the safety of India is concerned. I don't expect that we shall have to encounter another Xerxes, or leave our bones in an Afghan Thermopylae".[38] But he was under pressure to act, not just from Salisbury, but official opinion in India, which preferred to see the signs of the ominous and oppressive in Russia. The Governor of Bombay mirrored this inner haunting, by merging the image of tribal chaos on the Baluchistan frontier, with the menacing picture of Russia advancing towards India, to suggest the horror of the imperial predicament, facing in the same time and space, fears of barbaric destruction, and the threat of external invasion. "Is it wise", he asked, "considering the progress of events in Central Asia, that the country immediately before us, should be torn by factions, and be the prey of the first strong power that should choose to seize it".[39]

Northbrook under pressure to counter the disturbing implications of the Russian/tribal story emerging on and across the Indian borders, chose the political alternative of British mediation to arrest the slippage of power, and restore the sense of control in imperial consciousness. Robert Sandeman, who had already successfully controlled the Baluch tribes on the Punjab frontier, was selected as the man to head the mission to Baluchistan, with the purpose of transferring the Marri-Bugti and Bolan tribes from Kalat's jurisdiction to British control, and structuring informal British adjudicating control to regulate tribal disputes. But Sandeman had no military force to back his mission, the extent of his political authority was not clearly defined, and the Khan of Kalat perceiving in Sandeman an adversary not an ally, exploited the ambiguities of the mission to stay aloof from negotiating any terms of settlement with the British. Sandeman was forced to return on a negative note, and Northbrook attempting to save the credibility of the idea of the mission, instituted a second one, this time supported by military force, and

Sandeman's status as the Viceroy's Agent clearly stated. This was the Viceroy's last act to rewrite the text of crisis with that of control, for he resigned soon afterwards, and the story of the new mission unfolded in the wake of the new religion of empire and nation preached by Disraeli and Salisbury.

The appointment of the volatile Earl of Lytton as the new Viceroy in 1874, signified the time of a new imperiality imagining its space in the extravagance of possession, and the restless urge to always transcend the boundaries of the actual by perceptual destinations, that signalled from the distances of desire and destiny. As Disraeli put it, the choice of Lytton was a symbolic gesture. "Had it been a routine age", he explained to Salisbury, "We might have made ... a more prudent selection, but we ... wanted a man of ambition, imagination, some vanity and much will and we have got him".[40] Lytton's perspectival reality signified the physiography of high Victorian imperialism. He came to India, handcuffed to a metaphysical reverence for empire, that sought to space self and identity in the desire of the other, by the elision of person and place. For him, Russian progress menaced imperial rule and its political summit. As he put it, his ambition was not merely one of "scratching the back of Russian Power, but of driving it clean out of Central Asia".[41] In this perspectivism, imperial existence called into being in relation to a rival 'otherness', structured a demand reaching out for the place of the other, that became the basis for a desired identity and image. The legitimacy of this remaking was sought on the psychological ground of fear and loss. Inaction against Russia, Lytton prophesied would confine imperial space in the tropic landscape of dread and danger where negation ruled; for "Hindoos as well as Mahomedans, both within and without our frontier", he claimed "will despise our power, and gravitate to the stronger Raj. ... the Government of India will probably find itself swimming in a bath of blood, and we shall require every armed man we can keep for the protection of our own throat".[42] The structure of attitudes and references, that made this hallucinatory landscape of fear imminent, was in Lytton's view, linked to the errors of perception connoted in the old 'Masterly Inactivity' theory, which had imprisoned the empire on the line of the Indus, abandoning the vantage points of initiative and aggression to the adversaries of British India. In Lytton's interpretive, the hesitancies and ambiguities of frontier imperialism over past decades, were signs of "a bourgeois policy" that had been "timid without being really prudent, and disingenuous without being really astute".[43] To reverse this sign of paralysis, Lytton exploited the psychologism of paranoia and power to insert new life in the imperial text.

Lytton's discourse sought to map the spaces possible for language to appropriate, in order to resignify the idea of empire as historical presence and providential will. As he wrote:

> "We know that the approach of the two great rival Powers in Central Asia has continued uninterruptedly for two centuries, and has made progress at an ever accelerating rate as if governed by the laws of attraction that rule material bodies. We know that the conditions which govern the relations of civilization and barbarism are unchangeable, and that every cause which has acted in past times to compel the advance of ourselves and Russia continues to act with undiminished force... Therefore we can calculate, as certainly as we calculate on the succession of the seasons ... that within ... less than a generation ... England and Russia will be conterminous in the East."[44]

This was the vision of vanity feeding on the inevitability of the idea of empire in shaping human history, and overwriting the space of the lesser and inferior in the language of dominance and dependence. Lytton's permanent anticipation of two contesting fields of rivalry, in which the imperial subject strives to transcend its insufficiencies, through the maturation of power in an exteriority, in which the form is more aspired than achieved, established in the defence of the imperial ego, the lure of spatial identification, and the phantasmic permanence of the mental I seeking its "lofty, remote inner castle"[45] of total ascendancy. This imagining, pregnant with correspondences of self and mastery, situated its narrative realization in the obsessive repression and recovery of space that constituted the object of desire. These connotations of self, space and desire implied a need and negation of the 'other', to empower structures of possession and dispossession. This imaginary perception, acting as a temporary dialectic of power, conceived the empire as a totality, emerging from the assimilation and absorption of fragmentary 'otherness', and particles of difference existing outside the identity of the self. In this remaking, there was no space for alterity, only the coercion of ideology ruled to represent the self in desired images of authority and identity.

Applying the concept to the concrete, Lytton was candid in his appraisal of the tribal gap, still separating British India from Russian Central Asia. In his aporetic vision, the tribes were physically present, but culturally absent; tribal territory was abstracted from history and divorced of meaning, and read as a metaphor for the empty, the silent and insignificant, waiting for imperial inscription to bring it within the spatial and temporal structures of the relevant, the rational and the real. As Lytton stated: "Potentates such as the Khan of Khelat, or the Amir of Cabul, are mere dummies or counters, which would be of no importance to us, were it not for the costly stakes we put upon them in the great game for empire which we are now playing with Russia".[46] Lytton would only condescend to consider tribal entities if they served the object language of empire making. This imperialism of the self, could only occur in the annihilation of distance and difference, that marked the space of the other. Captive to his own concepts, Lytton was unable to engage with the tribal world in its specific situational context, or to place the tribal sign in any position, other than that of a mere sub-text in the meta-narrative of empire. As he explained:

> "...in our present situation there is no such thing as an Afghan question, or a Khelat question. These have become mere departments of the great and anxious Russian question. The question is not a local, but an imperial one, not an Indian but a British one."[47]

The rhetorical appropriation of the tribal in the imperial, provided a preface for its empirical realization. Foregrounding the imperial perspective in his intended restructuring of the frontier, Lytton wanted to prioritize the control and coercion of the Afghans who were "ruled by a barbarian chief," and consistently guilty of addressing "the government of a great empire in ... terms of disregard".[48] Unwilling to tolerate the impudence of the inferior, and aspiring to substitute deference for defiance, in order to redefine Afghanistan in the model of colonial subservience, Lytton wanted to send a mission to Kabul, to force the Amir to accept the presence of British troops on his lands. In case the Amir did not comply, the negation of the mission would be screened by a secondary mission to Baluchistan, to institute forms of control in that country, which would "clip his claws"[49] effectively. In Lytton's reading, the subjection of the Afghans would address the problem of tribal compliance, deny the Russians access to the high Afghan passes leading to India, and create a new spatial margin for imperial power. But Lytton was unable to test his scheme, as Northbrook the departing Viceroy remained firm on the idea of intervention in Baluchistan first, and would not recall the second mission he had sanctioned under Sandeman's leadership. Lytton was also under pressure from Salisbury to give primacy to the Baluchistan mission, which he visualised as the "father of the Central Asian mission of the future", that would provide the opening for "English rupees to try conclusions with Russian roubles in the *zenana* and *divan*".[50] "The doctrine of non-intervention in Baluchistan," he emphasized to Lytton, "had been carried a great deal too far. It is absolutely necessary for our safety that it should be peaceful and dutiful. If Beloochistan is well in hand, the importance of the Amir to us is terribly diminished".[51] Salisbury was reining back imperial spatial boundaries from Lytton's extravagant siting in the Afghan hills, but he was also proposing a perspectivism implicated in the displacement of the 'other' to secure access to an image of identity that would signify new heights of power and purpose.

Lytton reluctantly consented to the start of Sandeman's second mission to Baluchistan in the spring of 1876. The time of this new mission was Sandeman's moment to write the tribal chapter into imperial history, and establish the boundaries of licence and leadership, within which he could structure the realms of personal power. His intended remaking, coincided with the expressed reality of an inner surrender in tribal consciousness. The sign of this tribal retreat from the mental reaches of autonomy and the sovereign self, was visible in a communication from the tribal chiefs to Sandeman, which read: "If you wish to settle the country, you must either annex it or depose the Khan".[52] Psychologically the tribes were poised to capitulate; decades of internal war had led to negative self-assessment and a crisis in confidence, that created a want for external mediation to resolve inner fragmentation. The battered tribal psyche was colluding in the creation of the 'master-slave' dialectic that legitimated the imperial power principle. With tribal consent, Sandeman stripped the Khan of real power, by decreeing that in future the British government, would assist Kalat to maintain control in a manner consistent with the rights of his subjects. Additionally the tribal chiefs were to be treated as a separate group in their relations with imperial authority, and their privileges protected. Moving to the next stage, Sandeman issued a proclamation in August 1876, formalizing the text of tribal submission to British power. It proclaimed the Government of India as a permanent court of appeal in all civil, financial and revenue cases between tribesmen and themselves. Both Lytton and Salisbury objected to Sandeman's overt negation of tribal independence, and the conspicuous substitution of British power in the place of native authority. Lytton was perturbed by fears that the ostentatious inscription of British power in Baluchistan would make the Amir hostile, and complicate Kabul's redefinition as the forward point of British imperial influence. Further, he was caught between the desire to parade the phenomenon of tribal submission, and his instinctual withdrawal from any close engagement with the primitive, the tribal and inferior in human ontology. As he wrote to Sandeman:

> "I have no objection to the reaffirmation and recognition of the barbarous rights of these Khelat *Sirdars* ... because ... the *Sirdars* constitute at the present moment, a powerful British party at Khelat whose confidence it would be very imprudent to alienate. But you must bear in mind ... that ... in such a state as Khelat the intervention of a government such as ours cannot consistently with its dignity, be more frequent or more trivial, than that of *deus ex machina* in a Greek drama, whose intervention is confined to great occasions and exerted for great purposes".[53]

Lytton's equation of tribal alterity with inferiority, symbolized in the fear of contact and contamination with the lowly, mirrored the tensions of the imperial self desiring to master its opposite, and at the same time wishing to exclude it from the space of interiority and perspectival self-imaging. This ambiguity made imperial identity the place of splitting, between the real and unreal, mystifying the self in fables and fantasies of assumed superiority.

Lytton's wish to structure intervention in a manner that would limit tribal demands on imperial time and attention, that could be better expended in engaging with higher subject matters of empire making, led him to instruct Sandeman to revise the text of imperial involvement, scaling down its degree and direction. Salisbury agreed with Lytton, that imperial writing in Baluchistan should be guarded, discreet, suggestive not of intimacy but merely a response to an exterior crisis, marginal to the empire. The Secretary of State was attempting to mask the move, to signify it in terms of what it was not, as defensive armoury against possible Russian antagonism at this new sign of imperial reconstitution. Under pressure, Sandeman rephrased the terms of control, to reduce the verbal presence of the Government of India, without actually contracting the actual measure of political control. He revised the text, substituting the term 'Political Agent' in the place of 'Government of India',[54] leaving the Agent as the final arbiter in tribal political space. A permanent military presence to support the inner chart of power, with continuing control over Kalat's external affairs, confirmed the imperial imprint in strategic areas of tribalism, signifying ends and beginnings, the eclipse of autonomy and the start of abjection. To mask the text of conquest, Lytton instructed Sandeman to obtain a tribal request for British military occupation in Baluchistan, so that the empire would not seem to be oppressing a "reluctant and helpless prince".[55] In this imaging, the truth was masked in make-belief, to mirror the myth of the moral, as the imperialist sought cover while taking over, appropriating not just territory, but the means of perceiving such appropriation. On 26 December 1876, Sandeman's revised proclamation became the basis of a new Treaty, which was signed by Lytton and the Khan of Kalat at Jacobabad.

III

The symbolic and spatial touching of imperial and tribal frontiers occurred on the representational ground of the exotic, the exterior and the excluded. Early exploratory suppositions had discovered in Baluchistan an alien frontier of the savage 'other', making its iconic landscape a pathological world of hallucinatory fears, dominated by threats of bestiality, and the signs of predatory, murderous instincts. This landscape of unreason had to be suppressed, and structured in the language of imperial representational remaking, to construct the narrative of self and space in the place of difference and divergence. The appropriation of the tribe in the idea of the barbaric, was an originary gesture of exclusion that determined the structure of imperial historicity. The conceptual siting of the tribe outside the boundaries of permitted norms, allowed the ideology of intervention to masquerade as the ethics of redemptive rewriting in the space of the immoral. It mirrored the slippage of morality into history and politics to place the 'other' in structures of meaning and making, that corresponded to the imperial representational presentation of tribal reality as error that needed erasure, to bring it within the margin of what was acceptable and normal to the self. In this imaging of the tribe, the negative was foregrounded and pressed into ideological service, to assist the reduplication of the self in terrains that belonged to another.

If the tribe as text symbolized the sign of the savage 'other' which had to be reduced to servility, the narrative of Tsarism mirrored the image of the rival 'other,' to be mimicked more than mastered. The temporal and spatial structures of the second imaging, dictated the moment and manner of engagement with the first plane of representation denoting the tribe. The rival 'other', perceived within the dominant experience of anxiety, mirrored the surface realities of despair, desire and destiny. It led to the search for an image, as the appurtenance to power, in the space of the exterior, situated in the tribal gap still separating the two empires, that now metamorphosized into the site of meaning and making, the object of desire and space of destiny. The symbolics of spatial rewriting here, transcended the limits of the purely empirical, to signify in the abstract, a metaphysical dividing line, between rival passions, envy and anguish. As the Duke of Argyll put it, the inner meaning of the projected geographical line of separation, was bound up in its perception as "the boundary line of our jealousy, as well as of Russian aggression".[56] This perspectival connotation, mirrored the distortions of desire, seeking to be another, striving to annex the surface realities of imaged ascendancy, to world the self in the consciousness of power, that would duplicate the text of impression and intent associated with the other. In this mimetic rewriting, empire making was played out in the optics of the 'Great Game' with Russia, in which the language of rhetorical opposition was consumed by the symmetry of imperial desires. As a Russian newspaper *The Voix*, put it: "The real object of Russia in Central Asia ... is precisely the same as that pursued by England on the other half of the continent".[57] The identity of opposites in the 'Great Game', laid bare not adversaries of opposed ideas, theories and systems, but merely players absorbed in mimicking language, image and character, that mapped the boundaries of discourse and desire in which the game occurred. Tribal space entered this game, as the human playing field, across whose primitive body, the inscription of European empire making could be written, as fable and fantasy of the authorial dream.

NOTES

1. Quoted in J.W.Kaye, *Life and Correspondence of Major-General Sir John Malcolm*, Vol. II, p. 455.
2. Quoted in George DeLacy Evans, *On the Practicability of an Invasion of British India*, pp. 13-14.
3. T.H. Holdich, *The Indian Borderland*, p. 104.
4. R.Hughes Buller, *Imperial Gazetteer of India*, Baluchistan, p. 3.
5. T.H.Holdich, *The Indian Borderland*, p. 103.
6. Dufferin to Count Corti, 31 December 1887, *Dufferin Collection*, MSS.Eur.F.130/26, Vols. D&F.
7. D.Bray, *The Brahui Language*, Part II, p. 10.
8. H.Pottinger, *Travels in Beelochistan and Scinde*, p. 58.
9. C.H. Masson, *Narratives of a Journey through Kalat*, p. 420.
10. H. Pottinger, *op.cit*, p. 314.
11. *Ibid.*, pp. 313-314.
12. Quoted in R. Southey, *Gazetteer of Baluchistan*, 1891, pp. 53-55.
13. E. Schlogintweint, *Kelat the Brahui Kingdom on the Southern Border of Iran* 1876, p.9, L/P&S/20/B.297.
14. C. H. Masson, *op.cit.*, pp. 419-420.
15. Extract from R.Temple's Report on the Independent Tribes of the North-west Frontier of India, quoted in T.H.Thornton's *Memorandum*, of 18 November 1867, *Parliamentary Papers*, Afghanistan, 1878-79, L/Parl/2/88, p. 27.
16. *Baluchistan Census Report* 1901, p. 9.
17. G.N. Curzon, *Persia and the Persian Question*, Vol. 2, p. 260.
18. G. DeLacy Evans, *On the Designs of Russia*, pp. 55-56.
19. John Macneill, *Progress and Present Position of Russia in the East*, Third Edition, pp. v-vi.

20. *Ibid.*, p. 107.
21. G. DeLacy Evans, *On the Designs of Russia*, p. 23.
22. Armenius Vambery, *Western Culture in Eastern Lands*, p. 154.
23. S.S. Thorburn, *Asiatic Neighbours*, p. 128.
24. A.W. Hughes, *The Country of Balochistan*, p. 117 & p. 120.
25. J.Jacob, *Memorandum on Sind Frontier Proceedings Since 1846*, 9 August 1854, Quoted in *Frontier and Overseas Expeditions from India*, Vol. III, p. 49.
26. J.Jacob, *Memorandum of Proposed Arrangements in case of a British Force Being Stationed at Quetta*, 1856, *Parliamentary Papers*, Central Asia, 1878-1879, Vol.77, p. 122.
27. G.S.V.Fitzgerald, *Minute* 16 March 1875, *Political and Secret Correspondence with India*, L/P&S/7/1.
28. Quoted in B.J. Moore-Gilbert, *Kipling and Orientalism* p. 75.
29. *Ibid.*, p. 76.
30. Mayo to Fitzgerald, 25 November 1871, *Mayo Papers*, ADD.MSS.7490, No.268, Vol.45.
31. R.B. Phayre to Merewether, 20 October 1869, *Baluchistan Blue Book* I.
32. Report by Naib of Dadur to the Khan of Kalat, quoted in Fitzgerald's *Memorandum on Khelat*, 16 March 1875, *Political and Secret Correspondence with India*, L/P&S/7/1.
33. Northbrook to L.Mallet, (private), 7 June 1874, *Northbrook Papers*, MSS. Eur.C.144/22.
34. Disraeli, Debate House of Commons, May 1876, T.C.Plowden *Precis of Correspondence relating to Affairs in Central Asia, Baluchistan and Persia*, 1875-1877, pp. 87-88.
35. *Ibid.*
36. H.C.Rawlinson, *Memorandum on the Reorganisation of the Western and Northwestern Frontier*, 28 July 1877, *Political and Secret Memoranda*, L/P&S/18/A17.
37. Salisbury to Northbrook (private), 17 July 1874, *Northbrook Papers*, MSS.Eur.C.144/11.
38. Northbrook to Mallet, 31 May 1874, *Northbrook Papers* MSS.Eur.C.144/22.
39. G.S.V. Fitzgerald, *Memorandum on Khelat, op.cit.*
40. W.F. Monypenny and G.F.Buckle, *Life of Benjamin Disraeli*, Vol 2, p.1251.
41. Lytton to F.Haines, 10 December 1876, *Lytton Papers* MSS.Eur.E.218/18.
42. Lytton to Salisbury, 17 May 1877, *Lytton Papers*, MSS. Eur.E.218/11.
43. Lytton to Lord George Hamilton, (private), 3 June 1876, *Lytton Papers*, MSS.Eur.E.218/18.
44. *Minute by the Viceroy (Lord Lytton) on The Progress of England and Russia in the East*, 4 September 1878, *Parliamentary Papers*, Afghanistan, 1881, Vol.70, Part I, p. 151.
45. Jacques Lacan, *Ecrits*, p. 5.
46. Lytton to Sandeman, 29 September 1876, *Lytton Papers* MSS.Eur.E.218/18.
47. Lytton to Salisbury, (private) 2 June 1876, *Lytton Papers*, MSS.Eur.E.218/18.
48. Lytton to Salisbury, 5 June 1876, *Lytton Papers*, MSS.Eur.E.218/18.
49. Lytton to Disraeli, 16 July 1876, *Lytton Papers*, MSS.Eur.E.218/18.
50. Salisbury to Lytton, undated, *Lytton Papers*, MSS.Eur.E.218/3B.
51. Salisbury to Lytton, (private), 5 May 1876, *Lytton Papers*, MSS.Eur.E.218/3A.

52. Quoted in Lytton to Salisbury, 12 June 1876, *Lytton Papers*, MSS.Eur.E.218/18.
53. Lytton to Sandeman, 29 September 1876, *Lytton Papers*, MSS.Eur.E.218/18.
54. *Ibid.*
55. *Ibid.*
56. Argyll to Northbrook, 9 March 1874, *Northbrook Papers*, MSS. Eur.C.144/9.
57. Cited in T.C.Plowden, *op.cit.*, p. 12.

2

Form and Transformation: The Genesis of British Baluchistan and the Semantics of Boundary Making, 1876-1905

Placing the Indian border on Baluchistan, had implied the promise of allowing the British to reinvent the idea of empire in the sign and symbol of expansion, energy and experiment. But the text was always vulnerable to inner and external perceptions of disquiet, which forced revisions and restatements on the making and meaning of the imperial narrative. The dystopia of loss, the chronic search for an authorial voice in the unstable annexes of alien rule, encouraged the polemical recourse to a range of tropes, conceptual categories, and logical arguments, to emphasize the gestures of imperial dominion and definition. Tribes and territories were descriptively appropriated, to locate the sign of empire in a rhetoric of comparison and conquest, that invested tribalism with savagery and negativism, to make it bear the moral weight of imperial discourse, to open both an ideological and political space for the desired mappings of imperialism to take shape and structure.

The narratives of late nineteenth century imperialism signified in political styles, structures of imagery and ideological values the self-consciousness of a time. Issues of destiny, society and direction were fused in historicizing codes of discursive writing, that placed the category of the human and history, within the phenomenal definition of man in terms of the experiencing self defined against the other. This stance involving otherness, distance, limitation, on the basis of which a structure, a logical discourse was sutured, served in the colonial context to establish the myth of a white supremacist history, from which the colonized object was excluded ontologically for having few of the merits of the conquering, surveying, and civilized outsider. Hegel's unchanging Orient, Darwin's combative manifesto for genius as genesis, and social genesis at that, sustained the premises of Eurocentrism in writing history and culture, as the totality of a single universal text, denying the presence of other histories and other meanings. In this totalizing text, meaning worked through a form of metonomy, distinguishing between elements in terms of significance and insignificance, establishing the criteria for defining man according to categories of civilization and primitivism and their relation to history. This historicism provided the critical conceptual space, within which imperialism imagined its narrative ground in tribal Baluchistan. The permanent siting of the tribe in the interior of the savage, was political imaging drawn on the logic of an exterior controlling intention. As R.I.Bruce, when serving as political officer in Baluchistan, judged that for the Baluch: "Independence means bloodshed, desolation, risk and danger in every shape and form, and in the interests of peace and civilisation it is absolutely essential that they be brought under some paramount power".[1] Here the disfiguring and appropriative power of rhetoric, served the needs of imagery, that sought to conquer the space of the other with exclusionary and derisive structures of representation, to empower its resignification as the space of suppression, where the threat of primitivity was to be expropriated by the coercions of imperial command. The Earl of Onslow, Under Secretary of State for India, put it in Parliament, that historically it was the destiny of the tribes to be "absorbed in the great States that have grown up around them. I do not think any of us would predict any other destiny for the barbarous tribes of our North West Frontier".[2] This totalizing concept of history, working within the determined ethnocentricity of a Western imperial consciousness, could only create its meaning by excluding heterogeneity as signs of the undesirable and uncivilized, signifying the predicament of culture, not its purpose and promise. As Claude Levi-Strauss has pointed out:

> "And so we end up in the paradox of a system which invokes the criterion of a historical consciousness as a means for distinguishing the 'primitive' from the 'civilized' but—contrary to its claim – is itself ahistorical. It offers not a concrete image of history, but an abstract schema of men making history of such a kind that it can manifest itself in the trend of their lives as a synchronic totality ... history plays exactly the part of a myth".[3]

The tribal text in Baluchistan was read within these imaginary significations of history, in which the mythic and the empirical leaned on each other, to reangle the geometry of tribalism, to create new configurations of imperial spatiality, as the affirming symbol and statement of a homogeneous temporality.

I

Imperialising Quetta in 1876, was a form of metaphoric translation of the late nineteenth century search for space, that claimed the geography of another to write the history of the self. As Lytton expressed it, Quetta had revised the old premises of imperial structuring, and foregrounded the issue of engaging or disengaging with the tribal frontier as the locus and medium of a new architecture of power. Describing the trans-Indus tribal zone reaching to the Afghan border as a "broad belt of practically independent barbarism", Lytton elaborated that the "main question whether its chiefs and tribes shall constitute a bulwark to our power, or a thorn on our side, mainly depends on whether the predominant influence over them is exercised from Cabul or ... by ourselves".[4] The use of the barbaric label, signified both image and intent. In one sense it connotated through mimetic imagery "the vast, menacing, stupid powers of nature"[5] alluded to in Northrop Frye's archetype of the transrational primitive world, that exuded the threat of collapsing civilization. Additionally, the 'barbarian' was the stranger from another place, whose alien language signified the sinister dimension of the unknown and unreadable. This absence of the familiar, was the starting point for imaginary digressions into the realm of danger and dread associated with the tribe. Lytton presented the optics of this barbaric fear, as a predatory alliance between the tribes and the Afghan Amir, who was the "barbarian prince of a turbulent state",[6] that aimed at keeping the Indian frontier "smouldering like a ring of fire".[7] However the ultimate and most fearsome connotation of the barbaric threat was read in its dialogic relation with the Russian advance. As one imperial observer put it:

> "There are thousands of wild spirits in Central Asia, with everything to gain and nothing to lose, who only require a leader, and who would be only too eager for a raid into India; ... there are thousands under our rule who would be ready to assist them".[8]

This imaginary spectacle of savage barbarians, enthused by Russian leadership to prey on the fabric of the Indian empire, became the fetish of imperial anxiety, leading to a rhetoricized mentality permanently imbricated in suppositions of crises, conflict, and contradiction.

The discursive representation of the tribe as a barbaric threat to the temporal and spatial edges of the imperial construct, led to exploratory texts of displacement of the fear, bound in negative Freudian implications of repression, distortion, and negation. Lytton's perspectivism embraced two modes of disempowering the savage space of the tribes. In the first instance, he was determined to force the Amir to accept British political and military control in strategic points of his kingdom, to free imperial policy from external blackmail, and force the insignificant, but insolent Afghans to assume a subject position in relation to the British empire. Lytton's viewpoint signified the writing of history as hierarchy, whose temporal sign may be read in the sense of what Gilles Deleuze has described as referring to a "Self which possesses an increasingly vast and increasingly individualized field of exploration".[9] The second mode, also tied to the idea of self and space, was grounded in the concept of displacing existing political linkages between the trans-Indus tribes and Afghanistan, in order to reconstitute the border as an imperial margin. It should be "the constant aim and tendency of our policy", Lytton wrote "to detach them [the tribes] quietly but surely from the Amir".[10] Extension through exclusion, was Lytton's formula for curbing the savage impulse, and fencing its freedom within the political walls of the empire.

The Amir conscious of being cornered, as the British frontier edged upto Quetta, inadvertently aided Lytton's political agenda, by opting for open opposition. He preached *jihad* i.e. religious war among the Baluchistan tribes to incite rebellion against the British, and seemed to flirt with the idea of a Russian alliance by welcoming a Russian Envoy at Kabul, while denying permission to a British mission to enter the country. The Amir's seemingly subversive gestures, provided Lytton with a pretext for writing his text of dispossession. He declared heatedly: "A tool in the hands of Russia I will never allow him [the Amir] to become. Such a tool it would be my duty to break before it could be used".[11] On this imperious note, Lytton declared war on Afghanistan in December 1878. Taking advantage of early Afghan reverses, and the Amir's retreat from Kabul, Lytton secured Jallalabad, the Kurram valley and Pishin from Afghanistan. Subsequently when the new Amir, Yakub Khan negotiated the Afghan surrender by concluding the Treaty of Gandamak in 1879, Jallalabad was returned to Afghanistan, but not the districts of Kurram, Pishin and Sibi. The limits of these districts were to be eventually defined, and they were to be treated as Assigned Districts, for the moment, not permanently detached from Afghanistan. The ambiguity of this redefinition was part of the moral economy of an imperial vision, that sought to appropriate space, without seeming to do so. Thus, behind the overt hesitancy, Lytton was already proposing Pishin as the frontier of the future; he wrote to the Secretary of State that the extension of Baluchistan's border to Pishin would place British "military outposts within striking distance of Kabul and Kandahar."[12] Alfred Lyall, the Foreign Secretary, added his voice to the empirical advantages of retaining Pishin and Sibi; as he pointed out:

> "Pishin covered Quetta, and flanked all the roads leading to Kandahar and Quetta. Sibi commanded the Marris, pressed the Afghans back from the Baluch, and was of great importance in view to our communication with Dera Ghazi Khan".[13]

The discursive representation of Pishin and Sibi as objects of strategic desire, was accompanied on the ground by conscious attempts to recondition tribal awareness in imperially determined structures of meaning, that would exclude the signs of turbulence, turmoil, and the Amir's sinister script from the precincts of tribalism. Lytton directed Robert Sandeman, the newly appointed Agent to the Governor-General in Baluchistan to start the ideological indoctrination, by cultivating tribal chiefs and headmen with 'handsome presents' and 'cordial assurances' to believe and benefit from association with a powerful and magnanimous empire. Led by the same ideal of annexing tribalism to the imperial cause, Sandeman started to implement the process of what he described as bringing the majority of tribes under British influence, bound to the empire through their own interests. The object of reorienting the tribal mind, to desire an imperial presence was attempted through tactical pressure on tribal material interests, rather than an open exercise of power. In keeping with this strategy, Sandeman stood aloof from scenes of spiralling tribal violence in Sibi, scarred by the savage imprint of Marri raids from the neighbouring hills. By remaining impervious to tribal pleas for help, Sandeman was making the point that only tribes under British control would receive assistance, not those who acknowledged the Amir's authority or remained independent. In this manner, Sandeman sought to use distance and distress, to create a 'tribal need' for the British presence, in a form of purposeful obscuring of power and the will to dominate.

But before this experiment in psychological remaking could reach a conclusion, British reverses in Afghanistan and the massacre of the Kabul garrison in September 1879, ruptured the certainties of Lytton's political text. Further, a Liberal victory in the British parliamentary elections in 1880, and the consequent appointment of Lord Ripon as the new Viceroy of India, indicated an immediate post-mortem on the corpus of ideas associated with Lytton's extravagant, theatrical style of imperial structuring. Lord Hartington, the new Secretary of State for India, floated the idea of retreating to safety behind the Indus; the sense of experience contradicting expectation, led him to urge that forward positions like Sibi and Pishin signified expensive adventurism into the unknown; as he put it:

> "The chief objection I take to be the considerable force and expenditure which would be required for this ... extension of our frontier, and also the temptation to interfere in the internal affairs of Afghanistan, which would be caused by our proximity to Kandahar, and our facility of advance upon it".[14]

The withdrawal symptoms evident in Hartington's statement, however, were destined to falter on the highly coloured ground of Anglo-India's romance with the empire, which was a dream, a prayer a map, that could not be erased by mere empirical logic. In this imaginary, Pishin and Sibi were not just places; they were metaphors for the ultimate frontier of power, whose ambitious geography reached for the beyond, in distant Khelat-i-Ghilzai and the Helmund. And above all, they were signs of the combative empire, affirming image and interest through action and appropriation. A retreat from these places, signified in this reading, a reversal of the imperial idea and its displacement in the sense of the weak and ineffectual. As Henry Rawlinson warned, that by retreating, Britain would abdicate her position as a first rate Asiatic power, and must be content "hereafter to play a very subordinate part in the history of the world"[15] Frederick Haines, Commander-in Chief of the Indian Army, predicted that such a move would be read in India as a "weakness of will or military power".[16] This concern with representational reality as the index of power, signified the haunting of the imperial self by fears of transcience, that were symbolically resolved in the search for images and impressions, that would reflect the permanence of power.

This polemic that chose to wrap reality in association and supposition, was sufficiently strong, to influence the Viceroy Lord Ripon to argue the case for retaining Sibi and Pishin, on the ground, that they offered a stranglehold on Afghanistan by covering Qandahar, making the expense of war and occupation of Afghan country unnecessary in the future. In private, Ripon conceded that his support for retaining Pishin and Sibi, was intended to appease the anxiety of Anglo-Indian opinion, which confused aggression with strength, and perceived the spectacle of power as its substance. Hartington faced with growing opposition, postponed the withdrawal, while the Government of India, advised by Lyall played for time. London was informed that a sudden retreat from Pishin and Sibi, would jeopardize pledges of protection to local tribesmen, who would then become the victims of Kabul's revenge. At the same time, Lyall left the titles of the two places deliberately vague, in order to deny the Amir, and the tribes, any future claims to the sovereignty of the areas, and give Britain the space needed to defend her right to hold this corner of territorial advantage.

Lyall's denial of tribal sovereign rights, mirrored the epistemic violence of late Victorian ideology, which assumed that territories and resources belonged to those best able to exploit them. Tropes of primitivism and progress entered historical narrative to establish boundaries of empowerment, through exclusion and negation of contesting claims. The idea of the civilized West acted as a politico-ethical closure, that legitimated the dispossession of categories of otherness as natural and desirable. As Henry Rawlinson explained:

> "In the relations of the great European Powers with the half civilized chieftains of the East, the fine drawn distinctions of Western International Law are brushed aside as mere cobwebs when substantial and imperial interests intervene; and there is this to be said in favour of such a high handed course, that an honest deference to other conditions would be misunderstood by orientals and attributed to weakness".[17]

The *Times* wrote in a similar vein: "An uncivilized state has never been held to have a right to what we may term the full comity of nations."[18] John Westlake, a lawyer writing in the late nineteenth century asserted that sovereignty could only by exercised be civilized governments, and could not be based on the "consent of those who at the outmost know but a few of the needs which such a government is intended to meet".[19] This was the language of the self, seeking to structure boundaries of geography, culture, and law, that would deny the primitive, the oriental and non-European any proprietorship of political place and time. The question of Pishin and Sibi was addressed within this code of denial, that conceptualized the space of the tribal savage, as empty, virgin ground, on which the mark of imperial sovereignty could be inscribed, without violating any corpus of existing titles, as primitives could not by definition possess such civilized accessories. In this making which was an unmaking, sovereignty shadowed the right to conquer the barbarian, and redefine his spatial identity, without any reference to him. Applying this exclusionary model, that would prevent any tribal interruptions of imperial remodelling, the Government of India unilaterally sent a map to England, in 1881, in which Pishin and Sibi were included within the boundary of British Assigned Districts, signifying the final political mapping of these places as signs and symbols of an imperial spatiality, aspiring for geometries of distance and direction that would extend grounds and horizons of meaning and model.

The structured need in imperial ontology to always re-affirm its perceptual position in the space of the new, implied that Pishin and Sibi would signify not the sequel, but the start of a script on purpose and limits, within which representational meanings could be staged and structured. The tribes would figure as the medium, rather than the message of the text, that would be a reflection and reaction against the topology of predictions and perceptions, that haunted the imperial imaginary. Led by internal doubts and external dangers, the text worked within referents of the inside and outside, to establish a discursive link between two spaces, to mirror the problems of permanence within structures of the colonial relationship and the 'oriental mind', as well as the tense navigation of the idea of vulnerability, growing out of the ground of Russian Central Asia, to threaten the British imperial sign in the east. If India was the locus of the intimate enemy of the imperial self, Tsarist Russia was the distant adversary, and the possible union of these private and public terrains of disquiet, conjured the fearful future of annihilation, the dreaded end of imperial time. Apprehension of this apocalyptical reversal, empowered discourse to impose a certain order on reality, which blurred the line between the imaginary and the actual, to create a political-psychological text, implicated in presenting representations of danger to signify a future state of loss, which always threatened from distances of time and space, but remained absent in the present. This ambiguity of presence and absence, became the site for translating 'fear' in new territorial inscriptions of power.

In March 1884, the Russians occupied and annexed the oasis of Merv, bringing their imperial frontier to the brink of contact with Afghanistan. The Russianization of Merv, allowed the strength of the negative in British imperial discourse, to dominate the surfaces of perception. Merv was problematised as the ground of visible and hidden danger, that revealed and concealed dimensions of desire and deceit. On the surface level, it signified the geography of Russian imperial ambition, that proposed to exploit Merv as a 'stepping stone' for further advances in the direction of India. As a 'robbers den' in a 'hideous desert', Merv itself would provide "a motive, or an appearance of a motive"[20] as Lord Salisbury put it, to allow the Russians to move in advance of the position, to suppress tribal outrages. The visual perspective suggested an understanding of Russia's spatial redefinitions, as the prelude, that prefigured the uncertainties of crises, descent into doubt, and the expected dismemberment of the space of the self, from the violations of the threatening 'other'. Referring to the acquisition of Merv as the "gravest event" confronting the British empire in the East, there was Parliamentary concern that Russia would be encouraged to repeat the tale of Merv in Herat, breaching the Afghan wall that sheltered the space of power in India, dissolving the imperial "dream" into "some most terrible and bloody reality."[21] The Duke of Argyll read this predictive picture, as the end of civilization in the east, as the British had imagined and ordered.

The space of possible and probable views in which Russia's imperial geography was represented, moved from the surface to the subterranean, in suggesting another concealed vein of meaning bound up in significations of the 'oriental' for empire making, its inner language, and iconography of power. Nineteenth century European tropes of the Orient as the place of Eastern excesses, where Western reason tended to wither in the sensuality of instinct, provided templates for uniting external uncertainties, to inner distrust of the impressionable oriental mind, that preferred show and spectacle to substance and truth, allowing the new geography of Russian power to capture the oriental imaginary, through imaged significations of its political and military superiority. In discourse, the reality of the Orient was mediated through images intended to transfigure the objects of imperial obsession, to create a rhetorical world of conjectural danger and flawed consciousness, to mystify the narratives of power and prestige in which imperialism imagined its space. Lord Salisbury expanding on the ideational construct of the fusion between the exterior and interior forms of danger stated:

> "I believe that the great fault of our policy ... is that we have been much led by European modes of thought, and methods of warfare, and have paid too little regard to the peculiar circumstances

of the East. In Europe if the strategic position is sound, everything is safe; but it is not so in the East. There is an impalpable power which we know very little of, and which we are obliged to describe by the French word prestige – an impalpable influence which stretches like a shadow before the Frontier of every power, and in proportion as that prestige is great or small – it will spread forward its true domain far beyond the exact space that its arms embrace. Your frontier may be as strong as you please; your fortresses may be as impregnable as you please; but if the prestige of the Power coming against you is greater than your own, it will penetrate through that barrier ... it will dissolve the loyalty ... of those you rule, where loyalty and patriotism do not mean what they do here, and you will find that your fortress will dissolve and crumble under you, and that you are overthrown by the desertion of those who readily fly to the Power they believe to be stronger than yourself".[22]

Here, Salisbury was investing the Orient with qualities of character that barred it from entering the space of Western conceptual categories of honesty, patriotism, and loyalty. This exclusion, inferred by implication, that the ground of native character disfigured by unprincipled codes and conduct, would serve as the site of betrayal and desertion of the British imperial standard in favour of Tsarism, if its image of power would appear to promise more gains, advantage and profit. The threshold of danger associated with the native, also mirrored the anxiety of an imperial sensibility, implicated in a topology of power sustained by structures of subjection and servility, from within which it was feared, that the language of subversive reversal and danger would emerge, to contest the oppression of the imperial text. As J.Biddulph, Political Agent in Gilgit pointed out: "There must always be a number of people in India, discontented with our rule ... who are unsettled by the constant pressure of Russia, who ... out ... of a desire to be on good terms with what may turn out some day the stronger power, will always be ready to listen to Russian intrigues".[23]

Engaging with these significations of image, impression, and intent, that the imperial text could not escape, came a re-narration that sought to use tribes and territories on the Baluchistan frontier as a representational plane, to mirror the prestige of power as abstraction and actuality, to win the psychological and political war against the opponent. Acting on the premises of Salisbury's warning, that the tale of Merv would be repeated in Herat, if the idea of prestige was not impregnated in strategy, a new imperialism of railways and roads was envisaged for the frontier, that would serve as indices of a spatial and symbolic text, that would overpower the significations of the rival, to become certain of itself, in the place of power and prestige.

The geography of the text aspired to touch the extended, outer point of Qandahar, that now came to be identified with the assertive ideal of empire. But Qandahar was to be appropriated not through direct military conquest, but by running a rail link through Baluchistan, between Qandahar and the Indus valley, to bring this section of southwest Afghanistan under close British military surveillance. *The Times* debated that the Qandahar railway was the right reply to Russia, signifying aggression in a vein similar to that adopted by Russia:

"The railway was the most efficient arm of defence hitherto devised against Russian aggression, far more efficient than the conquest of Cabul, or establishment in power of a friendly Amir, for its effect when completed would have been to transfer our military base from the Indus to within 350 miles of the threatened point of attack namely Herat".[24]

Form and Transformation: The Genesis of British Baluchistan and the Semantics of Boundary Making, 1876-1905 43

The Pioneer Mail eager to use the idea of a railway, to remap the space of power and possibilities, urged that the Quetta railway "should be pushed forward through or over the Amran Range, so as to enable an army to be thrown into Kandahar at the shortest notice, and the line to be carried to that country, whenever the grand advance is ordered ... The occupation of Kandahar is not likely to ... strengthen our position by going there, so long as we are ready to occupy it in force from Pishin ... at very short notice ... as the first step towards taking over Herat".[25] The rhetorical sequel to Merv, was therefore, directing the structure of an imperial model that would mimic in order to menace, while implicating the text of the rival in representations, that allowed the rewriting of its own spatiality in perspectivisms of threat and loss, to situate the appropriative logic of its geography in the history of need, necessity, existence.

In June 1884 there was an official decision to extend the railway in Baluchistan from Sibi to Quetta, as the first phase of the linkage to the Qandahar border. The adoption of the railway foregrounded questions of political restructuring, in tribal territories that flanked its passage. As Agent to the Governor-General, Sandeman saw the imperial railway as a convenient platform for extending the local, tribal margins of his Agency. In his optics, the Kakars of Zhob and Bori (areas that dominated the northern approaches to the railway), were historically implicated in gestures of violent defiance and resistance to British power. Their Pathan label defined an identity that was a problem, grounded in the savagery of the tribal mind, and the fury of the Islamic fanatic. In this reading, the Kakars of Zhob, in particular, were guilty of following the leadership of a tribal chief Shah Jahan, who ruled by religious terror. Trading on his reputation, as a miracle maker, the Kakar chief held the tribes in a sinister spell of chronic anger and animosity against any foreign presence. As one imperial description put it: "...they are as a rule fanatics in religion, treacherous, revengeful, and totally untrustworthy: they hate all Europeans, and the life of a British officer entering their mountains is as insecure now as it was thirty years ago".[26] Sandeman tracing the adequation of this image to the real, drew on their history of responding to the Amir's call for *jihad* or holy war against the British in 1879, their subsequent indulgence in fanatical outrages that claimed the life of the British Revenue Commissioner in 1880, and their attacks on men and ammunition belonging to military outposts in Baluchistan, all through 1883-1884, to suggest the legitimacy of the pictorial problematic of horror and barbarity. By 1884, Sandeman was advising the Government of India to sanction a military expedition to Zhob, to eliminate the leadership of Shah Jahan and the *mullas* (religious teachers), who were politically implicated in preaching religious sedition on the frontier to subvert British power, and were also in collusion with the Amir to install local governments under Afghan control in Pishin and Zhob. Sandeman's dark, disturbing imaging of the Kakars, problematised the parameters of the Baluchistan Agency, as well as the safety and success of the newly sanctioned Qandahar railway, that would be exposed to Kakar ravages from the north. In the circumstances, the Government of India preferred to believe rather than not, Sandeman's representations of the Kakar Pathans as aggressive fanatics, disfigured by a predisposition to cruelty and treachery, since it made the imperial calculus of intervening and re-ordering tribalism easier. The Military Department was also keen to map the topography of Zhob, to explore the roads that led from there to Khelat-i-Ghilzai and Ghazni, that offered strategic control of the route through Central Asia and Kabul to India. Connotations of tribal savagery, made to appear more sinister when viewed within the discursive implications of a threatening Russian text, drew official approval for the expedition, that started out for Zhob on 15th November 1884, with Sandeman being accompanied by a mixed military and tribal escort.

Intimidated by military force, the less militant Kakars like the Panezais, Sarangzais and Dumars submitted to the British. But Sandeman reported that more violent groups, such as the Musakhels and Kibzais were actively opposing the advance of the force, under instruction from the *mullas*. From Zhob, Shah Jahan duped Sandeman by offering to surrender, when he was really buying time to remove his family and assets to safety. By the time Sandeman arrived in Zhob, he found the chief had already fled across the border to Afghanistan, and could only indulge in verbal retribution against the main target of the expedition. "The treacherous and fanatical conduct of Shah Jahan", Sandeman wrote, "is more determined than ever I was aware of, and if not checked, might in a time of trouble prove of the greatest danger".[27] However, Shah Jahan's withdrawal removed the backbone of Kakar resistance, and Sandeman was able to negotiate with a rival contender to the chiefship, Shahbaz Khan, to assume leadership in Zhob. The surrender, which included all the tribes that had defied the force, was structured on imperial terms; they had to accept British supremacy, agree to cash fines and furnish hostages as security for future good behaviour, allow British troops to be stationed in their country, and finally to sever all links with Afghanistan and their previous ruler. Sandeman defended the coercion of the surrender, by inter-texting the local and imperial narratives to suggest a new time-place point, in which, tribes would desire subjection in the guardianship structures of empire, to transcend their primitive, anarchic self, while unlocking new space for the guardians to appropriate in iconic inscriptions of power, prestige and purpose. As he put it:

> "The measures we are now taking to suppress [Zhob] are absolutely necessary to secure safety to the railway and frontier generally, and to preserve the friendship of the many influential Mohammadan chiefs of high position and their tribes, who are openly and actively our friends."[28]

From Sandeman's perspective position, the use of the term 'friendship', allowed the illicit smuggling in of the notion of consenting dependency, in which the reality of the hieratic imperial-tribal relationship was grounded. In contrast to Sandeman's disposition to mystify the imperial solution of the tribal problem in Zhob, *The Pioneer Mail* was less reticent in claiming the rewriting as "a very great success. Eight thousand square miles of country have been surveyed ... many of those blanks marked unexplored which [had] produced ... feelings of mingled shame and restlessness have been filled up, and ... a powerful tribe have learnt that the Sirkar Angrez is a reality and not a myth".[29] Implicit in this verbal assertion, was the Victorian compulsion to map the unknown, and bring it within perceptions of the known, so that the consciousness of power would find anchorages in the margin of the safe, the predictable, and accessible.

But expectations of the safe always foundered on the changeable ground of experience. Russia inserted another Merv like signification in the 'Great Game', by clashing with Afghan troops at Panjdeh on 31 March, 1885, and winning the place from them, in the course of delimiting the north Afghan frontier as part of an agreement with Britain, to draw an internationally accepted line of Russia's southern frontier. It appeared as if Russia had distorted the text of power sharing, which the boundary was supposed to symbolize, denying the British the level playing field that dialogue and distance had promised to structure. The trauma of Panjdeh led to a reconceptualization of content and form in imagining a frontier of the future for India. As Lord Kimberly put it in Parliament:

> "Frontiers drawn on maps, marked out by lines of posts, and sanctioned by promises on one side or protests on the other, will positively not serve any longer. The frontier of the future ... must

be a military one ... Authority has been given for the expenditure of five million sterling on frontier railways and military roads which are reckoned of immediate necessity".[30]

The commitment to a military frontier was sustained by the talk of war, and a Cabinet pledge that a Russian move to Herat would be treated as a cassus belli. On the Indian frontier, the idea of war was welcomed with feverish expectations. A correspondent from Quetta wrote: "We are on tiptoe of expectation here ... our nerves are jumpy ... Russia has encroached quite far ... any further advance may cause us to lose something more tangible than prestige."[31] The desire for war, expressed in language, signified the dangerous mental plane where consciousness interlaced with aggressivity, encouraged the repression of the rival within hostile, heated, premises of violence, anger and acrimony. Contrary to expectations, however, there was no war, as the Russians accepted arbitration, and the Afghans were satisfied in acquiring Zulfikar in place of Panjdeh. But the war of minds on paper and pen continued, to figure the threat of the 'other' in instinctual fears of impermanence, and the precariousness of power full of its own changing and haunted by its opposite.

In England, the newly elected Conservative Government of 1885, sought to harness the war mania in polemic and policy, to justify a more predatory imperial style. Salisbury, the British Premier, spoke of the Khwajak Pass and Qandahar as probable sites of future frontier remapping, and that no considerations of balancing the budget, or tribal susceptibilities should deter the spatial reach of this ambition. Desire to pursue the 'Great Game' in order to win, enslaved the imperial mind to the idea of a 'scientific frontier', to be drawn in the wilderness of the Baluch-Afghan borderland, that would defy invasion and interruption of its essential space. The architect entrusted with this new spatial definition, was F.Roberts, Commander-in-Chief of the Indian Army, who dreamed of the Hindukush as the most desirable frontier for India, but had to content himself with knitting the tribal margin along the western rim of Afghanistan into the forward militarised marchland of the empire. The fortification of this space, was intended to authorize a relation that would master and exclude the fear of loss and displacement. This fear, would be addressed by a continental approach to India's defence needs, by which Roberts envisaged giving the Indian Army an increased capability for aggressive action along the Quetta-Qandahar-Herat route. Militarised forts would cover the political surface of the frontier at select points, backed in the rear by a series of heavily armed cantonments, completely equipped with materials of war, forming the base line for action against the enemy. The inner and outer lines would be connected with railways and military roads on the one side, and on the other side with the great network of railway communications in India. By reaching for guarantees of permanence in a 'force' and 'fortress' mentality, Roberts was attempting to engage with space to master the dimensions of danger associated with the exterior, to supersede the consciousness of its menacing proximity in order to overcome it.

The spatial geometry of this frontier structure, signified by implication, the interruption of tribal space, to insert angles and degrees of imperial control, denoting a remaking of content and form, within the negatives of displacement, separation, exclusion. The coercion of this architecture of railroads and military command posts, would occur within the denial of tribal interests, that lay transverse against the surface of the proposed drawing. This meeting of the empire and tribe as two unequal and opposed configurations of consciousness, allowed the objectification of the tribal space as usable and disposable, for the gratification of the higher will of the imperial self. In this alignment of mind and meaning, charting a road was a way of entering and possessing, of metamorphosizing the space of the 'other' into the place of high strategy and imperial signification. It was argued for instance, that to exploit Quetta's strategic potential to cover the Qandahar border, it needed not just existing linkages with Sind, but also new road communications with the Punjab. The Foreign Department, consequently authorized the making of a new military road which would leave the Punjab at Fort Munroe, then curve in a westerly direction through the Bori valley to Pishin, cutting across the homelands of the Kakar Pathans in Bori, and the Khetran Baluch tribes who lived on either side of the Dera Ghazi Khan border. For the tribes, the road spelled disruption of established kinship and trading patterns that had formed on the axis of spatial convergence, not separation. The Khetrans in particular, now faced the prospect of being shut out from markets in the Punjab, and forfeiting kinship ties across the border. But Sandeman, always persuasive in resurrecting the 'horror' of the tribe, to suggest that their subjection was integral to the idea of safe passage along the road, meant that the Bori and Khetran valleys would be officially defined as part of British Baluchistan. Sandeman's style of political rewriting entered representational terrain, as the desired idiom of imperialising the evolving frontier structure. As Lord Connemara, the Governor of Madras reflected: "... it would ... be inconsistent to build up any wall of difficulty between Sandeman and the future".[32]

The coercive symbolism of the railroad in erasing tribal inscriptions, to map the signs of empire, was discursively presented, in Roberts's strident linguistic imaging of the promise and purpose of imperial remaking. To prepare for the day of trial with Russia, Roberts insisted, penetration and intimidation of tribal space was essential, "to bring these lawless, isolated and fanatical people under control ... we should punish outrage in such a severe and unmistakable manner as to make it clear that we are not afraid of them ... we should construct good military roads through the passes leading into Afghanistan by which troops could be readily concentrated at points dominating the unsettled and almost unexplored region lying between that country and India".[33] Here, the fear of the barbaric in the tribal sign functioned as the site of suppression and subjection, within the closure of intentional aggression, to refigure the image of empire in the transcendence of power. The road as a metaphor for the location of power in the depth of the tribal unknown, reached symbolic culmination in the provocative extension of the Sind-Pishin Railway through the Khwaja Amran Range to New Chaman on the Afghan side of the border. This forward act was implicated in the desire to discipline the tribal plane on which it was realized, as well as to structure the military surveillance of Qandahar, that would bring it within the geographic 'panopticon' of imperial space. In this angle of perceiver and image, empire became a matter of 'being tempted by space', to always transcend the limits and levels of perceived ascendancy. As Lord Dufferin, reflecting on the political significance of the new rail line, pointed out to Salisbury:

"The moment we pierce the Khwaja Amran Range with a tunnel ... in order to carry our railway twelve miles further towards a point which leads nowhere, it becomes evident that our policy is no longer that of guarding the entrance to our own house, or making a temporary excursion beyond, but that we are contemplating a permanent advance into foreign territory".[34]

The menace of the message signified in the railway, led the Amir of Afghanistan to remark that the British were now holding a pistol to his head. In this making and meaning, the metaphorical reality of the line worked as ideology, to situate imperial history in the Hegelian assumption of aggression as the proper function of human ontology.

As the framing narrative of imperialism, the conquest of space was the inner plot that could not interrupt its own logic, without forfeiting the very spirit of power it sought to capture from those it subjugated. In this emplotment, independent gestures from strategic tribal enclaves, could not be accommodated within imperial narrativization, as they signified a contesting reality in which representations of imaged authority would find no reflective surface. To engage with the tribal plane, to make it mirror the pretensions of empire, the topographic view of a strategic physiography combined with observation as 'guided vision' of the 'other', to place the tribal topoi in the cusp of expectation and reflection, that brought it within the ontological domain of imperialism. The empirical translation of this visuality, occurred on the strategic site of the Ghazni route from Central Asia to India, that acquired discursive prominence after the re-mapping of Qandahar. As *The Englishman* pointed out, that while the Khyber and Bolan covered the main approach routes to India from Kabul and Qandahar, yet the possibility existed of the "the enemy occupying a base at Ghazni, between the two great cities of Afghanistan and striking at the unprepared centre of our line through the Gomal Pass".[35] This strategic reading, brought the Zhob valley into the expansive diagram of imperial power, as it stretched in an east-west direction to the rear of the Suleiman Range, giving command of the Tochi and Gomal Passes on the Afghan side, while itself being easily accessible from Quetta. "The Gomal route", *The Times* observed, "abuts on the Ghazni road from Herat to Cabul, and should enable an adequate force on occupation of the country near Appozai [in the Zhob valley] to cut an invaders communication between the two Afghan fortresses".[36] Through such observation, the tribal space of Zhob was conceptually figured to create the strategic landscape of empire. Strategy translated into structure, as internal tribal turmoils in Zhob, provided a text for imperial censure and control. In Zhob, the existing Chief Shahbaz Khan, whom Sandeman had installed in power in 1885, was facing a critical challenge to his leadership from a rival chief Dost Mohammad, who sought to establish his rule by violent intimidation of his rival's supporters. The carnage of tribal violence in Zhob, allowed Sandeman to predict the onset of anarchy and chaos for the remaining frontier from Pishin to Afghanistan, and to warn that the defence of the 'Kabul, Ghazni, and Candahar line' in case of war with Russia depended on the ability to control the tribes who were a "source of permanent danger to the Indian empire".[37] The darkness of danger with which Sandeman always chose to invest the tribal image, suggested that his primary object was not to interpret, but to legitimate a representation that would condone the negation of tribalism, as a way of subjugating it, in the logic of imperial mapping and meaning. The new Viceroy, Lord Lansdowne coming from the perspectival position of engaging with the tribes from the summits of mastery and authority, declared that allowing the tribes freedom to dominate the Gomal would be a confession of weakness, "utterly unworthy of a great power".[38] Within this structure of attitudes and references, a punitive expedition to Zhob was mounted in 1889, to erase the disfiguring imprints of tribal form, and occupy strategic heights of the valley to inscribe the spatial text of empire.

Sandeman's imperialisation of Zhob was marked by the restitution of his old protégé Shahbaz Khan to the leadership, as a way of bringing the tribal political interior within the steering compass of imperial navigation. He also elicited a petition from the local leadership, requesting the presence of British political and military protection. This signified closure in the colonial trope of native inadequacy and dependency, fixing the tribe in the place of lowly misdemeanours, where myths of imperial guardianship and correction could be imagined.

Sandeman chose to signal the intent and idiom of imperial rule, by selecting the strategic position of Appozai as his headquarters, which gave him command of the Gomal Pass and access to the surrounding Pathan tribes who could now be coerced at will. Most of the local tribes, the Mandokhels, Waziris and

Sheranis read the message, and accepted Sandeman's terms to take service payments and keep the Gomal open for British needs. But there was one digression from this picture of submission. The Kidderzais, a section of the Sherani group, decided not to comply with Sandeman's arrangements in the Gomal. This gesture of resistance, vilified them permanently, confirming their place in imperial discourse as culprits who kept alive the robber mentality on the Pass, frustrating the imperial text of order and stability. In April 1890, Sandeman pressed for a punitive expedition against the tribe. While Lansdowne was considering his proposal, the Kidderzais offered to submit, in return for the repeal of a fine of Rs. 10,000 imposed on them, after the expedition of 1889. But Sandeman warned of damage to the imperial image, "If having once put our hand to the plough, we were to hold back,or ... refrain from taking any step which would make it appear that we were afraid of our own measure for opening out and pacifying the Gomal Pass and neighbouring countries."[39] Imprisoned in perception and prejudice, of tribal defiance constituting a graveyard for imperial ambition, Sandeman could only contemplate the fear of force as the desired medium for tribal subjection. Lansdowne assented, and sanctioned the expedition in 1890, "not so much on its merit", as he confided to James Lyall, Lieutenant-Governor of the Punjab, but because Sandeman was "difficult and dangerous to thwart".[40]

As military coercion followed, the Kidderzais paid a new fine, accepted British military posts, and watched George Stuart White, military commander of the expedition march his troops to the Takht-i-Sulaiman, the sacred peak of their mountain homeland, in order as White put it, "to teach a useful lesson to the people ... and ... effectually roll up the curtain of obscurity which has hitherto shrouded this fabled throne".[41] This symbolic and spatial violation of the tribal interior was intended as 'exposure', to collapse the invincibility of impregnable mountain terrains, on which the tribes defended their consciousness of being unconquerable. The military march therefore, served as the site of a psychological address to the sign of resistance in the tribal imaginary, seeking its inner negation through the force and fear of the real and unreal. White's 'lesson' to the tribes, through the Kidderzai example, was not to contest the imperial sign. As desired objects of control, tribes could only enter the narrative margin of empire, through constructed plots of resistance, recalcitrance, and ultimately reduction in the tracings of possessive power.

Dimensions of desire and destiny continued to converge as the inscription of subject positions, altered the pictorial of tribal space, to mirror the cartography of empire. By division and displacement, the idea of the tribal threat, was manipulated to structure the ground of empire, that shifted between margins of meaning to annex new spatial directions. Sandeman now urged, that in order to hold the new British position in Appozai, acquired after the second Zhob expedition,[42] he needed to control the direct routes to the Derajat through Sherani country. Although Sherani country was geographically "Punjab and not Baluchistan".[43] Sandeman wanted control of all the Sheranis, because one section of the tribes the Larghas were indulging in "habits of murdering and robbing"[44] unchecked by the Punjab authorities. Anticipating Lyall's objections from the Punjab, and anxious to insert a 'scientific frontier' between the two regimes, Lansdowne opted to divide the Sheranis, by placing the Larghas under Punjab and the Barghas with Baluchistan. The division rested on denial of an identity, for as Sandeman himself pointed out:

> "The distinction between the Bargas and Largas is not sufficiently real ... The whole tribe is very closely connected together by ties of blood; and there is nothing to prevent a criminal (say) from Barga taking refuge in Larga ...".[45]

Lansdowne also confessed doubts as to the legitimacy of the act of partition, whether the presence of two sections in the same tribe was sufficient "to warrant their being placed under separate administrations".[46] In this remaking, the sectional connotations of Sherani tribal identity was used to suggest the idea of divided space, that could be marked by dual imperial inscriptions. Here, the representation of reality, mirrored the making of a point of view within which the tribal topography could be exploited, for stretching and defining the boundaries of local power, and its accessory texts.

Beyond the Sheranis, stretched the stairway of the Gomal, that beckoned as the ultimate frontier of empire that would be won not just against the tribal factor, but also against inner dissensions of imperial models and meanings. The plane of high imperial imagining was unproblematic; it mirrored the logic of using tribal space belonging to the Waziris, Mandokhels and Ghilzais to situate the frontier of fate on the high Himalayan peaks, to capture the physical and spiritual remoteness of the mountains in the act of boundary making. The second plane, involving structure and model, for adding tribal content to imperial form, reflected the trap-ridden ground of inner tensions and conflicts, that required resolution on the balance of meanings derived from the complex of image, intent, and interest, that problematised the mapping of an imperial boundary within the referents of local administrative ambitions.

The paradigmatic nature of the problem derived from the contrary angles of perception associated with the political views from the Punjab and Baluchistan. For Sandeman, opening the Gomal Pass was part of a larger picture to secure the Derajat entrance, by holding both ends of all the passes leading from Afghanistan to India.[47] This was Sandeman's imperial argument for proposing to bring the Gomal highway, the Waziris who used it, and the line of the Gomal River under his jurisdiction. For James Lyall, Sandeman's directional aims mirrored the "annexing tendency" of his "administration... this tendency ... follows naturally on the system ... he uses".[48] To stop Sandeman from putting "mat posts on the Gomal"[49] that would enable him to advance ever deeper into tribal Afghan country, Lyall proposed that Punjab should control the Gomal valley highway. But Sandeman pointed out that Lyall's text envisaged control of only the Pass, leaving tribal conduct beyond that point unchecked. With Baluchistan posts on the Gomal, Sandeman insisted, the Waziris would be compelled to keep order.[50] Sandeman was proposing a form of control that would signify a frontier not just as physical mark, but also as surveillance screen to monitor both proximity and distance, to establish it in the sign of encroaching power, conquering gaze, and appropriative will. Lansdowne drawn to Sandeman's point of view, rationalized that the wild behaviour of the nomads and the Waziris demanded, "that the country be effectively policed, and the easy going ways of the Punjab Government, are by no means suited to such a task".[51]

In 1891, the Government of India decided that the Gomal River between Kundar Domandi and Kajuri Kach should be the boundary between the tribal countries supervised by Baluchistan and the Punjab. Thus Sandeman acquired the wedge between the Kundar and Gomal rivers, that Lyall had sought to interpose between him and the Waziris. Sandeman had navigated imperial meaning to the moorings of his model, that mirrored not limits, but explorations of power.

II

The creation of imperial space within the economy of the free and unfree, to signify the domestication of 'otherness' as unfreedom, carried within its epistemic construct, the deeply rooted logic of the disempowered interrogating the premises of their loss. In the sequel to Sandeman's spatial redefinition of the frontier, the language of tribal dissent signified the 'other' margin, that defied closure in imperial tropes of war, pacification, conquest. The Amir reacting to the sign of the 'Zhob-Gomal' route as penetrating "to the heart of Afghanistan"[52], called for *jihad* on the frontier, and incited a large band of Waziris to attack the British post at Appozai. James Browne, Sandeman's successor in Baluchistan, expressed concern that the Governor of Qandahar was threatening to occupy Toba in the spring of 1893, to encourage the Achakzais to plunder the railway to Chaman.[53] H.Daly, Resident in Indore, interpreted tribal action as militant reaction to the loss of independence spelled in the making of the Baluchistan Agency, which they were now attacking by every Pathan principle of "intrigue and treachery".[54] The Durand Agreement with the Amir in 1893, by which the Amir relinquished claims on Chagai and Chaman, and agreed not to interfere in most of Waziri country, did nothing to calm tribal fears of imperial intention. Roberts himself was troubled, as he watched the Indian frontier move towards the Hindukush; he wrote: "The storm may overtake us before we can do anything to strengthen that frontier".[55] The expected danger finally dawned, as the Mahsud Waziris rebelled and destroyed the British boundary camp at Wano in 1895; just two years later there was a general tribal uprising on the frontier from Tochi to the Malakand.

The disturbing force of tribal insurgency now stalked the discursive engagement with the crisis, and the subjacent theme of the limits of frontier making within the conceptual implications of Sandemanism. Arguments evolved on dual planes of meaning, separated by desires to continue or discontinue Sandeman's interventionist text. Northbrook accused the Government of India of being inspired "with a desire for wild schemes of annexation", that the tribes subjected to the spectacle of the annexation of Zhob, of forts dotting Waziristan and the Malakand, were provoked into rebellion as the only escape route from imperial captivity.[56] This censorship, not the celebration of Sandemanism, signified the wish to distance imperial rule from the dark and disturbing in colonial subjection, to preserve in the separation of space, the configuration of power that would not risk damage through tense encounters with the black thrusts of tribal desire.

Those more closely associated with Sandeman's text, looked for the production of meaning not in sceptical introspection, but in the sphere of authority and natural right, the sign of providence and the will to power. Roberts asserted, that the making of the new frontier addressed the savagery of tribal space: "The robber haunted No man's land", where, "every man's dwelling is a miniature fortress fortified against his neighbour", a "frontier not altogether worthy of a great civilising power".[57] Here the production of imperial space from the conquest of savage terrain, brought the frontier within the symbolism of the English empire, as the rule of right over the sign of error. The writing of horror inside savage spaces, legitimized the abolition of their independent text. As George Hamilton put it, "the tribes commit outrages because they trust to the impenetrability of their fastnesses"; and this condition could only be remedied by punishment and penetration of their homelands, that implied "interference with their independence", for there was no other way of "stopping outrage and securing the peace of our frontier".[58] From this warring spatial symbolism of tribe and empire, came the military action and language, that recontoured the savage frontier as the space that belonged to power, the 'terrible weapon of aggression', produced by the ultra Hegelianism of the imperial state model.

The suppression of the savage that added British Baluchistan to the Indian map, however, came to a close in the north and east, as tribal turbulence made the future of the 'forward' vision uncertain, troubled now by doubts that suggested closure to the framing narratives of war and conquest, in which the empire had inscribed its spatial text. The search for the new was suppressed in the anxiety to survive on ground already won, and the official decision to refrain from Sandemanising the Pathan borderland any further, implied that the empire's spatial gaze would need to focus on other perspectives and perceptions.

III

Turning from the violence and disequilibrium experienced in the 'production of imperial space' in the north and east, imperial cartography sought to transcribe 'space' into 'place' in the Perso-Baluch borderland, by reflective imaging, to make the desert desirable in the mirror of imperial perception. Reflection, as deliberate ideological strategy, shifted the position of questions and answers belonging to the framing narrative of the 'Great Game' to create a new problematic of the Russian danger, that suggested the need for other gestures, routes and directions to map and measure the locus and limits of probable danger. The visual and verbal engagement with this sense of danger to the premises of the self, occurred on the site of significations derived from spatial signs of Russian presence and purpose in Persia. In 1889, Russian aggression now more than half a century old in west Asia, appeared to be entering the precincts of the unacceptable, by establishing a Consul-General at Meshed, from where Russian agents were despatched to Birjind, Tabas, Siesten to effect the political penetration of southeast Persia and the Gulf littoral, which figured in British representations as the forbidden outer rim of empire, whose formal-functional logic implied exclusion, separation, distance, from that which threatened the perceptual grounds of power. Emerging from this contextual surface, the language of anxiety summoned what Hegel called the "terrible power of negativity"[59] to overcome the constraining situation. Russian consular activity was read as a dark plot to eclipse the message of British ascendancy in southern Persia, and along the borderland with Baluchistan. A British newspaper correspondent caught the mood of despondency: "It is ... humiliating" he wrote "to find ourselves so thoroughly displaced in these southern districts... where a little activity could have planted our prestige in the minds of the governing and trading classes".[60] To this sense of pessimism, *Blackwoods Edinburgh Magazine* added a note of despair, stating, "The Czar has now got England by the throat, and can tighten the grip as occasion may arise".[61] There were other disturbing messages for the concerned observer. Writing in 1890 to Lansdowne, George Chesney, Military Member of the Viceroy's Council, alluded to "the profound change effected in the situation by the completion of the [Russian] Trans Caspian Railway", which had transformed the idea of defending Herat from a minor military operation against limited forces, to a formidable challenge against the Russians who could now concentrate there in force, owing to their newly completed railway.[62] George Nathaniel Curzon, probing deeper into the text of the railway, situated its meaning in wider and darker spaces of perception; he wrote:

> "In Central Asia, commerce is pursued with political objects, mercantile agents are not uncommonly diplomatic emissaries in disguise, and command of the bazaars is the conventional prelude to ascendancy in court. The railway has enabled Russia to flood with her manufactures the whole of northern Khorassan, and to beat down the barrier of Afghan obstinacy on the north. ... with every caravan that starts from the line at Askabad, at Merv, at Bokhara, to carry Russian manufactures to Meshed, to Herat, or even to Cabul a small accretion of political influence may

be traced ...The military and offensive strength of the railway consists not in its application to the purpose of attacking India directly... but in the absolute and now inevitable command which it has given them [the Russians] of places or regions that are commonly looked upon as outposts of the Indian Empire, that are certainly concerned in any scheme of trans-frontier defence. In other words, the TransCaspian Railway has placed it in the power of Russia, both with ease and impunity to occupy Meshed, to seize Herat ...to descend in force upon Balkh".[63]

The power of this imaging was not so much in historical representation as in a hermeneutic one, providing a means for understanding the hidden message, the secret code of Russia's inscriptional markings in west and central Asia. This meaning would transfigure perception, and structure spatial rewriting to mimic and menace the language of Russian purpose and propaganda.

Salisbury was now sufficiently concerned with the pictorial problematic of Russianization in Persia, to criticise the Government of India for having been too absorbed with the Afghan perspective and the optics of danger from the north west, that had obscured its vision of the gathering crises in the south west. He wrote to F. Lascalles, British Ambassador in Berlin: "The same circumstances and motives which might carry Russia into Afghanistan, might if she finds it too dangerous a venture, carry her into Persia. A successful occupation of Persia, reducing it to Russian vassalage ... might be very menacing to India. It can only be really frustrated by the construction of railways from the coast or... from Quetta... which should carry troops up to within striking distance of Meshed".[64] In giving birth to the idea of a railway from Quetta to Persia, that would 'trump the TransCaspian', and reverse the error of allowing the 'Shah to see Russia in the flesh' and the British at a distance,[65] Salisbury was making space for a new imperial temporality, in which the frontier of the future would be grasped in the sign of the conquering ego, the gesture of mastery.

As the railway became iconic of imperiality, it entered the tropic margin of the 'Great Game' with Russia, figuring as the language of remaking and recovering, the contested ground of play from an advantaged adversary. As Henry Drummond Wolff, British Minister in Teheran, put it to Salisbury in 1890: "My feeling is that the line would be a tacit ... answer to the advances of Russia so that it would give Persia a confidence she cannot feel so long as she can contrast the activity of Russia with our indifference. With or without the line to Meshed Russia is practically mistress of Khorassan from where she could at any moment overrun southern Afghanistan".[66]

In India, Sandeman was eager to exploit the idea of the railway to alter content and form on Baluchistan's boundary with Persia, wrapped in the verbiage of imperial image and interest. Writing to Salisbury that, "British honour and influence upto Siestan and on the Perso-Baluch frontier must reign supreme", Sandeman linked the realization of this political terrain with absorption of tribal tracts in west Baluchistan, (where he was already exercising informal control), that were in danger of falling under Russia's scrutiny, as facts, which the Government of India was disinclined to act upon and register. A railway through "friendly Baluchistan ... to Merv so as to give confidence to southern Persia... as well as our own Baluch chiefs"[67] was Sandeman's substitute annexationist form within which spatial rewriting could occur.

Lansdowne and later Elgin's Government, however, remained immune to the high imperial rhetoric of the railway, preferring to privilege the north west frontier in the optics of India's defence strategy, so as to avoid being crippled by "inconvenient obligations"[68] in remote, wild places of the political imagination. The Government of India was only prepared to shadow the idea of a railway, by opening a disused caravan track between Siestan and Baluchistan, as a modest, inexpensive way of threading British interests in south Persia. In 1896 the Nuski-Siestan route was officially opened: its ultimate referent was Russia and the desire to seize Siestan when "Persia falls to pieces";[69] and the immediate referent was the promotion of commerce as cover, to legitimate spatial arrangements and interpretations, that would bring tribal west Baluchistan within the structure of self-aggrandisement associated with empire.

The intention to make and mirror boundaries of the self on the 'otherness' of tribal ground, was visible in the immediacy of the frontier delimitations, undertaken to anchor the route in the safety of British controlled territory. Demarcating the Baluch-Afghan sector from Domandi on the Gomal River to Koh-i-Malik Siah, the first part of the boundary line from the Sarlat hills to the edge of the Registan desert, disrupted the economy of local Rakshani and Mingal tribes by leaving their agricultural lands on the British side of the border, and their pasture lands on the Afghan side.[70] This rectification was probably intended to partly placate Afghan sentiments, for the other key adjustment in boundary limitation, involved taking Chagai from the Amir, to exclude Afghan influence from this finger of land that connected Nushki, the terminus of the new trade route to Persia. The implication of the act of boundary making, in revising the content of a space, to make it signify a different message situated in the logic of imperial reason, was readable in the Government of India's observation: "The chief value of the country [Chagai] lies in the trade route by which it is traversed – a route which is likely to be of much prospective importance, as it will form the easiest and most direct line of communications between Quetta and eastern Persia".[71] In this text, the space of Chagai was read and represented within meanings linked to the imperial sign, excluding originary significations of tribal form and content, as minimal and marginal, to establish a spatial understanding in terms of presence and absence of imperial motives and measures. The logic of this definition through denial, was mirrored in the ultimate reconstitution of Chagai as part of the Agency territories of Baluchistan, with a local British backed chief serving as nominal head of tribal political affairs.

Like Chagai, Nushki, the critical hub of the new trade route to Persia, became the object of a scrutiny that sought to suppress, in order to configure space in words and meaning, suggesting the ontological opposition of tribal and imperial being, that required the subjection of the inferior in the superior. F.C.Webb Ware, the British Agent in charge of the new trade route, and A.H.McMahon, who had drawn the boundary, represented tribal Nushki as a meaningless place of horror and hatred, left to self-destruct on the plane of feuds and murders by their ruler the Khan of Kalat, who was only interested in revenue receipts from the area.[72] In this picturing, tribalism as the site of predation and greed, signified the danger of destruction to the new route, that was metaphoric of a journey to the place of imperial promise and plentitude, away from the dark, negatives of its place of inception. To allow the sign of the high to reach into the interior of the low, in order to absorb, amend and arrange its spatial substance, the tribal topography of Nushki would have to be resignifed in the form and content of imperial normative ideology. Webb Ware wrote from the site: "Under the present regime, Nushki can neither be pacified nor can it prosper",[73] and that the only corrective for this site of error, was to offer the Khan of Kalat a quit rent for his rights in Nushki. Hugh Barnes, Agent to the Governor-General in 1897, supported this view, while McMahon urged that without an imperial solution, the trade route would be stranded in anarchy, its message lost in negation.

This imperial reading of space and route, entered the margin of the permissible, as it synchronized with a change of Viceroys. In 1899, Elgin left office, and Curzon arrived as the new Viceroy, already ideologically committed to the need for re-positioning in southern Persia, by exploiting the topography of west Baluchistan. Under Curzon, the Government of India became more explicitly imperial in vision and vocabulary, advocating that the limits of responsibility should not be constrained by narrow economic readings, but explored "by other and far reaching considerations of imperial policy".[74] In this viceregal legitimation of expansion and extension as the desired norm, the proposal to acquire Nushki as part of imperial spatial revision, escaped critical scrutiny in the Foreign Department, where the Secretary seeking to identify with the sign of the times, stated: "As I am inclined to share the belief that the new route is a matter of imperial concern, I do not wish to be understood as definitely opposed even to annexation [of Nushki]".[75] In this structure of attitudes, tribal Nushki could not be allowed to intervene between the object of imperial desire and its possession. The expected appropriation occurred as the Khan of Kalat relinquished the district to the British in 1899 for an annual sum of Rs.9,000.

Nushki and Chagai, provided access to a political corridor stretching from Quetta to Persia, signifying new angles of dominion and definition. Implicated in a spatial language that mixed routes with rights, the revised cartography of imperial power in the west, ended the marginality of the desert and nomad along the Perso-Baluch borderland, to create a political space that represented the inclusive and exclusive symbols of imperial self-hood, its locus and limits. The symbolic power of this remaking was mirrored in Webb Ware's claim, that the route had awakened the Persians to the fact that, "the Indian Empire lies immediately on their borders".[76] At Askabad, the Russians mapped the route and its spatial framings on the perceptual plane of political redrawing for ascendancy, prestige and command. As the *TransCaspian Review* commented:

> "The Northern Baluch Desert has become full of life, and where mercantile movement hardly existed, there is now...an even road for the insinuation of English goods into the very heart of...Iran... More important is the political meaning of the road...An English fortress has risen on the very frontier of Persia, connected with Quetta by a road which...will of course soon be made a carriage road and then a railway ... which will decorate the Koh-i-Malik Siah will give great weight to the utterances of the English ministers at Teheran."[77]

The political signification of the route, and the new frontier of power it implied, however, exerted its own gravitational pull for drawing the Russians deeper into the 'Great Game' for imperial space and its extended expressions. By the end of the century, there were Russian engineers surveying south Persia for a new railway to the Gulf. At the same time Persia contracted a loan from Russia, as a result of which Russia became her sole creditor. Viewing the upward curve of Russian influence in Persia, the Secretary of State for India, Lord George Hamilton, reflected that the use of the Baluchistan option merely threatened to dissolve the residue of Persian independence, without actually arresting the spread of Russian power. There was also dissatisfaction that in 1896, the boundary on the Persian sector had been drawn too close to the trade route, leaving the main springs of water in Persian control, as well as the lands of marauding Baluch tribesmen, who operated from the Persian side of the border to raid spaces within Baluchistan. Since the Persian authorities preferred to tolerate this tribal activity, as a way of keeping the British imperial fringe permanently tangled in the toils of tribal disruptions, there was a matching sentiment in India, that the existing frontier structure needed additions and angles to shape a more coercive geometry of power and purpose.

Curzon's answer to the anxiety of dominion in the west, was to metamorphosize the trade route into a railway, as a final reply to the language of insolence and abjection, in which Russia was seeking to establish her text in Persia. Convinced that Russia was intent on building a railway through south Persia to the eastern end of the Gulf as "a menace and source of nuisance to the British", while Persia was "quite willing to sacrifice herself in order to humour Russian designs"[78], Curzon believed that the moment had come when Russia and Persia had to be told that Russia must halt, that if any foreign railway was to be built on Persian ground it would have to be British. "There is no aggression in this policy", Curzon maintained, "It is self protection in its narrowest aspect".[79] Displacing the old axiom of imperial understanding, that the north west frontier should be the locus of strategic rewriting, Curzon announced: "If any one thinks that Russia is going to march down the Tochi or the Gomal I must...take leave to differ".[80] "I would sooner have a railway from Quetta to Siestan, than I would have half a dozen lines in the trans-Indus section".[81] "Situated at the point of juncture of the frontiers of Persia, Afghanistan and Baluchistan", Curzon concluded, "the future of Siestan affects the destinies of all three countries".[82]

Curzon's revision was a radical remaking, that conceptualized the frontier not just as a fence to shut out the external, but as an experimental ground from where new perspectives of limits and lengths could be imagined, interpreted, and inscribed. As the critics of his scheme asked, if the presence of Russia in Siestan would add so much to British difficulties as to justify dragging a train across a useless desert, which left in its desolate state would deter any invader.[83] The answer to this query lay in Curzon and Hamilton's ultimate desire for the acquisition of Siestan, as "it would make an admirable frontier for India on the western side".[84] But realizing that Persia would not alienate territory to a foreign power, they visualised the Baluchistan railway as a political bridge, to the desired point of domination. Under pressure from this ambitious re-mapping, in 1902, a secret conference at the Foreign Office concluded: "We should...steadily prepare for an occupation of Siestan by extending the railway beyond Nushki and pushing our trade".[85] The India Council was now persuaded to accept the Baluchistan railway, and communicating this consent to Curzon in 1902, Hamilton noted with satisfaction that this "transaction would practically settle our claim to Persian Siestan".[86] Lord Cranbourne summed up the meaning of the move: "We are anxious for the integrity of Persia, but we are anxious far more for the balance of power".[87] In this ending, the Quetta frontier and railway entered a narrativization of power, in which the appropriation of one space was used to legitimate the absorption of another, to signify the hegemony of the imperial map and compass.

The metamorphoses, transfers, and substitutions implied in the making of imperial space in Baluchistan after 1876, signified the site of a new visual consciousness, where space was explored by reducing it to outline/plan, and redrawn on perspectival planes to reconstitute the depth of imperial space on the picture plane. This gave rise to the dialectic of the facade, as face directed towards the observer, the privileged side of boundaries, barriers, forts, ramparts and railways, figuring as recourse and resource against the fear of intrusive Tsarism in the west. The exterior form leaned against interior content, designed as a medium for colonization by signs, images and objects, that brought tribal spaces within the matrices of imperial power and purpose. Here, space defined by the inside-outside relationship figured as the ground of an imperial architecture, that sought to subjugate and repel by use, function, form. This remaking of imperial space from the violation of an existing space, belonged to the idea of dominance lodged in the narratives of armies, war, and political conquest. In this reconstitution, the space of the tribal 'other' as perceived by and for the 'I' began to evolve, as the place of self transformation, translation, transcendence. The imperialisation of Baluchistan occurring within this plane of perception and perception of place, was symbolic of the Cartesian Europe centred logos, actualizing its space in the rationality of its own meaning and logic; a logic of this kind, as Henri Lefebvre suggests, "is always merely a deceptive name for a strategy".[88]

NOTES

1. R.I.Bruce, *The Forward Policy*, p. 346.
2. *Ibid.*, p. 336.
3. Quoted in R.Young, *White Mythologies*, p. 45.
4. Lytton to Cavagnari, (private), 9 June 1877, *Lytton Papers* MSS.Eur.E.218/11.
5. N.Frye, *Anatomy of Criticism*, p. 147.
6. Lytton to Northbrook, 25 October 1877, *Northbrook Collection*, MSS.Eur.C.144/18.
7. Lytton to Salisbury (private), 1 April 1876, *Lytton Papers*, MSS.Eur.E.218/18.
8. H.Green, *Suggestions for the Protection of the North West Frontier of India*, 16 August 1866, *Parliamentary Papers*, Central Asia, 1878-79, Vol. 77, p. 116.
9. G.Deleuze, *Proust and Signs*, p. 87.
10. Lytton to C.U.Atchison, (private) 13 December 1877, *Lytton Papers*, MSS.Eur.E.218/18.
11. Lytton to C.Girdlestone, (private & confidential), *Lytton Papers*, MSS.Eur.E.218/18.
12. Government of India to Cranbrook, Secretary of State for India, 20 November 1879, *India Foreign Proceedings*, Secret Supplement, January 1880, No. 491.
13. A.C.Lyall, *Note*, 19 September 1880, *Lyall Papers*, MSS. Eur.F.132/36.
14. Hartington to Gladstone, 19 September 1880, *Lyall Papers*, MSS.Eur.F.132/36.
15. Quoted in E.Baring, *Memorandum on the Retention of Kandahar and Pisheen*, 7 October 1880, *Parliamentary Papers*, Afghanistan, 1881, Vol.70, Part I, p. 215.
16. F.Haines, *Memorandum on the Retention of Kandahar*, 25 November 1880, *Political and Secret Letters and Enclosures from India* (hereafter PSLE), L/P&S7/27.
17. H.Rawlinson, *Notes on the Viceroy's Minute of 4 September 1878*, 26 October 1878, *Political and Secret Memoranda*, L/P&S/18/A 20.
18. *The Times*, Editorial, 10 October 1878.
19. P.D.Curtin, *Imperialism*, p. 53.
20. *Parliamentary Debates*, Lords 10 March 1884, Hansard, Third Series, Vol. CCLXXXV, col. 1008.
21. *Parliamentary Debates*, Lords, 10 March 1884, Hansard, Third Series, Vol. CCLXXXV, col. 997.
22. *Parliamentary Debates*, Lords, 10 March 1884, Hansard, Third Series, Vol. CCLXXXV, Cols. 1008-1009.
23. Biddulph to Northbrook, 19 October 1880, *Northbrook Collection*, MSS.Eur.C.144/6.
24. *The Times*, 22 May 1885.
25. *The Pioneer Mail*, 1 June 1884.
26. H.Green, *Memorandum on the Rectification of the North West Frontier of India*, 30 December 1878, *Parliamentary Papers*, Afghanistan, 1881, Vol. 70, Part I, p. 172.

27. Sandeman to Foreign Department, 19 October 1884, PSLE, L/P&S/7/43.
28. *Ibid.*
29. *The Pioneer Mail*, 4 March 1885.
30. Quoted in *The Times*, 14 May 1885.
31. *The Pioneer Mail*, 1 April 1885.
32. Connemara to Lansdowne, 8 August 1890, *Lansdowne Papers* MSS.Eur.D.558/19.
33. F.Roberts, *What Part should India take in the Event of a War between England and Russia*, confidential, 22 August 1888, *Salisbury Papers*, loose papers, Hatfield House, (hereafter HH.)
34. Dufferin to Cross, (private), 24 June 1887, *Dufferin Collection*, MSS.Eur.F.130/8A.
35. *The Englishman*, 5 November 1889.
36. *The Times*, 24 November 1890.
37. Quoted in *The Times*, 5 January 1898.
38. *Parliamentary Debates*, Lords, 7 March 1898, Fourth Series, Vol. LIV, col. 797.
39. Sandeman to Lansdowne, 13 September 1890, *Lansdowne Papers* MSS.Eur.D.558/19.
40. Lansdowne to J.B.Lyall, confidential, 12 December 1890, *Lansdowne Papers*, MSS. Eur.D.558/19.
41. Quoted in *The Times*, 20 May 1891.
42. Sandeman to Lansdowne, 21 November 1890, *Lansdowne Papers*, MSS.Eur.D.558/19.
43. Roberts to Lansdowne, 12 December 1890, *Lansdowne Papers*, MSS.Eur.D.558/19.
44. *Ibid.*
45. Sandeman to Lansdowne, 21 November 1890, *Lansdowne Papers*, MSS.Eur.D.558/19.
46. Lansdowne to J.B.Lyall, 12 December 1890, *Lansdowne Papers*, MSS.Eur.D.558/19.
47. Sandeman to Lansdowne, 2 September 1890, *Lansdowne Papers*, MSS.Eur.D.558/19.
48. J.B.Lyall to Lansdowne, 28 July 1890, *Lansdowne Papers*, MSS.Eur.D.558/19.
49. Sandeman to Lansdowne, 29 July 1890, *Lansdowne Papers*, MSS. Eur.D.558/19.
50. *Ibid.*
51. Lansdowne to Cross, 23 September 1890, *Lansdowne Papers*, MSS.Eur.D.558/19.
52. Sandeman to Private Secretary to Viceroy, 27 October 1890, *Lansdowne Papers*, MSS.Eur.D.558/19.
53. *Memorandum of Information, Regarding the Course of Affairs beyond the North West Frontier*, January 1893, *Political and Secret Letters from India*, Part II, January-March 1893, L/P&S/7/69.
54. H.Daly to Northbrook, 29 November 1897, *Northbrook Collection*, MSS. Eur.C.144/19.
55. Roberts to Lansdowne, 12 July 1890, *Lansdowne Papers*, MSS.Eur.D.558/19.
56. *Parliamentary Debates*, Lords, 7 March 1898, Fourth Series, Vol. LIV, cols. 792, 781.
57. Quoted in R.I.Bruce, *The Forward Policy*, p. 327, p. 325.
58. *The Times*, 15 February 1898.
59. Quoted in H. Lefebvre, *The Production of Space*, p. 134.
60. *The Pioneer Mail*, 4 March 1889.
61. *Blackwood's Edinburgh Magazine* 'Russia's Advance Upon India', July 1889, p. 129.

62. G.Chesney to Lansdowne, 9 July 1890, *Lansdowne Papers*, MSS.Eur.D.558/19.
63. *The Times*, 10 October 1890.
64. Salisbury to F.Lascalles, 6 October 1891, *Salisbury Papers*, HH.
65. H.Drummond Wolff to Lansdowne, (private), 16 August 1890, *Lansdowne Papers*, MSS. Eur.D.558/19.
66. Wolff to Salisbury, 8 July 1890, *Salisbury Papers*, HH.
67. Sandeman to Salisbury, 23 November 1891, *Ibid*.
68. Cunningham to R.J.Kennedy, (demi-official), 26 March 1891, *India Foreign Department Proceedings*, (hereafter IFDP), External A, Nos. 42-411.
69. D.Fitzpatrick, *Note on Baluchistan and Persia*, 22 November 1899, *Political and Secret Memoranda*, L/P&S/18/A145.
70. A.H.McMahon, British Commissioner, Baluch-Afghan Boundary Commission, to Secretary Foreign Department, 16 June 1896, No. 296, Enclosed in Government of India's letter of 11 August 1896, to George Hamilton, PSLE, L/P&S/7/88.
71. Government of India to Foreign Department, to George Hamilton, (secret), 16 September 1896, PSLE, L/P&S/7/88.
72. A.H.McMahon, *Memorandum on the Country South of the Baluch-Afghan Boundary Between Nushki and Persia*, 21 June 1896, PSLE, L/P&S/7/88.
73. F.C.Webb Ware, *Report on the Nushki-Chagai and Western Sinjerani Districts*, 1897-1898, Enclosed in Webb Ware's letter of 18 June 1898, to Agent to the Governor-General in Baluchistan, (hereafter A.G-G.in Bal.), *Curzon Collection*, MSS.Eur.F.111/364.
74. D.Fitzpatrick, *Note on Baluchistan and Persia*, 22 November 1899, *Political and Secret Memoranda*, L/P&S/18/A145.
75. W.J.Cunnigham, *Note*, 26 October 1898, IFDP, Secret Frontier, November 1898, Nos. 346-366.
76. F.C.Webb Ware, *Report on the Nushki-Siestan Trade Route* 1900-1901, p.12, Enclosed in Webb Ware's letter of 17 August 1901, to McConaghey, *Curzon Collection*, MSS.Eur. F.111/ 375.
77. Extract from *TransCaspian Review* 8 August 1897, IFDP, Secret Frontier, October 1897, Nos. 306-318.
78. Curzon to Salisbury, (private), 12 July 1900, *Salisbury Papers*, HH.
79. *Ibid*.
80. Curzon, *Note*, 15 March 1901, *Hamilton Papers*, MSS.Eur.C.510/8.
81. Curzon, *Note*, 20 May 1901, *Ibid*.
82. Quoted in India Office Political Department *Note on Persian Railways*, 3 July 1911, *Political and Secret, Memoranda*, L/P&S/18/C124.
83. D.Fitzpatrick, *Note on Baluchistan and Persia* 22 November 1899, *Political and Secret Memoranda*, L/P&S/18/A45.
84. Hamilton to Curzon, 16 May 1901, *Hamilton Papers*, MSS.Eur.C.126/3.
85. Quoted in Hamilton to Curzon, 4 December 1902, *Hamilton Papers*, MSS.Eur.C.126/4.
86. Hamilton to Curzon, 17 September 1902, *Hamilton Papers* MSS.Eur.C.126/4.
87. *The Times*, 10 September 1902.
88. H.Lefebvre, *op.cit.*, p.128.

3

Image and Identity: Constructions and Misconstructions of Tribalism in Imperial Eyes

The imperialisation of tribal space, initiated the re-representation of its identity and imagery, in sign and symbol, to map the terrain of otherness, and empower the re-writing of spatial form and content. Categories of the exotic and the excluded, braided imagistic reflection with rhetoric to suggest the forbidden, dangerous iconicity of tribalism, that provoked curiosity and censure. Mental topographies of subject-object, interior-exterior, truth and error, mirrored the tropic divide between imperial and tribal forms, signifying hierarchies of mind and meaning, mapping distance and dimensions of mastery and servility. The imperial text as a site of cultural control, propagated a perspectivism that was interest related and partial, in its representation of the object of scrutiny and command, i.e. the tribal, in order to fix, arrest and enclose him under the sign of the 'other', to normalize his subjugation in the horizon of meaning and being. Knowledge as the proxy of power would transform tribal space into the place of the written word, the rule of history, the order of imperial inscription and redemptive remaking, with the tribe/primitive crypted in the abyss of unreason, chaos, and destruction.

Trapped at the margins of civilization, the tribal landscape offered a reading of itself as Europe's other, as the prehistory of mind, of evolution arrested in time. The genealogy of this consciousness reached back to Plato and Aristotle, who contended that primitive people could only exist well as servile instruments of free men.[1] In this assumption, the concept of the primitive was beginning to be shaped by aggression and objectification. To the negative significance of the primitive in classical minds, medieval Christian Europe added its own figural dimension of the diabolical and demonic, so as to view all primitive pagans and non-Europeans as souls to be saved, and infidels to be conquered, rather than people with customs to be described. The primitivist concept acquired another layer, as medieval imagery engaged with Enlightenment reason and eighteenth century voyages of discovery, to locate the primitive outside Europe conceptually and cartographically. Confronted with the cannibal or primitive warring band, that seemed to defy both the rational and the human, Enlightenment thought retreated to the idea of the unnatural, the monstrous to typify the savage of the species witnessed in strange shores. Reading this perceived difference in human types as genetic, David Hume, the 18th century philosopher suggested," Such a uniform and constant difference could not happen in so many countries and ages, if nature had not made an original distinction betwixt these breeds of men".[2] In France, Montesquieu's *Persian Letters* was setting up the image of Europe as the 'scientific' and 'progressive'[3] continent. Discourse and discovery balancing against each other, were siting the Enlightenments' alternate 'other' in the geographically remote and exotic primitive.

In post-Enlightenment society, translations of difference still remained anchored to the dichotomization of self and other, in the Nietzschean sense of point and margin, centre and periphery, the moral and amoral terrain of human being. But it acquired a more coercive dimension, as it became part of the imperial world-picture in the nineteenth century, signifying structures of mastery and servility, connotated by the expansion of the European nation-state to sites of colonial power and privilege. Within this structure of signification, and its closures in terms of oppositions and hierarchizations, that which did not conform to the teleologies of Western reason, history and progress had to be edited, censored, and suppressed. Distorted within this angle of perception, verbal inscriptions of the disempowered margin, tended to be signatures of the politically dominant on the social body, of those excluded from the exercise of constructing their own identity and image.

The negative difference of the tribal/primitive was shaped by the register of resemblance and analogy, reflected in Darwinian evolutionary constructs, with its linkage of the primitive with the inferior, and the savage with the animal. Charles Darwin's horror of the Fuegian as a "savage who delights to torture... offers up bloody sacrifices...", and his celebration of European man who had "risen ... to the very summit of the organic scale ...may give him hopes of a still higher destiny in the distant future",[4] created the dominant codes of cross-cultural comparison in the nineteenth century. It legitimized structures of Western thought patterns, which would appropriate the task of global image making to serially arrange man on a linear scale of bio-cultural evolution. In particular the Darwinian pre-occupation with the nearness of man to apes, the Malthusian struggle for existence, the idea of survivals, located the savage/civilized model in an evolutionary sequence, where the primitive functioned as a fossil, a residual trace of an older natural order, signifying the shadowy, moribund past which European man had left behind in the time of pre-history.

Social Darwinists like E.B.Tylor and Herbert Spencer, used the Darwinian paradigm to geneticise the code of human history, linking the operation of race to patterns of bio-cultural difference, that shaped the textures of human space. Tylor's easy ethnocentrism maintained: "the educated world of Europe and America practically settles a standard by simply placing its own nations at one end of the social series and savage tribes at the other, arranging the rest of mankind between these limits according as they correspond more closely to savage or cultured life".[5] Here, the savage was the point of the past, waiting to acquire its missing apex of progress from the West. For Spencer, the idea of progress belonged to the mass of acquired traits, that became hereditary genetic blue-prints, to determine the savage and civilized categories of humanism. The alliance of reason and discipline created the archetype of the higher human form, while their absence resulted in the primitive type, captive to the irrational and animal instinct. In Spencer's *Types of Lowest Races* the savage was typically "Dark skinned and small of stature... unclean, promiscuous and brutal..."[6] It was a verdict which would determine the parameters of primitivist-tribal representation, implying biological backwardness and stunted growth, suggesting that the primitive was typologically wretched, with an added dash of diabolicalness.

Degrees of mental progress were measured in terms of distance from primitive reflex action. Tribes, women of inferior rank, children and criminals were metaphorically equated through similitudes to savages, or departure from civilized norms, as the servile matter of humanity. Figuratively the primitive did not mirror the innocence of nature, but marked the shape of its savage distortions. The romanticism of Rousseaus's noble savage was metamorphosizing in the Social-Darwinist imaginary, into the darker

Hobbesian version of primal man caught in the toils of endemic conflict. Analogies of the childlike, criminal, and savage, to signify the concept and category of the primitive, proved particularly seductive and persuasive to the imperial sensibility, seeking a definition of the native that would imply subjection, not just in terms of self and other, but as error, deviance, unreason. A subject-position at once immature and half-grown, governed by the instinct to crime, could be construed as the site for exercising paternalistic control in the classic tradition of Victorian authoritarianism, of the adult European ruler guiding and correcting the errant, childlike native, while masking this control as the civilizing mission, the redemptive text of the 'white man's' imperial burden. Social Darwinism captured the distortions of Western mirroring, that imaged the unfamiliar and unknown as ancestral darkness, the primitive time in which the alienated 'other' of European man was trapped. It was implicated in Europeanizing the concept of culture, gestating the problem of the centre defining the margin, perceiving the 'other' as reflection and refraction of the dark recesses of the instinctual self that had to be suppressed and denied.

I

Influenced by the story of Victorian evolutionism, and the supremacist perspective of an imperial race, colonial representations of tribal Baluchistan were structured on a cluster of core ideas, that stressed the autonomy of reason, and the universalistic nature of meaning. The visual possibilities of this determinism by 'race, moment, milieu', suggested the categories, reflections and analogies through which the empire read the tribe, subordinating the substance of the real to propagate its model, that would function as self-evident law, reconfirmed through the form. History and ethnology were searched to create pictures of the mind, that captured the tribal figure in gestures and geometries, that reconfirmed the distances of conception and misconception, separating the imperial from the tribal. M.L.Dames, author of *A Historical and Ethnological Sketch of the Baloch Race* and also Political Agent in the Baluchistan Agency, suggested a metonymic condensation of the word Baluch to signify ethnicity and a typology of violence. Noting their resemblance to warriors of the *Shahnama* on account of their preference to dismount and fight on foot at close quarters, Dames inferred a probable Persian ethnic affiliation, and original geographic location of the Baluch near the Black Sea, where they served in the ranks of Kai Khusroe, the sixth century Persian ruler's army. But the raiding activities of the Baluch forced the Persian ruler Nausherwan to lead a punitive expedition against them, which probably set in motion the first exodus of the Baluch from northern Persia to Kirman. Subsequently, the military power of the Ghaznavids, followed by the strong centralising government of the Seljuk Turks, rendered the Kirman-Siestan region unprofitable for raiding, forcing the Baluch to migrate eastwards. By the fourteenth/fifteenth centuries, these raiding/migrating Baluch bands reached Baluchistan, and colonized parts of it; the Marri and Bugti tribes in the valley of the Suleiman Mountains near Sibi, the Jamalis and Umranis in the Nasirabad tracts, and the Rakshanis, Sinjeranis, Damanis and Rekis along Chagai and Western Sinjerani country.[7] The story of this tribal colonization was a narrative of conflict, that not only traced the literal punctuations of victory and defeat to establish possession, but also expressed the symbolism of violence in the tribal imaginary, as the celebrated terrain for confirming the heroic and epical in tribalism. Dames's translation of popular Baluch ballads tracing the emerging tribal contours of the Baluchistan-south Punjab frontier region, represented the central configurations of Baluch culture in terms of war, reprisals, and revenge, staged on a wild and hostile landscape, where the savagery of man and nature acted as mirror and montage to affirm images of destruction, loss, negation. The darkness of this picture was captured in the epic ballad of the Rind-Lashari (two Baluch tribes) war in the course of the sixteenth century, soon after the Baluch entered India through the Bolan and Mulla passes. Mir Chakar, chief of the Rinds quarrelled with Mir Gwaharam, the chief of the Lasharis, on the bases of passions and interests, related to rival desires for the same woman, the social prestige value of horse racing, and the economics of livestock possession. Acting on this surface of perception, the Rinds engaged on a horse racing exercise with the Lasharis, and distorted the actual result to claim a false victory. The outraged Lasharis retaliated by killing a herd of camels belonging to the tribeswoman who was the object of the Rind chief's desire, and under his protection. This provoked the latter to embark on a war of revenge, that entered Baluch history as the Rind-Lashari conflict, which lasted for thirty years, at the end of which a remnant of the Rinds survived in Punjab, while the Lasharis were completely destroyed. This corner of historic memory subsequently became the site for mediating the archetypal warrior hero, i.e. Mir Chakar Rind, whose leadership captured an image and concept of violence, that coded the symbolic space of the tribe as the originary sign of nature, gesturing the sensual, physical, and the fearful symmetries of power. As Dames noted, Mir Chakar was brave and a 'semi-savage', who instinctively provoked his cousin Jaro to kill his own son, simply to test whether Jaro would keep his oath to kill anyone who touched his beard.[8] Chakar's lapse, and the moral aporia of the Baluch in their choice of Chakar as iconic of the legendary leader, made the tribal figure a being of 'crude passion',and his history a mere repetition of "vivid scenes of war and rapine",[9] as Dames put it. In imperial readings, the tribe was being moored in history and anthropology, as the savage territorial machine, a pre-moral relic. Denys Bray, exploring linguistic significations in Baluchistan wrote in the Census of 1911, regarding the meaning of the Baluch word *tuman*:

> "The very name *tuman*, the Turkish *tuman* 'the ten thousand', almost seems to imply... a tribe on the war path, warring first with the alien people that stood in its way, and warring later with any rival *tuman* that disputed its spoils.".[10]

Dominated by archetypes and their repetition, the tribal past in Bray's estimate, stood outside the ground of real history, approximating merely primitive behaviour patterns feeding on crises, contradictions and the anxieties they engendered.

The tribal system designed to always reconstitute itself on its own ruins, made use of scission to frustrate fusion, to preserve in its composition, the ethnological predisposition for the migration of power, thereby impeding its central concentration; to sustain the nomadic rites of leadership and territorial signs, that would inscribe and revise identities, on political ground being made and remade in the language of material desires and demands. Confronted with the presence of division, and the power of the fragmentary in the tribal political view, Dames sketched a picaresque description:

> "The composite tribe [Baluch] or tuman is built up of several clans. Within the clan the members are supposed to be of the same kindred, and as a rule the nucleus of the *tumans* consist of a few clans ... which consider themselves to be closely connected by blood. These have served as a centre of attraction for other less powerful unattached clans which have lost their original tribes either through internal quarrels or through the tribe having been defeated and broken up. The new tie is not always a very strong one and such members of a tribe are the first to leave it if it is defeated, and look for a more powerful protector. Sometimes mere discontent with the chief, or an internal feud, is sufficient to drive a clan from one *tuman* to another.[11]

Dames was depicting the lacuna of tribal political ground, and its mirage like quality, that reflected images of power for the moment, unable to acquire permanency or transcend the purely episodic in their assertion. The explanation for this lack, was linked to ethnological descriptions, that suggested the Baluch were typologically wretched and unable to overcome their limitations. Imperial translations of the word 'Baluch' to mean the bad and naked, affirmed the notion of the minimal tribal world exiled from ethics and culture. The linguist, G.W.Gilbertson, profiled the Baluch character by dissecting the term 'Baluch'. Taking the small word *luch* to mean 'bare' i.e.naked, he suggested that the term was an abbreviation of the compound word *luch-bahadur*, which signified a thorough paced villian, a scamp and a vagabond. He therefore concluded that in the Baluch "we have the desert scamp...of whose shortcomings we hear so much".[12] To legitimize his evaluation he referred to Dames's observation: "Robbers they [the Baluch] were and to some extent still are: to be successful in raids and cattle thefts was a title to esteem, and *rahzan* or highwayman was a title to honour".[13] Like Gilbertson, Colonel Mockler writing on the Baluch in 1895, asserted that the Rind Baluch "whose name signifies a turbulent, reckless daring man",[14] had never acknowledged the authority of any ruler and professed to owe obedience to no one. As such, the reality of the Baluch in imperial verbal terrain, stood arrested within the enclaves of primitivism and nature. The Baluch tribe was iconic of the beast in man, and the sign of ungoverned nature. Translating a Baluch war song, that internalized nature in poetry, Dames tried to establish the connection between the wildness existing within the Baluch and outside him, in trees and rocks, rivers and rainstorms. The Baluch imaginary tied to nature as a metaphor for the tribal self, recounted in ballad:

> "The mountains are the Baloches forts: these hills are better than an army. The lofty heights are our comrades, the pathless gorges our friends. Our drink is from the flowing springs, our cups the leaf of phish, our beds the thorny brush, the ground our pillow. My horse is my white sandals. For my sons you may take the arrows, for my bretheren the broad shield, for my father the wide-wounding sword."[15]

The poetics of this tribal experience and concept of nature, that contradicted the Western perception of nature as object to be mastered and manipulated, traced the difference of identity in language, entering the space of Europe's other as the contradictory, the uncivilized and the wild.

On the surface of imperial consciousness, the Brahui mimicked the Baluch in his savagery, but he was more obscure, fettered in ignorance, and lacked the predisposition for productive labour. Exploring the ethnicity of the Brahui in the *Baluchistan Census Report* of 1911, and in his books *The Life History of a Brahui* and the *Brahui Language*, Bray came to view them as a primitive enigma. Etymological evidence suggested linkages with west and central Asia; "The Brahui", Bray wrote were the "ba-ro-hi- 'people on the hill' or as they put it be-ra-hi 'people without roads' or the men of Biroea, ancient Aleppo."[16] The Syrian origin was favoured by the ruling house of Kalat, as it fed the myth of a descent from the Prophet's uncle Mir Hamza, who lived in Aleppo. But as Bray pointed out, Brahui tribal names suggested a wider catchment area. The Mingals for instance were probably the Mins of the Behistan inscriptions, while the Sarparras could be identified as descendants of Strabo's Saraparae, a Thracian tribe whose name was supposed to be derived from their custom of decapitating strangers.[17] In this ethnographic reconstruction, the Brahui was already emerging as heir to the horrors of savagery.

Bray would not admit language as evidence of ethnicity in the case of the Brahuis, as their dialect belonged curiously to the Dravidian language group; but there were no other cultural similarities with the races of south India. The other possibility, of Brahuis possibly forming a component of the pre-Aryan, possibly Dravidian Mohenjo-daro civilization which had included parts of Baluchistan, Bray dismissed as untenable on acount of the civilized-savage dichotomy; as he pointed out:

> "And in all human history there are few greater contrasts than between the highly developed city-civilization of Mohenjo-daro and the wandering tent life of the hill Brahuis. Sir Auriel Stein faces the difficulty with imaginative candour. In the Brahuis he sees not indeed the descendants of the ancient settled race who founded the civilization, but the descendants of the semi-barbarous peoples on the fringe, its poor relations as it were. And he points to the Brahui hills above the plains of Mohenjo-daro, bleak, barren affording the invader neither attraction nor room for settlement, as just the ground where a nomadic fringe of the city-civilization might be left undisturbed, throughout the ages, long after the cities had been blotted out."[18]

The perception of the Brahui as the primitive in history, seemed to synchronize with his present, that was permanently captive to the limiting boundaries of the nomadic and natural, in patterning his existence. As Bray described:

> "The Brahuis are essentially a pastoral people, breeders of sheep and goats; in the more favoured part of the country they rear horses and cattle. Lazy and unenterprising they make poor agriculturists. The extremes of heat and cold and the general poverty of their country necessitates periodical migrations ...but though nomads in this restricted sense, they cling with a strange tenacity to their somewhat inhospitable country. They ... have no liking for the trammels of regular discipline ... The Brahui ... is childishly fond of show ... His faith is by no means fashioned according to the strict letter of Muhammadan orthodoxy ... To this day belief in evil spirits, who may be warded off by charms and exorcised by sacrifices of blood and the frenzy of the devil dancer is all but uinversal".[19]

Bray's Spencerian image making, uncovered the Brahui as the stereo-typical native who was childlike, indolent, unable to function as the instrument of his own elevation. The poverty of the tribal condition therefore signified what was lacking, that which was incapable of development, a stunted form of species survival excluded from the curve of history as the progress of man.

The Pathan pictorial extended the descriptive domain of tribalism deeper into the realm of the unacceptable. It mirrored the base "primitivity", that was "to them a second nature – their polygamy, their blood-feuds, their sanguinary wars of succession"; the Pathan problematic, signified the ultimate contradiction of race and nature, that configured frontier space as the intractability of "irreclaimable desert and the eternal mountains ... and the equally irreclaimable faithlessness and treachery of the Afghan character... Their homes are caves ... their lurking places are the rocks whence-armed ... they pick off with deadly aim any well-to-do passer by".[20] Further as George Hamilton put it, that unlike the Baluch, the Pathans were a source of inexhaustible fanaticism. A Pathan was always ready to reinvent himself as a spiritual soldier, eager to eliminate the non-Muslim infidel, so as to achieve a place in paradise, and enter the narrative of the heroic in tribal myth and fable. The oppositional and adverserial in Pathan consciousness, were decoded in terms of distrust and suspicion, a rhetoric of the emotions, inherited from Europe's long perception of Islam, as the external enemy, signifying the frontier of force and fear against Christendom. Describing the attitude of the Pathan tribes in the Zhob area of Baluchistan, R.I.Bruce, one of the Political officers wrote: "They only knew of us by reputation as *faringhis* or *kafirs* (infidels), whom it was the duty of all good Mahomadens to slay with the sword.".[21] In the imperial visual spectrum, the Pathan mimicked the violations and violence of the anarchist in Europe, like a spectre of destruction, existing outside the moral category of the human. His character and conduct betrayed the compulsion to plunder and rob, not from the crisis of circumstances, but from choice as an ethnic trait. Alluding to the moral malformation of the Pathan type, C.E. Bruce described the mental attitudes of one such group of Pathans – the Achakzais:

> "...it is popularly believed that when an Achakzai is stricken in years and getting past work, he cannot woo sleep unless he pilfers something from his own house and hides it away.".[22]

Another Pathan section, the Kakozai Badinzais were foregrounded in imperial writing as "real aristocrats of the profession of cattle lifting. Their father Kako once made an ecstatic flight through the air with a gobbet of flesh through his teeth; and to the Kakozais this pious legend is proof positive that burglary is a highly respectable calling for Kako's descendants".[23] In this summary, the Pathan image was trapped on the negative surface of passion and greed, implicated in the error of defining his interiority in the language of terror and moral lapse.

II

The ethnographic mapping of the Baluch, Brahui and Pathan tribal types as the 'other' of human morality and reason, was reaffirmed in administrative, archival reports that tended to locate tribal economic and political man in the compass of nature and need, working within the codings of the sinister and sensual to defend territory, tribe and title. In charting the tribal scene, imperial reports proliferated with case studies of feuds and raids, as primary social strategies for maximizing material gains. The language of structured violence implicit in feuding and raiding texts, promoted the idea of tribal space as natural space, absorbed in a dark Hobbesian struggle for survival in a scene of scarce resources and rewards. In official reconstructions, tribal man seemed permanently sentenced to enact the Darwinian saga of primitive man's brutal existence in nature. He was the disfigured predator, stalking the land for food and shelter, poised for violent action to defend or expand his survival ground. The fusion of the harsh and natural in the tribal model, made it a metaphor for the survival of the fittest philosophy, drawing curiosity and censor as the exotic and the ex-centric in human space and time.

Raids and feuds as fulcrums of the tribal behaviour model, monopolised the text of official writing; they coded the flows of tribal desires that enveloped the physical and political. Perceived as regulators of tribal social metabolism, raids and feuds were political and economic statements, that differed in time and execution. The raid appeared as a finite act of violence, operated for immediate political effect, or to enlarge the material holdings of a group by removing assets from an enemy group. In contrast, official reports depicted the feud as a medium for keeping alive the pathology of social conflict, unrestricted by the passage of time. The ground of the political feud mirrored the interiority of the tribe, where passions for power and privilege within the hierarchical text of the tribe were pursued. In its economic orientation, however, the feud tended to be spatially mapped, as extrinsic phenomena unfolding on the in-between spaces, separating tribal territories. The economic connotations of the feud, were translated in imperial writing as biological survival responses, linked to niche competition in a poor material environment.

Observing the feuding scape, from a time-place perspective, it seemed that the specific material premises of feuding structures differed in relation to local ecological variables, which dictated the ratio of agricultural/pastoral resources in the tribal economy, and the availability/non-availability of permanent sources of water. The spatial operation of these factors, which operated with greater or lesser intensity in a particular micro-area, usually determined the lifespan of individual feuds. Nomadic pastoral tribes like the Marris and Bugtis in north-east Baluchistan, with little agricultural income and low water resources, were seen as most susceptible to the feuding psychology, as they lived almost permanently on the frontier of want and scarcity, and their social adaptation conformed to configurations of violence, that signified the terror and tensions of survival in the wilderness of nature. The stairway of the tribal structure, with its tiers of sections and leaders, with well defined responsibilities for assuming the vengeance liablity, arising from the killer-victim script of the feuding narrative, provided a structured arena for the dialectic of violence to form and deform the tribal body. From the *pira/paro* of the Baluch and Brahui tribal structures, and the *kahol* in the Pathan case, that functioned as primary self-help groups in cases of offence against any of their members, the principle of retaliation reached to upper tiers of the tribes, i.e., the agnatic sub-section whose members lived in close proximity to each other, and shared land and water rights, who were required to redress any victimization of their members, unavenged at the lower levels of segmentation. If the killer and victim belonged to different tribes, the principle of vengeance would dictate the phenomenon of the inter-tribal feud, that would fester in time and space. In strategy and structure therefore, the feud perpetuated a vision of tribalism, implicated in an ideology of force that was total and terrible in its domination of mind and matter.

A closer scrutiny of feuds in the arid zones of Baluchistan, served the purpose of revealing their scarred imprints on the self of tribalism, revealing a poverty of form, content, and imagination. The asymmetry of subjugated groups and subject groups, structured the feuding complex in north-east Baluchistan, where aggressive, mobile semi-nomadic tribes like the Marris, Bugtis, and Kakars preyed on sedentary, settled tribes like the Shadozais and Lunis, for land and livestock. Occupying the centre of this feuding map was the Marri tribe, whose collective narratives mirrored the fury and fear, of the disconnections and deterritorializations, actualized by the exercise of feud. The origin of the Marri psychology of feud, was partially traced to physical lack, where nature as a limiting boundary to economic development, created an endemic crisis of scarcity, that coded the desire for forceful territorial gains from neighbouring tribes. Comparing the stony surface of Marri tribal areas to that of uninhabited deserts, where water was scarce and the cultivable land did not exceed three per cent of the total area, imperial description perceived in the Marri tribal psyche, the negative imprint of the wilderness in its most sinister and savage form. Placing him in the category of hostile nature, imperial mirroring imaged the Marri as a biological imperfection, carrying the code of the harsh world he inhabited. As one account put it:

> "Their [Marri] country consists for the most part of rugged hills destitute of water...an ideal robber stronghold ... The Marris are inveterate robbers. Their hand is against every man and every man's hand is against them. They lead a nomadic life and have no villages, except a few mud forts, and, with the exception of those members of the tribe who live about Mandai, depend very little on agriculture".[24]

DIAGRAM OF MARRI TRIBAL LIMITS IN RELATION TO NEIGHBOURING TRIBES.[1]

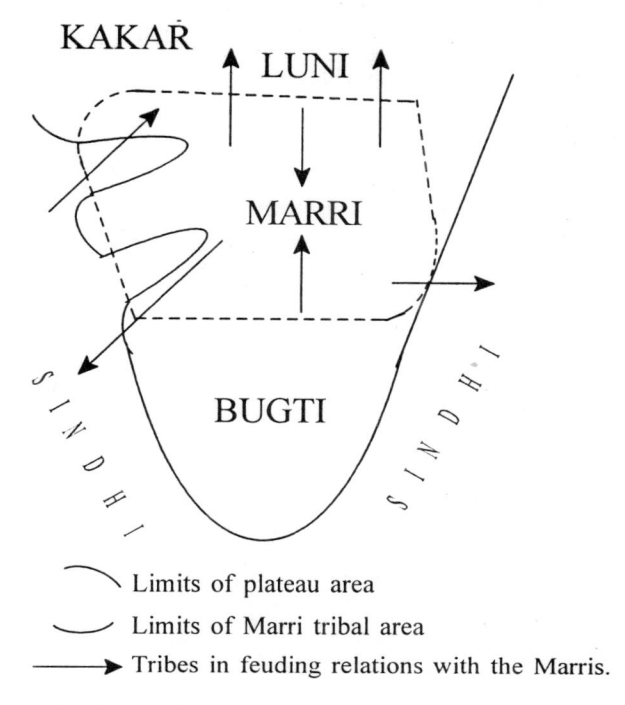

```
         KAKAR    LUNI ↑
                  ↑ ↑
                  ↓
                 MARRI
                  ↑
       S                     S
        I                     I
         N       BUGTI       N
          D                 D
           H               H
            I             I
```

⌒ Limits of plateau area
⌣ Limits of Marri tribal area
⟶ Tribes in feuding relations with the Marris.

1. Model based on F. Barth's 'Competition and Symbiosis in North East Baluchistan', *Folk*, 6,1,1964.

The discovery of the robber in the Marri type, encouraged the criminalisation of tribal conduct, sustaining the Victorian euphemism that what was criminal in London would pass as the norm of the native in the empire. This negative reading, seemed to receive further legitimation from a self-declatory statement by the Marri tribe, expressing its self-conscious world view; as the Marris announced:

> "We are the enemies of all our neighbours. We do no good to anyone, nobody wishes us well, let us then afford every encouragement to strife around us, let us give passage through our country to anybody who seeks it to injure another, whichever side is injured or destroyed matters not to us in any case we shall be the gainers".[25]

The Marri voice was making visible the pathology of the savage mind, trapped on the surface of its own egoistic desires for aggression and appropriation of the space of the 'other', symbolically resolved as the enemy of the self, whose elimination was legitimate and desirable. This narcissistic accent of the Marri tribe was a position of desire, the first signs of which were the territorial signs, inscribed across the spatial map of 'other' tribes. As O.T.Duke pointed out in his report, Marri tribal territory was the heritage of a warring past. Their lands in Kahan, Philawar, Nissau were won from the Hassanis between 1759-1780; Quat Mandai and Badra were taken from the Pani Pathans between 1839-1842, followed by the possession of Kohlu valley from the Zarkhun Pathans. The legacy of this warfare was a state of permanent feud with neighbouring tribes. Memory and meaning sustained the primacy of feuds in Marri ontology, and when the British engaged with the tribes after 1876, they found the group at war with the Shadozais and Lunis (Pathan tribes). Under mounting pressure from Marri depredations, the Lunis retreated from parts of their tribal territory like Bagao and Chamalang, which according to British records degenerated into violent wastelands, where life was always on the brink of extinction from the

Marri reign of terror. Thus the bleakness of the natural terrain in Baluchistan, was always deepened and darkend by tribal imprints signifying desolation, void, absence.

Twinned with the Marris, were their neighbouring Baluch tribes the Bugtis, who were part of the horror of the tribal nightmare, that the British recorded. The Bugtis entered official description as the malefic tribesmen who:

> "Occupied the angle between the frontiers of the Punjab and Upper Sind ... The Bugti country is rugged and barren ... The regular occupation of the tribes was...plundering, carried on systematically and on a large scale. Every man in the tribe was a robber ...usually at war with the Marris, and perpetually plundering their neighbours".[26]

Athough menacing as individual tribes, the peculiar danger of the Marri-Bugti equation, was linked to the periodic alliances between them, when they put a moratorium on hostilities, to engage in joint depredations against enemy territories, in the hope of causing more damage and reaping richer rewards from victims. Between 1860-1880 the Marris and Bugtis entered British records for raiding the Punjab, Sind, and Kalat frontier, as well as the hill country of the adjacent tribes with great ferocity, spreading absolute 'desolation and terror'. Reflecting on the human and political cost of the Marri-Bugti raiding assaults, Robert Sandeman wrote: "... the attack by the Marris and Bugtis on the Shadozai chief of Thal Chotiali in which two of the latter were killed, was rapidly followed by the late attack on the Dombkis ...in which eighty of the tribe were killed, makes me despair that affairs are reaching a crisis, and that I cannot ... hope to preserve the peace of the Punjab frontier ... which is greatly exposed to Marri and Bugti depredations.".[27]

In imperial eyes, the Marris and Bugtis as authors of carnage, were guilty of forcing the boundary of the human to retreat so as to reassert the reign of the natural, the barbaric, the instinctual on the social map. Tribalism was now a sign of the desperate in the human; it was savage through geography and temper; it signified the threat of barbaric negation, that justified its suppression and subjection within the matrices of the imperial and ethical.

The signification of feuding violence in defining and dissolving boundaries of desire and power, in the tribal territorial context, could also be read in the social codings of the west Baluchistan area, bordering on Persia, where the desert provided sinister cover for a marginal existence, that carried the imprint of the inhuman, the tragic and the desperate. This western corner of Baluchistan, extending from the highest point of the Malik Siah Koh to the Mashkel Lake or Hamun, was the barren setting for an unsettled tribal existence unable to transcend the limits of scarcity, and the oppression of force, in determining models of social behaviour. The reality of feuding configurations here, were depicted in imperial representations as species specific adaptation in an arid environment, mirroring the Lamarckian notion of the mutation of behaviour into hereditary instinctual traits. In this perception, the labyrinth of sandy hills that honey-combed the region, was the natural space for the outlaw, the fugitive from civilization. The desert which signified the emptiness outside existence, could only accommodate marginal life forms, that depended on the violence and violations of preying on the material patch that belonged to another, in a world apart from their own. Worlding the desert from his own cultural space, the imperial observer, perceived the sandy hills as 'ideal hideouts for robbers', existing far from the reaches of central government, making it a 'veritable Alsatia for the border outlaw'. The poverty of material life here, was disfiguring and daunting enough to make the possession of a few date palms, the object of desire and subject of discord. T.H.Holdich, while drawing the Perso-Baluch boundary, recorded the desperation and desolation of the desert feud. He wrote, that at the edge of the Hamun which was a salt swamp in dry weather, and a shoreless sea in times of flood, were a few scattered date groves, inadequately cultivated, ragged and unproductive, which from time immemorial had been the bone of contention between two local tribes. Identifying these tribes as the "wild and lawless Damani tribes of Eastern Persia and the desert bred Rekis of Baluchistan", he continued to describe how "raids and reprisals blood feuds and wayside murders have been hatched in these wretched groves, until matters had reached an acute fighting stage, when our government stepped in and decided to have a Persian boundary."[28] As a nomadic, predatory tribe the Damanis lived purely by the psychology of capture, and their annual descent into Reki territory to raid the date harvest, causing dispossessions and feuding destructions, signified the lapse into a damaged existence, where the desert had claimed the human in its sinister script of sand and scarcity.

The decimations and disconnections of the feuding narrative, also scarred tribal fields in neighbouring Chagai and Nushki. Here a victim-predator picture was drawn to adequate representation with reality. In Chagai, the Sayyids, a group with religious status on account of their descent from the Prophet, were portrayed as passive victims of the predatory Sinjerani Baluch from the Helmund, who coveted camel grazing tracts in the area. The feuds which followed from this opposition of interest and intent, exterminated the Sayyids, except for a small fragment, centring the Sinjeranis in the new spatial angle they desired, thereby effectively altering the boundaries of power and powerlessness in favour of the aggressor and intruder.

The idea of possession through dispossession, that structured feuding narratives, entered the spatial texts of tribes in neighbouring Nushki, in terms of territories lost and won, without punctuation and stoppage. Official summaries of this dark spectacle of attrition and appropriation, mentioned the Mandai Baluch as the original inhabitants of the area, who were so weakened by internal rifts, that they were unable to defend themselves against the depredations of the Barech Afghans from Shorawak. Consequently, the Mandais sought assistance from a nearby Baluch tribe, the Badini Rakshanis. The two tribes combined to drive out the Barech raiders, but in the aftermath as the British Political Agent, Webb Ware described: "The Badinis then proceeded to establish themselves in Nushki, quite regardless of the feelings of their host".[29] British records in 1899, further documented the unscrupulous appropriation of Mandai lands by the Rakshanis, to the point that the Mandais ceased to exist as an independent tribe, being forced to merge with another branch of the Rakshanis, i.e., the Jamaldanis in order to survive. In this official picture of tribal history as horror, the Rakshanis imaged the darkness of political cannibalism, feeding on betrayal, oppression and elimination. Again, there seemed to be no margin of redeeming virtue in this emerging story of tribalism.

The ground created by feuding force, was however never stable; it was always the victim of changing passions of time and mind, and the Rakshani usurpation itself came under siege from new ambitions and aspirations from across the border. This threat materialized in the form of the powerful and aggressive nomadic tribe, the Zaggar Mingal Brahuis, whose chief decided to migrate from Kalat to Nushki, to take possession of the waters of the Kaiser stream. Under pressure from largescale Mingal incursions, the Rakshanis had to give way on the water, and lost in addition the clear alluvial plain lands known as *dak* country, stretching from Nushki to Shorawak. Describing this dispossession, Webb Ware wrote: "The Mingals from time to time added to their possessions...largely by forcibly exacting compensation for bloodshed in the frequent quarrels which followed their arrival. The *dak* lands which this tribe claims comes under this category".[30] Webb Ware was suggesting the immorality of possession in the tribal scheme, where boundaries on the land were drawn in blood, where life resembled man's ape like ancestry in the forest, unmediated by a higher reason and vision.

Nomadism, that appeared central in the dark turns of the feuding narrative, was decoded as the sign of racial malformation, which effectively subtracted the primacy of the spatial dimension in textualizing feuds, although the objects of tribal struggles, i.e. land, water and pastures, indicated the inner predicaments of survival, rather than genocidal preference. In official views, tribal nomadism was represented as a behavioural norm, that had become hereditary by generations of application. A tribesman was therefore born with this genetic coding and its aggressive implications. Nomadism was a racial heirloom, whose premises were guarded by the power and prejudices of the savage temper, an inferior consciousness trapped in the margin of the pre-social, the backward, and the limited. Official reports described the 'natural disinclination' of nomads to engage in regular work of any kind, preferring instead the vagaries and risks of an unsettled existence, with no boundaries of permanence and plenitude. Advancing a biological argument for the norms of nomadism, Webb Ware wrote in 1899: "In my Administrative report for last year, I stated that the nomads of the district were characterised by an utter want of enterprise, added to which they were lazy and had little inclination to better their condition, and that in the few cases where I had induced them to start *karezes* (water wells) I had found that they were content to win a bare existence from the soil and disinclined to persevere". He found these nomads would only do a few days work digging water wells, and then "finding manual work irksome, and the nomad instinct asserting itself, they incontinently threw up their work and wandered off to pasture their flocks forty miles away". In Webb Ware's conclusion, this reflexive retreat on the part of the nomads from the ground of legitimate work, discipline and self-advancement, proved that it was futile, "to expect the nomad population ... to abandon all at once their roving habits engendered by years of wandering and to settle down quietly to agricultural life".[31] In this judgemental description, there was an implicit assertion that agriculture was the norm, while pastoral nomadism was a deviation from the socially correct anchorages of life. From the boundaries of this perspectivism, it followed that nomadism implied the errors of the human map, that could not be easily erased, without reversing the genetic coding within which it survived. As a racial imprint, it was almost immune to cultural re-writng, and would therefore persist as the unacceptable inscription of backward indolence, in the evolutive script.

If the primary sign of feud was the position of territorial desire, supplementary signs designating other directions, limits, and latitudes of interest, signified an investment of the social field with desires for chieftaincies, titles, and privileges of status. As imperial records suggest, all the tribes, Baluch, Brahui and Pathan, served as mediums for trapping the flows of ambition and anger, that coded the gestural language of political feud. The linear sign of the tribal chain, following a combinatory logic of hierarchically designed sections and leaders, functioned as a site for the desiring subject to always reinvent its own political ground, by seeking to move upwards, to the apical summit where power and privilege dominated. Edging close to this point, that signified mastery of the tribe, traced the field of desire in which feud was conceived. The Marris offered a version of this feuding inscription, in the graphic language of oppositions, that sought to subvert tribal schemes of power, leadership and alliance. In 1875, the succession of a new chief, Meherulla Khan, appeared to signal an interstitial time, suggesting political ambivalence at the centre, that could be exploited by the ambitious minded, seeking to limit the boundaries of the chieftaincy, before its consolidation by the new leader. Mir Hazar Khan, the leader of the Langav subsection, and also titular *wazir* or prime minister of the tribe, acted as the nucleus for aspirants seeking to grow politically at the expense of an uncertain centre. Meherulla Khan aware of this inner threat, abolished the position of *wazir*, so as to reduce Mir Hazar's official role. But this proved a pyrrhic victory, as it allowed feud to overpower the spaces of conception and misconception, where the passion and paranoia of the political psyche ruled. In this contesting zone, the desire for power was represented as the sign of feud, manifesting as ravaging raids and murderous killings, dissolving familial and sectional boundaries, to resignify the tribe as archaic anarchy. This imaging entered official description, where the feud was apprehended as crises, threatening the boundaries of order in the disorder of its flows. Expressing concern, the Deputy Commissioner wrote in 1892:

> "Matters recently reached the stage when Mir Hazar and all the headmen were on one side with the actual control of the tribe in their hands, while on the other hand Nawab Meherulla Khan stood practically alone and unsupported; as a natural consequence, existing feuds between sections of the tribe were allowed to continue unchecked, the contending factions of the tribes made use of their feuds to further their own cause, and the internal state of the tribe was drifting from bad to worse".[32]

To reverse these inner connotations of feud, the British sought to erase the originary cause of rupture, by restoring the title of *wazir* to Mir Hazar Khan. But the chief, Meherulla Khan preferred the schismatic ground of feud, to the political safe territory of compromise and concession. In order to keep alive the language of feud, he chose to accuse Mir Hazar Khan of poisoning his son. The imperial administration read this move, as the opening lines of a blood-feud chapter, that needed to be suppressed through corrective intervention. On this judgement, the British decided to eliminate Mir Hazar Khan completely from the tribal framework, allowing the chieftaincy to reclaim its lost ground, not in the idiom of tribal adequation of leadership with strength, but as a sign of imperial patronage to reinscribe the chiefship as a secondary, and subordinate voice, in imperial articulations of power and its subtractions.

The paralogisms of political feuds and their conclusions, may be surmised from the narratives of the Raisani Brahuis near Quetta, and the Pathans of Zhob, that like the Marri text, figured in imperial representations as stories of the savage code that invoked pleasure in pain, measured life in its negation, substituted absence for presence. In the case of the Raisanis, the Rustomzai section of the tribe desired separation and independence from the main tribe. This ambition for redefinition on the part of the Rustomzais, signified the alteration of existing boundaries of power within the tribe, implying loss and reversal for the Raisani chief, whose authority would lapse over a major tribal section. To prevent this remapping, the Raisani chief started the offensive by confiscating Rustomzai landed rights near Quetta, as well as blowing up their fort. In retaliation, the Rustomzais shot a Raisani tribesman in Quetta, and the sectional chief Allyar Khan openly declared in 1895, that he would avenge the injuries inflicted on his section by the Raisani chief. Hugh Barnes, Agent to the Governor-General in Baluchistan, judged these positional exchanges as the dangerous language of feud that sought annihilation as its end statement, that needed the restraining discipline of the imperial code, to be rescued from the brink of the chaotic. An imperial solution was now inserted in the tribal scheme, to arrest any inner answer to the question of schisms arising on the body of tribal political desire, by restoring the old pre-feuding boundaries within the tribe. The Rustomzais were given back their confiscated lands, and Allyar Khan was recognised as *sirdar* or leader of the Rustomzai section, on the condition that he acknowledged the overall supremacy of the Raisani chief in the tribal scheme.[33] In this representation and resolution of feud, imperial optics sought essentially to quarantine the tribe, against the diachrony of its own desire-identity linked contradictions, to disallow the history of the new from being written, by imprisoning the tribe within positions of the past. The feud was the gap which allowed the empire to write the history of the 'other' as the narrative of the self.

In the case of the Jogezai Pathans of Zhob, feud was again visible as break and rupture, but this time within the more narrow enclosure of the *sirdar khel* or the ruling family of the chiefship. The Jogezais were a subsection of the Sanzar Khel Kakar tribe, and their chief was regarded as nominal head of all the Kakars in Baluchistan, since the time of the eighteenth century Afghan emperor Ahmad Shah Abdali, who had conferred the title of *badshah* on the group leader. This investment of the symbolic and real in the configuration of chiefship, overcoded the position with a surplus value, transforming it into an object of permanent desire, that would form and deform the language of feud and its text of terror. In 1854 when the existing chief Rashid Khan passed away, his son Shahbaz Khan was ousted from the succession by an older cousin Shah Jahan. This usurpation split the ruling family into two rival feuding factions – Nawab Kahol to which the new leader belonged, and Ishak Kahol to which his dispossessed rival belonged. In the war of attrition which followed, the Ishak Kahols abandoned normal tribal affiliations to support non-Kakar tribal groups with whom the Nawab Kahol were embroiled in conflict relations. By way of retaliation, the Nawab Kahol blinded Dost Muhammad, a member of the Ishak Kahol, who took revenge by killing Jullundar, Shah Jahan's eldest son. The Pathan philosophy of *badal* or counter revenge had turned a political feud into the blood feud, that accepted no time horizons in its evolving story. Sandeman, as Agent to the Governor-General, perceived this extreme language of the Pathan feud, as the ideological errors of Islamic fanaticism and the savage instinct. Shah Jahan was imaged as a sadistic twisted figure, whose political reputation had been won on false religious propaganda that sought to establish him as a miracle worker and holy man, in order to secure submission through the terror of the sacred. He was also guilty of working in concert with religious *mullas* to preach *jihad* or holy war against all opponents, to fan tribal xenophobia in defence of his political domain. Sandeman proposed to disempower him by force, to expose him as a false prophet, whose powers would not "arrest the progress" of British arms in his country, and whose charms would be of "no avail against the bullets of our troops".[34] This was the language of intervention as intimidation, to overwrite tribal space in the control and command dictation of the imperial code. Sandeman led two military expeditions in 1884 and 1889, to crush Shah Jahan, and install Shahbaz Khan as chief of Zhob, on terms of loyalty, signifying dependency on the British, thereby effectively reversing the sign of the tribe as the unrestricted site of uncoded desire.

Supplementing the territorial and titular inscriptions of feud, was a more interior and intimate text, tracing ritual sexual aggression. As Deleuze and Guttari have suggested: "Beneath the conscious investments of economic, political ... formations, there are unconscious sexual investments, microinvestments that attest to the way in which desire is present in a social field, and joins this field to itself as the statistically determined domain that is bound to it".[35] Women as objects of sexual desire and derision, whom tribal men sought to dominate, exploit and possess, formed the body on which the language of feuding desire was imprinted in a sexual-social vocabulary. The sexual signification of women was stored in their biological roles as providers of descendants, in order to secure male lines of ownership. inheritance, and status-identity. This merging of the sign of the sexual and social in the female person, uncovered the concept of marriage as mirror and mirage, reflecting without resolving the dualisms of the sensual and mercenary, in the ritual gestures of bride-price and adultery, that marked and mapped acts of union. Narratives of marriage occurred in the margin of tribal consciousness that denoted women as commodities, or non-persons to be bartered in transactions between men, to secure new alliances, or as compensation to settle disputes. In this connotation, women functioned as a form of tribal currency, that circulated visibly in the social field as the exchange principle of the bride-price contract, which was central in all marital negotiations. Bride-price constituted a cash transaction between two families, according to which a woman was bought/sold by her male guardian for a sum of money, varying from Rs.300 to Rs.3,000, as well as other assets like livestock, depending on the paying capability of the family. The overpowering significance of this economic text could be read in its breach, where any departure from or denial of the bride-price contract, was the signal for terminating the marriage alliance structure, in the negation of the feuding sign and its blood code. As in the reported case of two families of Aliani Marris who entered a marriage alliance in 1886, with the bridegroom agreeing to pay Rs.100 in bride price, and give his sister in marriage to a male member of the bride's family, the contract miscarried soon after the marriage, as the bride passed away, leaving not mourners, but contesting voices anxious to limit material loss. The groom demanded his bride-price back, while the bride's family demanded the completion of the contract to give his sister in marriage to their group. Passion and paranoia drew this opposition to its feuding destination, when the groom was murdered by the brides's brother; in retaliation the victim's family took the life of the assailant's brother to equalize the field of injuries.[36] This translation of bride-price into blood feud, as the reports represented, implicated tribal ideology in marginalizing women in perception and reality, to exploit their presence or absence, as pretexts for writing texts of profit and loss in the language of feuding excess.

Exploring the dehumanizing spectacle of tribalism further, imperial reconstructions pointed to the crude and cruel, in the sign of adultery, that affected the making and meaning of sexual partnership, social possession and symbolic desire. Central to this inner consciousness was the disempowerment of women, that created the matrix within which gestures of erasure and symbolic substitution occurred. On the social graph, a woman was sold in marriage to make money, defend the tribal gene pool, and serve as free domestic labour. As one tribal proverb put it: "A wife does more work than a couple of bullocks, and with luck will breed enough in a few years to pay for her bride price thrice over".[37] In this association of the woman with an animal, was the negation that suggested she was a non-person. This view that sought to erase the idea of women as individuals, designated them as male possessions, so that their conduct was judged not in relation to themselves but the men to whom they belonged, husband, father or brother. The fictive servility of women and mastery of men, were symbolically coded in the tribal ideology of *izzat* and *sharm*, honour and shame. In tribal belief, this implied that the attribute of *sharm* or sexual shame, was latent in all women, but it impinged directly on the man's honour or *izzat*, when his wife, sister or daughter was guilty of committing adultery. Traditionally a husband or one of his own agnatic group had the right to avenge adultery, with the blood of the guilty couple, or at least the wife; this blood-price would wipe out the debt of blood-feud obligations. But if preferred, he could take compensation from the seducer which was usually a cash sum, varying from Rs.300 to Rs.1,500, depending on the ability to pay. After taking compensation, the husband usually divorced his wife, who was then turned out of the district and consigned to the care of a headman, in another district. The latter would keep her, until he could sell her in marriage again. He would then deduct the cost of her upkeep from the bride price, and the balance would be returned to her former husband.[38] Looking at a tribal woman therefore, Denys Bray commented that she was sentenced in her life time to be a mere "drudge about the house, a beast of burden on the march, in the courts a chattel in dispute, and too often a thing of dishonour".[39] Women as objects of derision and subjects of violation, re-drew the tribal narrative within the text of the savage, where being and becoming was mirrored in the sign of force.

In the space of imperial representation therefore, the regime of force and feud directly resulted from the savage inscription. Tribal desires, deceits, and devestations, signified fallen positions, the overwriting of the human code by its opposite. Tribalism was now a metaphor for illegitimate sensuality; it signified base passion, as described by Kant: " [For men] are full of savage and unreclaimed desires, of profit, of lust of revenge", which unmediated by culture make "all things dissolve into anarchy and confusion".[40] On the imperial plane of representation, tribal nature appeared simply as a flow of biological nature, signifying the margin of petrified reason, and the malignant topos of the anti-human, where vengeance and resentment marked not the beginning of justice, but its becoming and its destiny in the social formation.

III

Feud as the document of tribal barbarism, that mirrored the idea of the equivalence between damage and pain, seemed to embrace the Nietzschean allusion to "punishment as a means of instilling fear...punishment as festivity, that is, as the violation and humiliation of an enemy finally overcome; punishment as a means of producing a memory...for the person on whom the punishment is inflicted ...punishment as a form of compromise with the natural condition of revenge."[41] The image of feud as a celebration of cruelty, was at its most pervasive in travel accounts, where tribal ground was mirrored as the theatre of dark terrors, signifying the oppression of the moral void, that negated the idea of the good. Charles Masson, an early traveller, described feud as a form of Nietzsche's punitive debt structure, that opened the space for coding payment as pain, in the blood of the body. As he wrote:

> "Blood feuds once created, can hardly be extinguished and the tribes in their conflict, balance the accounts of slain on either side. A regular debtor and creditor account is kept, and the number of men and women ... for whom satisfaction in blood is required is carefully treasured in memory. The value of human life is but slightly appreciated in Baluchistan, if we may judge from the frequency of murders, and the apathy which attends their perpetration. No tie of consanguinity is sufficient protection from the perfidy of unnatural relatives. The domestic history of the greater portion of the chiefs of the several tribes furnishing a surprising and disgusting recital of crimes and treasons, and there is scarcely one whose hands are not imbrued with the life blood of his kinsmen".[42]

Feud as memory signifying revenge, as a contractual code regulated by ruthless force, as the experience of animal pleasure in all destruction, summarized the tribe as malefic and macabre, in the English traveller's imaginary, the dark otherness that preyed on human victims.

The European gaze drawn to the sinister strangeness inhabiting the tribal corpus, perceived in the sign of feud, the gestural language of primitive fury that sought to gratify the sensuality of victory and revenge, by torturing and tormenting spaces of the enemy body. Mapping the ferocity and frenzy of the tribal disposition, Ferrier, a French traveller passing through Baluchistan in the mid-nineteenth century described the nomad Baluch "as savage ... wild beasts, which like them rove through their deserts ... To observe laws like other nations, to work ... or obey a master, are things to them impossible ... they are as proud of their crimes as we are of our good actions."[43] He continued, that tribes embroiled in feud, "scent it like a pointer...They are without pity, and if unarmed will tear each other like tigers with their nails, bite with their teeth, or strangle one another without the least cry".[44]

Continuing the theme of horror in which western/imperial representation sought to locate the reality of tribalism, G.P. Tate travelling down the Indus in the 1890s, brought his own strain of Victorian perspectivism to record the tribes who lived in the 'silent wilderness' beyond the river. Habits of savagery were stressed, and the gruesome was foregrounded, to picture the tribe as the exotic other, for a readership expecting the unexpected, and a self-conscious imaginary anxious to perceive itself as the limit, beyond which stretched the barbarian world of moral aporia and extinction. In Tate's reconstruction, the tribal story was symbolic of the primeval nightmare in which reality was the dreadful pursuit of base human desires to hoard, kill, dominate, indulge and satisfy to the limits of power and lust. He wrote:

> "Horrible stories were told over camp fires of revengeful murders in the balancing of feuds: and of the means adopted to render it unlikely that the captives taken and enslaved should ever desire to be taken to their homes. In 1891 I saw two pillars of earth that were declared to contain the remains of two men who had been tied to stakes and entombed alive. These men had been the owners of two exceedingly fine asses which were coveted by the chieftain of their tribe. The simplest way of satisfying desire was to take possession of the animals and the chieftain did. But the owners of the animals had the audacity to resent his action. They watched their opportunity and made off with the asses, and being pursued and captured were made a stern warning to others of the rights of authority. It was argued that the chief had been rather lenient with them since just before the pillars were completed over their heads, these misguided men who had dared to assert their right to their own property, had been stunned by a blow from an axe handle".[45]

In this predatorial gratification of desire, the misuse and abuse of the victims' bodies was symbolic of the extraction of pain as surplus value, where boundaries of possession were marked by fear and torture, to create the dystopia of loss, captivity and enslavement. As Tate implied, the body as the descriptive ground of horror, led the idea of the 'tribal' back into the shadowy crypt of its gothic interior, where only madness and murder lived.

IV

On the register of imperial narratives therefore, the darkness of the tribe, the structure of its temporality was at one with the whole question of identity, within a political theatre of blood, of vendetta and venom. Discursive interrogations of tribalism had uncovered the broken ground of splintered psyches, collapsing into the chaos of the turbulent unconscious. The idea of the tribe stood implicated in the power of the negative for violence, terror, and permanent aggression against life; tribal space was both the weapon and sign of this struggle. Placed in this angle of the moral breach, the tribe entered the imperial imaginary in the Nietszchean perspective of the ethical binary. The idea of the ethical as positional in Nietszche's proposition, confirmed the self as moral and right, with the immoral and error being invested in the difference, that characterized categories of otherness. The imperial eye contemplating the alien and the strange, resolved the perceived difference of the tribal narrative metaphorically as dangerous, diabolical and deluded. This imaging was the primary point of subjectification. Thus the tribe metamorphosized into the primitive, the anarchic and savage, as it entered the reflective planes of imperial observation, document, and fable, with the image signifying the reality patterned into it, from the optics of analogy and metaphor. Tropes of the natural and animal, allowed the negative to function as ground and horizon of tribal being, legitimating the imperial violation of its interiority, as mastery of the human and moral over the servile and base. This was representation as subversion; it was as Homi Bhabha has suggested, "...a mode of negation to manipulate representation. ... a form of power that is exercised at the very limits of identity and authority, in the mocking spirit of mask and image".[46]

The perspectival subject implying character of imperial representations, captured the tribe as the horror of history, as the primitive consciousness that found pleasure in pain, suggesting that the tribal world was ontologically lost, existing as an irredeemable savage triangle where the eye, the hand and the flesh mapped the terrors of the cruel mind. Here, language as epistemic aggression was seeking to negotiate the identity of the 'other' as oppositional, as the antithesis of civilization, malevolent, terrible, sinister, the natural subjects of imperial censor and the coercion of conquest. The epistemic perspectives of such imperial representation, were constituted in terms of 'affects' or interests. By dehumanizing the tribal image, by verbally reducing it to a dark trace of arrested evolution and reason, imperial discourse was securing its alibis to invade and interrupt the 'otherness' signified in the tribe, to structure the plane of colonial subjection by establishing margins of dispossession, where tribal alterities could be silenced, and sentenced to embrace the text of imperial rewriting. The Darwinian 'other' was used as excuse and explanation, to image the tribe as the natural object of European mastery and manipulation. Imperial history would act as mirror and metaphor for the Hegelian notion, that the savage could only exist in servile relations with the civilized. In this disfigurement of the 'other', the true became the fable, where language entered representation to confer significations, that enslaved the signifier to the conceptions and misconceptions of 'difference' as error, exception and exclusion.

NOTES

1. A.Sinclair, *The Savage a History of Misunderstanding*, p. 11.
2. Quoted in M.Bernal, *Black Athena*, pp. 203-204.
3. Quoted in *Ibid.*, p. 204.
4. J.A.Boon, *Other Tribes, Other Scribes*, pp. 40-41.
5. G.W.Stocking, *Victorian Anthropology*, p. 162.
6. *Ibid.*, p. 234.
7. M.L.Dames, *The Baloch Race : A Historical and Ethnological Sketch*, p. 49 and R.C. Roome & C. Walton, Military Report on the Nushki, Chagai and Western Sinjerani Country, 1904, pp. 48-53, MSS.Eur.F.111/386.
8. M.L.Dames, *Popular Poetry of the Baloches*, p. xxiii.
9. *Ibid.*, p. xviii.
10. D.Bray, *Baluchistan Census Report*, 1911, p. 162.
11. M.L.Dames, *The Baloch Race*, pp. 4-5.
12. G.W.Gilbertson, *The Baluch Language*, p. vii.
13. *Ibid.*
14. E.Mockler, *Origins of the Baloch*, p.30.

15. M.L.Dames, *The Baloch*, op. cit., pp. 49-50.
16. D.Bray, *The Brahui Language*, Part I, pp. 35-36.
17. *Ibid.*
18. *Ibid.*, p. 42.
19. *Ibid.*, pp. 4-5.
20. *The Times*, 7 February, 1898.
21. R.I. Bruce, *The Forward Policy and its Results*, p. 143.
22. C.E.Bruce, *Notes on the Pathan Tribes of Baluchistan, The Bruce Collection*, MSS.Eur. F.163/57.
23. *Ibid.*
24. *Frontier and Overseas Expeditions from India*, Vol.iii, p. 58, p. 73.
25. O.T.Duke, *Report on Thal Chotiali and Harnai*, p. 128.
26. *Frontier and Overseas Expeditions from India*, Vol.iii, pp. 73-74.
27. Sandeman to Political Agent, Jocobabad, 17 April 1874, India Foreign Proceedings, K.W., Political A, May 1874, Nos.137-139.
28. T.H.Holdich, 'Perso-Baluch Boundary', *The Geographical Journal*, Vol.9, 1897, p. 416.
29. R.C.Roome and C.Walton, *Military Report on the Nushki Chagai and Western Sinjerani Country*, Secret, 1904, p.171, *Curzon Collection*, MSS.Eur. F.111/386.
30. *Ibid.*, p. 176.
31. F.Webb Ware, *Report on the Nushki, Chagai and Western Sinjerani Districts*, 1899-1900, p. 15, *Curzon Collection*, MSS. Eur.F.111/374.
32. Deputy Commissioner, Thal Chotiali, to Agent to the Governor-General in Baluchistan, 7 October 1892, India Foreign Department Proceedings, External A, May 1898, Nos. 54-64.
33. H.S. Barnes to Secretary Foreign Department, 22 November 1897, IFDP, External A, December 1897, Nos. 9-16.
34. Sandeman to Foreign Department, 23 December 1884, *Political and Secret Letters from India*, L/P&S/7/43.
35. G.Deleuze and F.Guttari, *Anti-Oedipus*, p. 183.
36. *Administration Report of the Baluchistan Agency*, 1893-1894, p. 60, *Selections from Records*, v/23/65/317.
37. *Baluchistan Census Report*, 1911, p. 115.
38. *Manual of Customary Law*, p.386, p. 349, *Political and Secret Department Library*, L/P&20/B.297.
39. *Baluchistan Census Report*, 1911, p. 115.
40. Quoted in N.Smith, *Uneven Development*, p. 4.
41. F.W.Nietzsche, *The Genealogy of Morals*, p. 61.
42. C.H.Masson, *Narratives of Journeys in Kalat*, pp. 420-421.
43. J.P.Ferrier, *Caravan Journeys*, p. 432.
44. *Ibid.*
45. G.P.Tate, *Frontiers of Baluchistan*, pp. 7-8.
46. H.K.Bhabha, 'Foreword', in F.Fannon, *Black Skins White Masks*, p. xxiii.

4

The Coercion of Power: The Discourse of Discipline in Resignifying the Tribal Margin

Visions of the tribal 'other' inscribed on surfaces of imperial observation, provoked new framings of social space in gestures and directions signifying high and low, included and excluded, the legitimate and illegitimate. The imperial observer acting as the site of knowledge and power, used the strength of subjective representations to structure a field of relations, governed by the dialectic of 'command and demand', to impose the space of order upon that "chaos which precedes the advent of the body".[1] Through trace, mark, intention, tribal man would be retimbered to signify a correction, from within the imperial point of view. Savage inscriptions, the transgressions, the disorders and the deformations they implied, entered the discipline of a vision, that allowed the observer to recode, regiment, and regulate, the correspondence between representation and perception of the disorderly, unruly and erroneous. The optics of this visuality, involved arrangements of bodies in space, control of activity, models for imposing homogeneity and anti-nomadic procedures, that would fix and isolate the observed, in subject-positions of the passive and disempowered. Situated in the hegemony of gaze and ground, imperial optics compared with what Paul Ricouer described as a "vision of the world in which the whole of objectivity is spread out like a spectacle on which the cogito casts its sovereign gaze."[2]

The actualisation of this vision, depended on the fabrication of a punitive space, allied to the function of discipline as dominance, as a 'new micro-physics' of power, intended to cover the entire social body. Anatomically, this disciplinary terrain belonged to the corpus of Foucauldian perspectives on the coercion of power, and its site of operation, the human body. As Foucault suggests:

> "The historical moment of the disciplines was the moment when an art of the human body was born, which was directed not only at the growth of skills, nor at the intensification of its subjection, but at the formation of a relation, that in the mechanism itself makes it more obedient as it becomes more useful, and conversely. What was then being formed was a policy of coercions that act upon the body, a calculated manipulation of its elements, its gestures, its behaviour. The human body was entering a machinery of power that explores it, breaks it down and rearranges it. A 'political anatomy', which was also a 'mechanics of power', was being born; it defined how one may have a hold over others bodies, not only so that they may do what one wishes, but so that they may operate as one wishes".[3]

Imperial inscriptions in tribal Baluchistan, occurred in this coercive language of power, tracing the topos of a disciplinary society, preoccupied with surveillance, observation, control, to create the space of its strategems and needs. In this space, the presence of the 'other' facing the ego of the imperial self, was the penetrable body, the vulnerable flesh, an accessible symmetry. The violence of its reduction was situated within the demand to shape an apparatus, where the individual body would be fragmented to a part of the whole, defined by its place in the new imperial machinery of control, its behavioural dispositions made to submit to the rulers' recodings of the permitted/unpermitted dyad, in short to deny its originary identity to enter the chorography of imperial terrain. This remaking, that claimed the tribal body as an object of regulatory control, evolved as discourse and diagram, as ideology and imprint, to create a meaning and a model to annex and administer social figurations signified in the 'other'.

I

The hand, authorship, and originality of the new disciplinary text in tribal Baluchistan, belonged to Robert Sandeman, the first Agent to the Governor-General in Baluchistan, from 1876 to 1892. Sandeman's migration from the army to political service[4] made him partial to models of control that captured 'the military dream of society', to replicate on the tribal plane the mechanism of the perfect army, the docile useful troop, the discipline of the regiment in camp and field. As one contemporary observer remarked about Sandeman: "His instincts were always those of a soldier, rather than a civilian; his methods were of the rough and ready order, and as such commended themselves to the people who were not yet prepared for a full draught of civilization."[5] The inference that the savage in the tribe, was only capable of perceiving the basic language of the command-obey signals connotated in the sign of the soldier, placed him at a fixed point of 'evolutive time', willing his primitivism to function as resource and recourse in the empire's war to win subservience to peace, order, silence. For Sandeman, writing social discipline was an act of mimesis, making the political mirror the military, duplicating and deploying its central coercions and subjugations, to implement the penal mapping of the human body.

The dominance of the military icon in redrawing tribal terrain, was dictated by representational views of its wild interiority, where the act of political discipline required aid from the sword, to place the social body in the museum of imperial order. Through metaphor and analogy, language in imperial discourse, became an ally of the vigilance of a vision, that desired the permanence of the military presence as guarantee and guardian, of social rewriting in tribal space. Central to this text, was the idea of recoding combative tribalism to police its own interior, under the surveillance of the military eye, to ensure compliance of the model to the ruling apparatus of empire. This intended migration of the tribesman from primitivism to policing, it was imagined, could only occur if the savagery of the tribe was permanently suppressed under the weight of military power. Fearing a divorce of the military from the tribal, in the aftermath of the second Afghan war, when economies in the Military Department threatened troop reductions on the frontier, Sandeman wrote anxiously to Alfred Lyall in the Foreign Department in 1880, "I need not say that the troops are the backbone of all political arrangements and without their moral support I am badly off".[6] Linking this need to the specificity of the tribal situation, Sandeman argued that sedentary tribes like the Tarins and Shadozais could not be used to police enclaves of tribal savagery, associated with the predatory aggressions of the Marris, Bugtis, and Kakars, without military supervision, as the former were victims of the latter, that carried by implication, the threat of setting "the wolf to guard the sheepfold".[7] Sandeman's visualising reappeared in language and logic, from General S.Edwardes's (commander Quetta District) observation, that replacing tribes for troops in local military posts would be like "baiting the jungle for tigers".[8] This metaphoric reduction of the tribe to the beast, was part of a verbalism that sought to smuggle in the primacy of the military ideal in civil government, by suggesting an understanding of the tribal problem within connotations of violent discord, and limitless aggression, to conjure the tribal scene as some primeval forest of fear, that needed negotiation in the hunter-hunted pairing, to make the sinister serene.

Sandeman's desire for a military framing to hold the body of his social text, proved difficult to deny from an imperial perspective, that needed to structure the colonial view in orderly angles, whose symmetry would not be impaired by the unruly and unpredictable, that would disrupt its point and purpose. Consequently, the Military Department decided to retain troops in Quetta, Pishin, Sibi, Thal Chotiali and Quat Mandai as symbol and sign of the presence of power, that would intimidate and intern the savage temper within the walls of 'discipline and punish', to shape the 'docile body', the willing instrument of imperial rule.

The mechanism within which colonial rewriting occurred, to anchor civil order in the graphics of a military model, was designed to signify opposition to the savage tribal machine that it replaced, so as to mark the birth of empire as the norm of the new to which the old would have to capitulate. The geometries of power inscribed by the new on the old, produced a pyramidal social machine, approximating, what Gilles Deleuze has described as a "megamachine of the State, a functional pyramid that has the despot at its apex, an immobile motor, with the bureaucratic apparatus as its lateral surface and its transmission gear, and the villagers at its base, serving as its working parts".[9] The dominating head of this political pyramid was the Agent to the Governor-General, whose despotic functionalism embraced political, administrative and judicial ground, signifying a personalisation of power, as a kind of social and political self-centring, to symbolize the authorial and arbitrary, in the space of colonial disempowering and dispossessions. As Jim Biddulph, appointed Officiating Agent to the Governor-General in Baluchistan in 1882, verbally mapping this domain of power put it:

> "We have no codes or regulations in our judicial proceedings, though we stick to our Indian rules where Indians are concerned. Each case in which the people of the country are concerned is dealt with on its merits, and our decisions would horrify the Lord Chancellor. Sometimes we hang a man for murder and sometimes we fine him for Rs.500. We are in fact the arbiters and enforcers of the local laws and customs, and the result is eminently satisfactory".[10]

This new inscriptive marking introduced the 'despotic' imperial machine, that would overpower and overcode the savage territorial machine, to achieve the subjugations that would serve the ends of the state, and the constellation of new formations that would assert the "imperialism of the signifier, the metaphoric or metonymic necessity of the signifieds, with the arbitrary of the designations – that ensures the maintenance of the system".[11]

The physics of the system operated within a gaze that provided a vantage point on the observed, endowing the eye with power to appropriate to itself, the capacity for visually mastering the infinite existence of bodies in space. This 'vision' or an 'inspection by the mind' as Descartes would suggest, operated as the perceptual site for excluding and suppressing, that which appeared to threaten the function of the imperial self and its observing eye in space, time, language. The link between vision and social power, turned on the optics of a gaze that merged seeing with surveillance, mapping with measuring, to trace the topos of discipline on the body of the observed, the object of scrutiny. As

Giovanni Battista della Porta has put it, the imperial eye was implicated in the logic of a visualism that dictated: "one must watch the phenomenon with the eyes of a lynx so that, when observation is complete, one can begin to manipulate them".[12] In this sense the gaze as the ground of perception and policy, replicated the power relations inherent in social discipline and the revisions it implied. As Matthew Edny explains: "The act of observation embodies the observers' physical (military, political, gendered) power over the observed; it also embodies a moral power in that it ... creates and normalizes the observed".[13]

Sandeman used the discipline of the gaze, to establish the empowered examiner and examined subject relationship, to move purposefully through the space of bodies to be re-arranged, regimented and regulated to signify the new place of docility and obedience. He instituted an optical regime that used vision as an ally of power, to place tribesmen in the constant surveillance of the 'panoptic machine', the coercive scrutiny of a gaze that was relentless and meticulous, in probing the interiority of tribalism, making it always more visible in order to control, command and correct. Sandeman always preferred to see with his own eyes the majority of disputed tribal cases, problems and predicaments, to advantage his own rewriting on the ground of the known and visible, while disadvantaging the observed on terrains of growing vulnerability to the coercive eye, which guarded all exits from the domain of discipline. As one tribesman referring to the oppression of the gaze put it: "There is no use in fighting Senaman Sahib. He knew everything and turned up everywhere".[14] And as Charles Aitchison, Lieutenant-Governor of the Punjab, 1879-1884, also remarked about Sandeman, "He knows personally all the ... leading men and has great influence over them...the people ... are learning respect for law and order...For this we have mainly to thank Sandeman whose personal influence ... is something marvellous".[15]

Through the use of the eye as the site of power and knowledge, Sandeman was refiguring the Napoleanic gaze that was invasive and possessive, seeking to shape and own its field of vision to secure the guarantees of authority, identity, and universality that structured its spiritual landscape. The philosophy of the gaze carried the imperial codings of society in its stated text:

> "You may consider that no part of the empire is without surveillance, no crime, no offence, no contravention that remains unpunished, and that the eye of the genius who can enlighten all embraces the whole of the vast machine without, however the slightest detail escaping his attention".[16]

The drawing of imperial space within a specific 'logic of visualisation' that sought to subjugate or repel the transgressions/disorders of the tribal existent, had the advantage of multiple view points, seeking to reframe the body of the observed, in Sandeman's optical regime of mapping, minding and making. These additions to the surveying eye, were located in the functions of five Political Agents, who managed the administrative and political requirements of local government. Drawn from the Indian Political Service, the Agents were specially selected on the basis of character and motivation. As Sandeman explained: "The success of the administration of this part of the frontier depends on the individuality of the officers under me, and their special fitness for the work".[17] Transfers were infrequent in the service, so as to encourage the Political Agent to become familiar with tribal behaviour, in order to observe, record, and train tribesmen on the high ground of imperial morals and manners. The Political Agent was expected to study tribal conduct in order to curb it. This implied that control and transformation of behaviour, would occur as condition and consequence of the accumulation of knowledge, as a dimension of power over the body of the 'other'. Archival information would direct strategic interventions to erase savage inscriptions that offended imperial sensibilities, to constrain the gestural movements of the tribal body, to make it the silent recipient of the disciplinary text. In this manner, the tribesman would be tied to the Political Agent in a relation of power, that would envelop his body and mind, resignifying it as the place of exercise and expectation of imperial demands, definitions, and designations.

In becoming the target for a new mechanism of power, the tribal body was entering a disciplined social terrain, where it would function as the object and instrument of its own control and subjection. This new role definition for the tribal person, was expected to materialize through the employment of tribes in local levy services, designed to guard minor security posts evacuated by the military, to provide a native platform for supporting the colonial apparatus of domestic order, and engage in routine duties like carrying the post and collecting local taxes. The system of levies as a technique of internal peace and order, sought to implement the mechanism of the perfect army, of disciplined troops, always obedient to the political will. Internally the problem of architecture was to structure a form of detailed, hierarchical control which would operate on the surface of the social body, to situate it in the optics of a visuality implicated in surveying, directing, and ordering, to shape the 'disciplined' social view desired by the imperial observer. To evolve the form and content of the new social vision, Sandeman was able to draw on the traditional tribal unit in Baluchistan, with its combination of sections and leaders, that provided an internal chain of vertical command, based on the unilinear delegation of authority. Sandeman used this internal hierarchy to institute a leadership chain, extending from the tribal chief through the headmen of different sections, in order to create a graded service system, with well defined figures exercising authority across sectional and tribal categories, to fabricate a social reality grounded in self-surveillance and self-control.

The economy of the scheme turned on the use of the tribal chief as a political artery, to circulate imperial control in all parts of the tribal social body. In the past, the tribal element had been used in its broadest sense to domesticate wild spaces of the northwest frontier. Herbert Edwardes, Commissioner of Peshawar had advocated its use in the Punjab after the Sikh Wars, while Eastwick introduced, and John Jacob extended a tribal service system in upper Sind between 1839 and 1858. But Sind and Punjab officials tended to pay money to tribal individuals likely to be implicated in raiding activities, rather than tribal chiefs, as a way of arresting the frequency of raids. Such payments or bribes never served as permanent answers to the tribal problem, as raids would be duplicated by other tribesmen eager to win subsidies in return for abstaining from such violence. More seriously, the cash handouts created new figures of wealth and power in the tribal system, that threatened to erode the status and authority of the tribal chiefs, carrying by implication the danger of leaving the tribal body headless and more un-governable. The depression of the tribal chief, that haunted this system of payments, was mirrored in the Bugti chief's confession in the aftermath of the tribal raids that battered the frontier between 1848-1853, that he no longer had the power to check the mentality of plunder. "I did all I could", he said, "and when I found myself helpless I sat in my house and let things take their course".[18]

Sandeman altered the dialectics of the payment structure, to empower the payer in relation to the recipient. The mechanism he used to signify the new reversal, involved selection of the tribal chief as the only legitimate figure, who would receive a subsidy in return for a commitment, to keep his entire tribe from violently invading the boundary lines of British defined interests and needs. As one close admirer of Sandeman put it: "The keystone of the radical change which was introduced by Sandeman was the recognition of the hereditary chiefs...and exacting their responsibilities...and allowing no crime to go unpunished".[19] Sandeman had experimented with this model in 1867, on the Dera Ghazi Khan frontier of Punjab, when he paid the Marri Chief, Ghazzan Khan, an annual sum of Rs.600, to employ forty tribesmen, to keep open communications between Baluchistan and the Punjab, and abstain from raiding the southern Punjab frontier. The success of this measure, encouraged the Government of India to expand the scheme in 1872, by increasing the subsidy for employing Marri and Bugti tribes to Rs.32,040 annually, under Sandeman's direction. In 1876, when Sandeman acquired control of the Baluchistan Agency, the structural principle of tribal service was further exploited and expanded, to accommodate the developing infrastructure of local government.

In grafting a tribal vein within the corpus of colonial rule, Sandeman engaged in re-imagining the space of the tribal chief, as an intermediate site, from where imperial perspectival positions could be conducted to the interior of tribal social territory. As part of this conceptual re-wiring, the chief was assigned to a functional place, where he had to enlist in fighting the empire's battle against feuds and raids. This migration from a tribal text of meaning to a colonial one, occurred on the newly architected ground of imperial subsidies and status, calculated to transform the 'warrior' leaders of tribal culture, into obedient instruments of the empire, their usefulness increasing in proportion to the measures of docility and servility they imbibed in their person. The new colonial markings on the body of the chiefly figure, appeared in the guise of status i.e. headship of a levy service, to police the tribal pictorial in the imperial interest; and as privilege, in the form of personal political payments to align chiefly interest and intent with the disciplinary angle of imperial optics. An example of this remaking in text and tactics, was the case of the Marri Chief Meherulla Khan and his son, who were awarded personal monthly allowances of Rs.730 and Rs.320 respectively, in order, as the Foreign Department explained:

> "...to train up the son of the Marri Sirdar to habits of command and a position of importance in his own tribe ... and a knowledge that it is in his interest to prevent plunder and to act in accordance with the wishes of government".[20]

In this visuality, the tribal chief was being made to serve as the ground of discipline itself, exceeding the limits of a figurative function on the premises of the disciplinary terrain. The iconography of the political chieftain, was being resymbolized to signify the art of control and compliance, in which imperialism sought to mirror its subjugations and suppressions.

Organizing the tribal brickwork to structure the colonial panopticon, involved the rigorous partitioning, and hierarchical structuring of society, time and space. Tribal chiefs were assigned the task of implementing the differential distribution of individuals, on the basis of who they were and what rank they should occupy on the ladder of tribal service. Appointments to positions of *ressaldar*, *jemadar*, and *duffadar* were controlled by tribal chiefs working in concert with the *mukuddams*, or section heads in the tribe. The rule to be followed in making such appointments, was that *ressaldars* were to be selected from the families of tribal chiefs; *jemadars* were to be drawn from the families of important section heads; and *duffadars* from families of less important section heads. This dynastic and hierarchic model of leadership, served as a surveillance screen, that brought tribal space within a scrutiny that was alien, intrusive, mechanical in the circularity of its function. Structured on a rule that measured status, and hierarchized in terms of values, the social levels and labels of individuals, the model introduced through its value giving measure, the constraints of a conformity which had to be achieved. Empowering the principle of a rule to be followed, created a differential space, segmented into sections and supervisors, heads and bodies, arranged in subject-object formations to simulate the distortions and divisions of the disciplinary ideal.

The technology of power used to create the disciplinary society, sought to control the individual, by exerting pressure on his interests, advantages and disadvantages. To divorce the tribal being from the violence of his natural desires, required indoctrinating his person in the work ethic. Forced to work and tempted by the bait of gain, tribal man was resituated in a system of interests, which would automatically sever him from his anarchic, animal appetites. By reconstituting the tribesman as 'homo economicus', Sandeman believed he would permanently pledge the tribal conscience to the imperial cause. Advocating that the empire should turn employer, he wrote: "The system I would urge of giving employment to the tribesmen and enlisting their interests in ours, has been the guiding principle, by following which a way has been discovered out of the many difficulties by which I have been surrounded".[21]

To manufacture the ground of economic interests on which tribal consent to the imperial order would rest, Sandeman introduced the mechanism of cash incentives that would serve as good conduct payments. The efficacy of monetary investment in recoding the tribal temper, drew on the referent of primitive lapse and character malformation. As Theodor Hope, Member in the Foreign Department, put it: "The Baluch is eminently an avaricious savage, and his pocket when you can get at it is I believe the most vulnerable point he possesses".[22] Payments tended to shadow this idea of the negative in which the tribe was bound, exploiting it as the site of pressure on which compliance could be won. The mapping of tribal payments was indexical, tied to a register of imperial suppositions on the savage content in tribal forms. Semi-nomadic tribes, implicated in histories of violence, holding strategic valleys and mountain passes, like the Marris, Bugtis and Kakars were singled out for substantial payments, to keep them fenced behind the wall of monetary gain erected by imperial rule. Sandeman's discursive reflection made clear, the strategic nature of imperial payments. Discussing the subject of payments to the Marris, he wrote:

> "The Marri clan are to this frontier what the Afridis are to the Peshawar frontier. If the Marris are well in hand, the peace of the Bolan Pass and other trade routes is secured, as also is the safety of the Punjab and Sind frontier".[23]

In order to tempt the Marris to cross the borders of anarchy, and enter the space of order, Sandeman awarded them Rs.5,490 per month, in return for which the tribe would maintain twelve posts, manned by 163 tribesmen, to safeguard communications between Sibi, Harnai and Thal Chotiali. Their close neighbours the Bugtis received similar good behaviour money of Rs.1,390 per month for guarding the Dera Bugti road. Others like the Kakars who dominated the Chappar Pass, as well as sections of the Bolan and Harnai routes were assigned nearly Rs.1,000 per month, to provide horsemen on guard duty in the vicinity. In the Quetta-Pishin area, poorer sections of the Achakzai Kakars, chronically implicated in raiding violence along the Khwajak Pass route, qualified specially for the payments, as they had the power to paralyse the trade between Shikarpur and Qandahar, that usually passed through the Khwajak and the heart of their country. In assigning the Achakzais Rs.20,004 per month, for providing 110 tribesmen to secure the safety of passes leading from the Khwajak Amran Range to Pishin, i.e. the Baluchistan-Qandahar frontier, Sandeman was guided by the consideration, that the Achkazais were "not only a powerful tribe but also notoriously a troublesome one".[24] Here as elsewhere, the payments were addressing the dark powers of the tribe, suppressing its fury in the currency of civilization to arrest the horror of its significations.

Through the machinery of payments, a space was created that carried the message of 'Pax Britannica'. The translation of the message however, was determined from the perceptual premises of that which seemed to threaten its inner language and liturgy. This dread, or fear overcoded the message with regulations and restrictions, to create the space of prohibitions and repressions. Haunted always by the savage in the tribesman, escaping from control to overwhelm the signs of civilization, imperial rule coded its spatial message in the power of the norm, that would preside as referee, determining the permitted/forbidden categories of behaviour. The idea of the norm was used to structure the penal implications of a 'tribal responsibility' principle, that governed the working of tribal payments and services. Drawing on the binary division and branding of behaviour as normal/abnormal, harmless/dangerous, normative judgement sought to measure social conduct in terms of distance and proximity to imperially determined social mannerisms and morals. The coercion of the norm, dictated the repression of a mass of behaviour judged as falling outside the line marking acceptable, normal conduct. Establishing the concept of tribal service within the judgemental gaze of imperial social psychology, the colonial text emphasized that "service payments were intended to give the tribes a direct interest in behaving in an orderly manner, for tribal service must depend primarily on the good conduct of the tribe".[25] The tribal chiefs were to understand that access to the system of imperial remuneration, was based on the condition, that "the peace of the country and freedom...from raiding is strictly maintained...in the event of any serious raiding the whole is liable to be stopped".[26] In cases of theft, robbery or murder, headmen were required to provide information on the offender, surrender him to the government if possible, or pay the cost of the damage done. But if chiefs or headmen themselves were involved in injurious acts, they would forfeit their service. By the power of its gestural markings, the colonial intention signified its desire to intern the violence of savage inscriptions, within the bounds of the illegal and abnormal. 'Good conduct' implied action that would conform to the parameters of a 'normative vision' of human conduct, that relegated the feuding/raiding mental structure of the tribes, to the margin of the deformed, that defied and denied the normal. The definition of normality became essential, in shaping individuals to the requirements of colonial institutional power. It allowed tribal action to be surveyed in a comparative field, where the eye of the norm dictated the recoding of behaviour acceptable to the rules of imperial reason, while denying the validity of tribal social inscriptions. The discipline of the norm, worked on the tribal body through the penalties embedded in the 'tribal responsibility' text, that traversed the social anatomy to create points of pressure and pain as a means of regulating tribal gestures, habits, and movements. Trapped in this field of normative observation and the coercions it signified, the tribesman was made to assume responsibility for the constraints of power, and embrace the discipline imposed upon him; he had to inscribe on himself, the power relation in which he became the instrument of his own subjection.

While the colonial machinery of power evolved on the suppression of the tribal primitive formation, it continued to be haunted by that which it sought to eclipse, in order to erect the self. This may be inferred, from the urgency to represent the reality of the emerging colonial terrain in Baluchistan, as a residual, corrected diagram of tribal formation, re-articulating within the matrices of imperial meaning and model. In official language, levy posts were represented as "rallying points for the tribe as a whole",[27] not just the names on the pay roll, thereby denoting the idea of service, as symbolic of old tribal identities, refigured on new ground. In order to keep in place, the tribal masks of imperial rule, J.Ramsay, one of the later Agents to the Governor-General, reflected that the structure of collective service 'gave vigorous' life to the concept of the tribe as a social collective, since service duties would serve as reminders of the original functional purpose of the tribe, as a common platform to regulate political and social interests.[28] In 1889, at a tribal *durbar* in Quetta, Dufferin spelled out the duplication of the old boundaries of tribalism in the graphisms of the new colonial model. "We desired", he announced, "in all that we are doing to respect your rights, to have regard to your traditional customs...Wherever... possible...we have relied on the machinery of your own tribal councils... and institutions"[29] to govern political relations. The verbal merging of the old in the new, was given spatial structure, by assigning tribesmen to serve exclusively in areas of origin and domicile, to preserve tribal boundaries of identity within the service structure, that signified a form of reterritorialization, implicated in the compartmentalization of the conceptual ground of tribal power and performance. This imperial preoccupation with the reading of the model, its textual latencies, and the sublated content of tribal form, mirrored the logic of political writing designed "to mask the will to power", as Lefebvre suggests "and the arbitrariness of power beneath signs and surfaces which claim to express collective will and collective thought",[30] to conjure away the violations of erasure and overwriting.

The ultimate reduction of the tribal sign in the iconography of imperial power, perception and place, was implicit in the Foreign Department's concluding observation on the coded asymmetries, within which, messages and meanings of authorial form, subjugated group, probing eye, and exposed body, moved from consciousness to structure, to signify the primacy of the imperial category in political space. As the Foreign Department claimed:

> "Levies are tribal bodies under tribal authority, and not commanded by British officers...Such bodies have however a tendency to pass insensibly under the control of government officers, especially when such officers are appointed 'to inspect them', and the basis of tribal responsibility remains in theory, after it has ceased in practice."[31]

The fact and fiction of tribal engagement in defining the political space of empire, belonged to the order of spatial mapping, in which fabrication rather than representation, ordered the production of meaning; where the verbal did not meet the actual, but offered instead a site of ambiguity, in which more than one framing could be selected, to narrativize the content and form of the disciplinary drawings in tribal society.

Tribal service, mimicked a more military style of architecture in those areas bordering on Afghanistan, the Northwest Frontier Province and Persia. This branch of service known as the Tribal Levy Corps, was intended to function as a para-military border patrol unit, mainly along the Zhob valley and Chagai frontier, to guard the main points of entry into Baluchistan. E.F.Chapman, Quarter-Master General in the Indian Army, 1887, situated the structure within the concept of using tribal power to defend the lines of empire; he wrote that the service:

> "rests upon a system under which we look forward at an early date to identifying the tribal inhabitants of the border regions with ourselves in closing it to an enemy's advance, while the avenues leading directly through it to the points, which to us may become of great importance, are opened out for forward movements whenever this becomes necessary."[32]

In this visuality, the tribesman was being refigured in the image of the pliant soldier, ready to be used by the empire in another war. Enemies were found in the guise of Waziri raiders on the northwest, hostile Afghans to the northeast, and marauding Perso-Baluch tribes on the west, against whom the Corps could learn to manoeuvre, and imbibe the regimented discipline of the army. They wore uniforms, carried arms and served under a British commanding officer, to complete the impression of a corps trained for army combat duty. But behind this primary signification, was a secondary one, inserted by Sandeman into the functional text of the Corps. On his directive, men chosen for the service were nominated by tribal chiefs, and headed by members of the chiefly families. Further, the corps was also at the disposal of Political Agents, for enforcing internal order, or eliminating disobedience to chiefly authority. Sandeman wanted the Corps to complement the function of the Levies, to bring the interior of tribal non-conformism within the corrections of the disciplinary gaze, implemented by the policing eye of the Political Agent, and his accomplice the tribal chief, to structure the landscape of control imagined in Sandeman's textual perspective. In short, the Corps now situated on the intermediate ground between army duty and civil order, was required to function within dual referents, produced by a system of power, which sustained its own reality of antagonisms, by choosing to interpret signs and symptoms on the basis of political need and ideological compulsion.

By 1890, Sandeman had in place, a network of services and payments, designed to erase the savage inscriptions of the tribe. The system had the effect of reforming the content of tribal space to conceal the aggression of imperial re-writing, and at the same time, constituting a repressive space, as nothing in it escaped the surveillance of power. Through form, function and structure, imperial power and the tribal body were at once bound together, and kept apart through distinctions of being, nature, substance, that the system sustained. Intimacy and mastery acted on the savage sign to overwhelm its contrary language, and contain it on the plane of the permitted. Decoding the tribe, in favour of the disciplinary text itself, was a way of arresting those undesirable and unpredictable gestures of raids, feuding aggressions, and furious forays in the space of imperial interests, by creating a timetable of duties and obligations, which would fix tribesmen in the role of obedient subjects. The main aim of this disciplinary power, was to function as an anti-nomadic technique to combat the signs of chaos and confusion, which defined the anchorages of tribalism, in order to recompose pictures of turbulence, within structured imperial view points of order, obedience, and obligation.

The production of manageable subjects through 'a certain policy of the body', extended across planes of political purpose to reach the punitive point of judicial sanctions. At the junction of plane and point, the imperial apparatus of control, assumed a self-legislative and authoritative judicial function. The order of law in the imperial formation, allowed the observing subject to engage in a judgemental gaze from the vantage point of absolute privilege, to guarantee and police the correspondence, between the exterior world and interior representation, to exclude anything disorderly or unruly. Within this perspectivism, the language of law, expressed the imperialism of the signifier that produced its signifieds i.e. "regime of terror",[33] as Deleuze puts it, to subjugate the old social body, disorient its meaning and limits, to create the place of new repressive inscriptions. The mechanism for allowing this law to invade the social corpus, was structured on fragments of tribal customary code and the punitive text of the Frontier Crimes Regulation, that chose to represent coercion as control. In this making, the 'form' mimicked the tribal *jirga*, or council of tribal elders, that used to dispense justice in the traditional order.

But the content of the form, signified the optics of a regime, bound in the vice of regimenting and regulating all shapes and surfaces of reality.

The tribal shell that would hold the corpus of imperial law, was structured on a three tier system. At the level of the base unit, two or more tribal headmen and *sayyids* (religious leaders) were appointed to the adjudicating tribunal, where the disputant parties also nominated an equal number of their own representatives. This adhoc *jirga* functioned at a local level, to address family and sub-sectional disputes, serving the colonial requirement of a primary filter, to trap strains of social violence at the source. The intermediate tier, operating above the base line, was represented by the Standing District and Joint Jirga, which was composed of permanent tribunals drawn from tribal chiefs and section leaders, with space reserved for a mandatory British official presence. Empowered to decide cases affecting the administration of two agencies or districts, or relations between major tribes, the Joint Jirga functioned as a major instrument to regulate and regularize wide angles of the provincial map, to resignify it in the ruling ground of imperial prescriptions and prohibitions. At the head of this adjudicating pyramid, was the Shahi Jirga, composed exclusively of tribal chiefs and Political Agents, which met twice annually at Quetta and Sibi, to deliberate on difficult, unresolved cases, like major tribal blood-feuds, that threatened to overwhelm spaces of order with the significations of disorder they connotated. Appeals beyond this level, were lodged with the Agent to the Governor General, whose decision was final and binding on controversial, crisis ridden episodes and moments of tribal experience.

The strategic logic of the *jirga* was defined by Robert Sandeman:

> "A tribal *jirga* ... possesses many advantages. It commands the confidence of the tribes themselves, and the decisions thus given are therefore treated with great respect. Each case is thoroughly sifted ...The investigation gives us an insight into the condition of the tribes, and is a guide in fixing such fines and conditions as circumstances demand".[34]

The *jirga* was therefore designed to function as the site of knowledge and power, that would operate directly on the individual tribal body. Sandeman's stated purpose to use the *jirga* as a recording screen to compile an exhaustive inventory of the social body, signified the coercion of knowledge, that would be the basis for the formation of an individual, adequate for the productive requirements of imperialism, and its accessory techniques of control and subjection.

The neo-archaism of the tribal *jirga*, promoted by the imperial state machine, was constrained within a margin of compulsions and coercions, that ensured its identity as an enclave of compliance in the place of empire. Sandeman assisted this recoding of tribal form to serve the power plan of imperial rule, by linking the efficacy of the *jirga* to the system of services and payments belonging to the Levy Service. Elucidating the coercion of the concept, Sandeman wrote:

> "The system of hearing and deciding cases by *jirga* is greatly influenced by the Service given to the *sirdars* and their tribesmen....should a tribe neglect...to produce a tribesman before a *jirga*, the service given to the tribe can be stopped, and the pressure thus produced... is eventually sure to produce the desired result. Again... should certain members of a tribe oppose the execution of a *jirga* settlement, they can be coerced by the withholding of their service. ...if a *sirdar*...should obstruct the settlement by *jirga* of any quarrel, effective pressure can be brought to bear on him, by the stoppage in part or whole of the service enjoyed by him. It is always possible to inflict severe punishment ... by withdrawal of service ... Under the *jirga* system the primary responsibility

for, and the odium necessarily attendent upon the decision of civil and criminal cases is thrown upon the individual *sirdars* and their tribes. ... The *jirga system* is in practice local self-government. The system, however hinges upon tribal service".[35]

The penalties structured in the model of the *jirga*, that threatened margins of material interest, made it iconic of the coercion of power that commanded bodies, prescribing and proscribing gestures, rituals and reactions, to produce the space of "blind, spontaneous and lived obedience".[36]

The repression of imperial law coded in the social order versus disorder pairing, extended its disciplinary reach through the imposition of the Frontier Crimes Regulation of 1901 in Baluchistan, signifying a frontal legislative assault on the inner recesses of border violence. Within its text and conventions, the Regulation signified what Deleuze reads, as the cruelty "bricked into the State apparatus which ... organizes in tolerates or limits it in order to make it serve the ends of the State and to subsume it under the higher superimposed unity of a Law that is more terrible".[37] The Draconian structure of the Regulation, empowered the Political Agent to mimic the tyranny of the dreaded despot. In his capacity as Deputy Commissioner, the Political Agent was allowed to withdraw any case from a civil court, and refer it to a *jirga*; in a criminal case he could impose sentences upto fourteen years of rigorous imprisonment; as well as, banish suspected fanatics and blood offenders from the district. At its most punitive, the Regulation allowed the Deputy Commissioner and *jirga* to take securities for keeping the peace, from families and factions, that seemed to carry the risk of involvement in blood-feuds at some future time. If a life was taken while such a security was in force, the group forfeited its securities. If tribesmen required to give sureties for good behaviour of a kinsman were unable to do so, they were sent to prison for a period. Here the field of punishment was being structured beyond the limits of the offence, to include surmise, suspicion, and speculation, as adequate ground for prosecution. Further, in the absence of the real offender, a substitute was sought in the figure of tribal kin or associate who would bear the burden of guilt, which implied the prosecution of innocence, burdening the social conscience with a hostage mentality, forcing the body to live in a margin of fear, if one of its parts malfunctioned. Here justice was disfigured as punishment and vengeance: "the vengeance of the voice, the hand and the eye, now joined together on the despot. ... Law is the invention of the despot himself".[38]

The evolutive model of the colonial legal apparatus in tribal Baluchistan, symbolized the psychologism of the Victorian addiction to the fiction of the family in texting order. Their symbolic designation of 'Reason' as the father, and 'madness' as the child or minor, may be read by way of analogy in the colonial text, where the imperial-tribal relationship, mirrored the head-body arrangement in space. On this perceptual plane, the colonial legal machinery may be comprehended as a substitute 'family' tribunal of responsibility, before which the tribesman stood as a guilty child, and in relation to which he was required to transform into a responsible adult.[39] This remaking, was encoded in the vision of willing tribalism to own the problem of social architecture, orienting itself on the bases of angles shaping the geometry of imperial conceptual space. Sandeman's intent of using a tribal envelope to convey an imperial message, signified a vision that sought to re-orient the tribal interior, in imperially induced dimensions of the legitimate and illegitimate, using the shell of tribal form, to blur the lines of the old and new. This interior recoding assisted by the terror of coercions, symbolized a mimesis not of aesthetics but of social power, that desired as its enduring inscription, the "passivity" that "must now become the virtue of the subjects attached"[40] to the imperial body.

II

The picture of tribal capitulation to imperial dictation, entered official archives, as the 'miracle' of Sandeman's inspired political touch. As one member of Parliament put it, the space of pre-Sandeman Baluchistan, was a "welter of confusion, bloodshed, a danger ... to its neighbours, and a hell to itself".[41] In its transformed post-Sandeman state, the space had become the place of political landscaping, framing views not of the savage, but his metamorphosized person, as compliant cultivator, and obedient soldier of the imperial system. The epistemic reversal implied in the imperial designation of 'violence' as the forbidden space of society, compelled the tribal imaginary to retreat into 'safe' margins of social function. Old imprints of feuds and raids were bricked under the cement of service and payments, leading to what was officially claimed as the revival of human traces in the space of its negation. As R.I.Bruce describing the birth of the new in the history of the tribe put it:

> "The Marris and Bugtis are rapidly extending their cultivation, and consequently depending less on their flocks, on the precarious livelihood obtained by plunder. Each succeeding year sees the cultivated areas increasing, new tracts brought under the plough. ... The policy commenced with the Marris and Bugtis has since been extended to many other tribes (Khetrans, Lunis, Shadozais...many branches of Brahuis, Baluchis, Tarins, and Kakars) with equally remarkable results, fully evidenced by the state of entire peace and prosperity the country enjoys, under the influence of which ruined towns are springing up again, agriculture and trade are rapidly spreading and increasing.[42]

Sandeman appeared to have led the tribes to the point of correction, that was the perennial hope of imperial philosophy; the realization of the wish, as expressed fervently by Salisbury: "We must gradually convert to our way of thinking in matters of civilization, these splendid tribes".[43] "The combination of punishment ... with civilization is particularly happy"[44], he had observed, for eclipsing the anti-human, and exposing the savage soul to the 'civilizing mission', connoting the moral empire, where illegitimacies of conquest and control could be symbolically resolved in the idea of redemption of the native soul. Placing the meaning of the model within the philosophy of the civilizing quest, and the idea of the ethical, a Member of Parliament, reflecting on Sandeman and the implications of his political re-writing stated: "In place of the wooden and effete system of law, he...did establish in Beluchistan another system, more human, sympathetic, and civilizing, which was imperatively demanded by the exigencies of the political situation". This "hearts and mind" policy of "peace and good will", he continued, had in ten years "completely transformed Beluchistan. When he went there it was a country distracted by blood feuds, inter-tribal warfare...lawless marauders robbing and murdering in every direction.... But by his tact and courage, sympathy and patience, he completely changed all this. The tribes were reconciled to each other and by the rule of the British government, murderers were punished, robberies were suppressed, ...order and tranquility prevailed everywhere."[45] This pictorial, that offered a view of the imperial presence as a new moral content in the savage depths of tribal being, belonged to a cerebral ideality, that regarded repressive regulation as the desired social signature of the ethical, the normal, and the civilized in human ontology. It was part of the prejudicial, discriminatory rhetoric of English India, that presented race, culture, history as the ground separating observer and observed, to insert boundary lines of identity in the space of self and other. In this spatial view, there could be a meeting but not a merging of boundaries. The boundary served as a conceptual line for imagining the other as raw nature, that had to be bound, restrained, acquired and commodified to situate him in the margin of the acceptable, and usable, from the viewing point of the imperial self. On this representational plane, the tribe imaged as raw but reformable, formed the subject for recovery and re-writing in the tropic text of the civilizing mission, that would discipline in order to define, correct in order to control, shape in order to own the mind and matter of the object in making.

The crushing of the tribal code on the imperial ground of remaking and resignifying, to insert a 'civilizing' conscience in the savage mind, was foregrounded in a decision awarded by the Shahi Jirga in 1896, on feuding conflicts between Marris and Lunis which had claimed a high margin of human victims. James Browne, Agent to the Governor-General at the time, believed that the ferocity of the feud, demanded that the main offenders, should serve not the seven years a *jirga* would sentence, but fourteen years rigorous imprisonment as decreed by the Frontier Crimes Regulation. But he wanted the *jirga* to pass the judgement, to make it symbolic of a tribal censorship of its own narrative, a denial of the savage inscription, to recontour image and identity on the moral maps of imperial drawing. On obtaining the consent of the *jirga*, to the disciplinary coercion that ruled his vision of correcting error, James Browne reflected:

> "In my opinion the National Parliament [*the jirga*] has now by its replies ... shown that it had advanced with the times, by recognizing and recommending that the British Government should, and must in such cases, inflict heavier punishments than any *jirga* could award. The *Sirdars* have wisely recognized that it was essential to place such powers in British hands, for the good of the country, and the repression of national conduct inconsistent with the better social conditions which time is gradually developing in Baluchistan.[46]

Within the optics of this observation, the tribal chiefs were visualised as 'hands' that would shape the remaking, presenting the tribal body as the tablet of imperial inscription, in which the power of the alien would preside, directing the denial of originary sites of identity, meaning, language. It mirrored, "a process generating a force", as Gayatri Spivak has observed, "to make the native see himself as other".[47]

Through mimetic copy the tribesman entered imperial inscriptional space, suppressing the savage voice of blood, honour, reprisals, in order to speak in the 'civilized' language of compensation, cash and monetary gain. Reports mirrored the migration of the tribal mind from the menacing to the mercenary. Officials noted that in the case of blood feuds, it was now a matter of routine, for *jirgas* to award *iwazana* (compensation) or *sharmana* (dishonour) money, for the aggrieved party who preferred to distance themselves ideologically from the concept of revenge killing, with its symbolic connotations of honour and duty, in order to realign with the principle of colonial regulation that promised money and materialism. The Frontier Crimes Regulation with its insistence on cash securities to manage conduct, coded money within meanings of desire, that remapped ambition and aspiration to signify in the place of the primitive, the new sign of 'homo economicus'. A mark of this making, was the surfeit of inflated cash securities that made their way into record books, as tribesmen came to view these bonds as new status symbols of prestige and rank. Perspectival alterations also led tribesmen to lodge false charges of murder and adultery, as *jirgas* gave high compensation awards to the aggrieved group. In 1917 a Brahui Jirga in Quetta,[48] acknowledged the creation of this margin of deceit in the tribal complex, by pointing at the pervasive practice of subverting the text of court and custom to make illicit monetary gains. The space of the illegal within the legal machinery of colonial rule, the mind of the mercenary that the civilizing mission mapped, mirrored a making that was an unmaking, signifying the descent of the tribe into a social depth, without the anchorages of old meanings, caught in a mimetic recoding that led to the point of the negative, the illegitimate, and immoral. This slippage of meaning and alienation within identity, was part of the ambivalence generated by colonial desire, where the tribal hybrid was conceived as the dark native shadow of the colonialists's presence, in order to suppress the message and memory of another space, that did not belong to the story of empire. The disfigurement of tribal content in the framing narrative of empire, signified the displacement of limits and levels of identity, to the "disturbing distance in-between", as Homi Bhabha has suggested, "that constitutes the figure of colonial otherness – the white man's artifice inscribed on the black man's body".[49] On this site of ambiguity, the question of identity became one of lack and absence, the de-formation of the interior, the dysfunction of the mind.

The site of suppression, on which the exterior silence of tribal being could be viewed, however, was itself subject to inner tremors originating in subterranean veins of disquiet. From the places of repression and ambiguity, appeared the signs and forms of a contrary language, by which dominant imperial practices of vision were resisted, deflected, or imperfectly constituted. Imperial rewriting in the political space of the tribe, where headship and roles of authority were determined, had the effect of structuring contradictions that disconcerted the premises of colonial formations. The concept of re-forming tribal chiefs to function as colonial collaborators within the network of service and payments, forced the leadership to navigate the dimensions of a duality, that led to the plane of intermediacy, dilemma, and dysfunction. Trapped in an ambiguity, he was unable to transcend, the tribal chief became not the mirror of the model, but its inversion, signifying from the in-between space of empire and tribe, the ontological question, as to whether he was "imposing the central order on the tribe, or defending the tribe against the state".[50] The translation of this ambiguity, as disconnections and dislocations in angles of leadership, may be inferred from the content of the Achakzai narrative, denoting intervention, subjection and subversion.

Intervention in order to invent, started in 1879, when Sandeman circumvented the existing model of Pathan tribal structure, in which authority was diffused among powerful section heads, to establish a figure of his choice, known as Aslam Khan Arzbegi, as the new chief of the Achakzais, through whom the colonial government would conduct business, and to whose authority Achakzai headmen would have to submit. The aporia of this remaking, was its denial of the tribal understanding of the leadership role, that belonged to the symbolism of power and performance in tribal texts, and was iconic of interior reflection, and recognition of the ability to lead. From this tribal view, the insertion of a chief handcuffed to the imperial perspective, was an inadequate figure to command the political allegiance of tribesmen. Tribal withdrawal from the colonial model, was mirrored in the paralysis of chiefly power, and its inability to control the rising curve of Achakzai raids in Pishin and along the Afghan border. By 1883, Oliver St.John, the Acting Agent to the Governor-General, was conceding anxiously that the new chief was unable to control the tribes.[51] The invention of authority in the colonial architecture, based on the negation of the tribal code, had become the object of reversal, by that which it had sought to disempower and marginalize. However, overlooking the signs of tribal alienation within the model, Sandeman repeated the experiment of bringing Achakzai poltical conduct under a central leader, by removing the existing nominee, and bringing in his place a new head, one Abdul Karim Khan to function as imperial agent and tribal chief. But Abdul Karim Khan chose to exploit the imperial appointment, to resignify the leadership within a margin of independence predicated on tribal power, in distinction from exercising authority as an appendix in the imperial political equation. To claim this space of opposition, the new leader strategized to function within the boundaries of Pathan memory and meaning tied to instinctual desires for freedom, uninhibited action, and release from external control. Architecting this unfettered, unregulated domain, which he believed would serve as his tribal support base, Abdul Karim Khan declined to arrest Achakzai offenders, left levies unsupervised, and resisted all forms of colonial control in tribal affairs.

The Achakzai message, which signified an interrogation of colonial power from the premises of tribalism, constituted a writing back, that was discursively represented in imperial document as the danger of defiance, that would breach the walls of order, system, discipline, erected to intern the spectral signs of primitive anarchy; the collaborator had turned insurgent, and was now a suitable subject for coercion. To discipline defiance, Sandeman removed Abdul Karim Khan from the central space of tribal power, confined him to a minor position in service near Quetta; promoted his cousin, Ghulam Haidar Khan to headship of the Toba Levies; and finally placed the Pishin levies under the command of district officers.[52] This was Sandeman's 'imperial' resolution of the contradiction that governed the ground of tribal leadership, stranded in the ambiguities of old and new definitions, instinctual and artificial texts and territories of perception and purpose.

The problem of the model was not just restricted to Achakzai resistance; it reappeared in troubling form on the register of Marri reaction, signifying the story of tribal repudiations forming below the surface of imperial structural signs. In the case of the Marris, colonial intervention collapsed the line between tyranny and authority in the tribal scheme. The chief who had formerly depended on income from tribal resources, i.e., percentage shares in communal land and livestock assets, and awards for adjudicating on tribal disputes, and was therefore forced to act within the consensus of the tribal model to sustain his position, found in the re-empowerment of the colonial system,(signified in the headship of the levies, personal allowances and land grants), the mechanism with which to displace tribal limits to the exercise of chiefly power. Functioning beyond the limit, from the site of surplus power, the Marri chief now emerged as tyrant of the tribe, exacting customary dues and penalty payments not just for himself, but illegally for the extended *sirdarkhel* or families related to the chief, for which there was no traditional tribal sanction. Underpinning this despotic definition, was the consciousness, that chiefly authority no longer needed tribal consent to hold its premises, as it could now depend on its role as colonial collaborator, to access the imperial power base, to govern or mis-govern the tribal interior. Tribesmen petitioned against this form of chiefly coercion, defining areas of loss, sustained by the forcible levy of fines, arbitrary exaction of penalties, and forcible seizure of livestock. The Baluchistan Government, however remained impervious to the language of loss, being foregrounded in tribal consciousness, as a result of which discontent transformed into migrating action, as large numbers of tribes started an exodus into Afghanistan, to escape the repressive inscriptions of the colonial regime.

The migrations signified a form of tribal censorship, of the form and content, of the colonially determined leadership model. This contesting sign of tribal consciousness, threatened to erase the disciplinary text of colonial power, as the migrations claimed the tribesmen, needed to serve on guard duty in levy posts. The growing picture of desertions and unmanned posts, was captured in official discourse as the crisis of obedience, opposition, orientation. As H.Wylie, Officiating Agent to the Governor-General, at the time of the crisis in 1898, reflected:

> "The Baluch tribes are united under one chief, whose orders they obey ... if therefore a body of Baluchis ... quits the country under the leadership of discontented persons ... the entire clan feels the chief's authority has been set at defiance, and the deserters have scored a point ... If nothing is done ...a general spirit of lawlessness and independence of all authority will be engendered."[53]

Here the language of discourse was sifting the site of tribal discontent, to represent 'distress' as dissent, that disfigured the topography of acquiesence, acceptance, and accommodation, which the remade tribal margin was expected to mirror in imperial suppositions. As a result, the recording of the migration, was embedded in inscriptional meaning and interpretation, that stressed its significance as denial and defiance, of a "code of pacification", which under the Raj as Ranajit Guha suggests, "was a complex of coercive interventions by the state and its protégés, the native elites, with arms and words".[54] Dimensions of discord, that threatened to negate the code, demanded immediate erasure. Thus observation as judgement, dictated and directed intervention in the Marri tribal scene, to remap the margin of chiefly power as the site of personal, not family privileges, to reverse the language of tribal alienation from the internal leadership structure, that was the political bridge between the plane of the tribe and the point of empire, to sublate the antagonistic in symmetries of purpose, plan, perspective.

III

As the meaning of the model slipped into the margin of resistance and repression, the tensions of the text, signified the problematics of manufactured power, the production of dominance, whose intervention as a dislocatory presence in tribal society, engendered a form of constant, if implicit contestation between the signification of the imperial sign, and its interrogation by the colonized in tribal accents. As the correction/coercion codings of the model, imagined a topography of power structured on the confiscation of the savage inscription, the site of erasure, had to be colonized in messages affirming the reach of the ruler. Thus, the destination of dissent on imperial terrain was the point of the negative, the space where it was disempowered as convulsions of the unruly, and represented in discourse as the plane to be reangled, to preserve the primacy of imperial picturing. Appropriation of dissent as the mark of the menace and sign of the contrary, made 'consent' the desired plane of imperial vision. This 'produced' image of consent took form in the silenced savage, the reproved primitive, now refigured to signify the disciplined corpus of colonial imaginings.

The philosophy to tame the tribe, that informed and deformed imperial visuality, implied a certain metaphysic of the interior, in which the savage temper, "that repressed cruelty of the animal man made inward and scared back into himself", became, "the creature imprisoned in the 'state' so as to be tamed."[55] In the discipline of the vision and its judgemental framings, the body of the tribe became the "stone and paper"[56] on which the new writing marked its figures, its phobias, and penalties that announced the verdict, and the rule that had been ruptured. The repression of the breach, that signified transgressions of the norm, forced the 'resentiment, that countervengeance' of the repressed into a state of latency, producing the silence of the exterior, that was claimed as the trophy of the disciplinary war against anarchy and confusion. As Denys Bray put it:

"Sandeman's mission was to bring peace where there was chaos, and thus to uphold the King's peace throughout the land, and to foster its development through indigenous agency on indigenous lines."[57]

The composition of peace, presented in imperial vocabulary, was structured on the metonymic absence of the tribal voice, its sound stifled in imperial tonalities maximizing the use/obedience pitch of tribal rhythms, to suggest a harmony of flows, that concealed the suppressed essences and energies, that constituted the melancholy of the subjugated and silenced. Signifying the mythic space of 'Pax Britannica' from the arbitrary reaches of its narrative play, the imperial sign entered the symbol of state as desire, imagining and fabricating realities, to privilege the view of bodies and boundaries, suggestive of the ordered symmetries of imperial perspectival space. The vision seeking to validate the site of its ascendancy, colonized the place of subjection with metaphors and tropes, to mirror a world of reason, laws, privileges, hierarchies, constraints, as "that which is firmest, most general, best known, most human, and hence that which regulates and rules".[58] In the space of this vision, the diagram of power translating as the disciplinary model, acquired direction and dimension as the 'bio-power,' or 'bio-politics' of populations, as described by Foucault," controlling and administering life, it is indeed life that emerges as the new object of power".[59] If the coercion of power was the representative language of the model, the object of its punishing philosophy was the body of the subjugated savage, whose 'negative' difference was marked as the inscriptional site to deform, splinter, and recompose particles of identity to re-image primitivity in forms and fantasies of colonial desire.

NOTES

1. H.Lefebvre, *The Production of Space*, p. 117.
2. Quoted in J.Crary, *Techniques of the Observer*, p. 48.
3. M.Foucault, *Discipline and Punish*, pp. 137-138.
4. Sandeman served in the Indian Army, between 1856-1866, and subsequently as Deputy Commissioner, Dera Ghazi Khan.
5. E.F.Chapman, quoted in T.H.Thornton, *Sir Robert Sandeman,* p. 300.
6. Sandeman to Lyall, 29 June 1880, *Lyall Papers*, MSS.Eur. F132/25.
7. F.Fryer, Deputy Commissioner Dera Ghazi Khan, *Memorandum on a Proposal to Substitute Local Levies for Troops now occupying Thal Chotiali*, undated, *Bruce Collection*, MSS.Eur.F.163/4.
8. Edwardes to Chapman, 23 February 1882, India Foreign Proceedings, External, P/1922.
9. G.Deleuze, *Anti-Oedipus:Capitalism and Schizophrenie*, p. 194.
10. Biddulph to Northbrook, 20 August 1882, *Northbrook Papers* MSS.Eur.C.144/6.
11. G.Deleuze, *op.cit.*, p. 215.
12. Quoted in J.Crary, *op.cit.*, p. 37.
13. M.Edny, *Mapping an Empire*, p. 54.
14. Quoted in T.H.Thornton, *op.cit.*, p. 311.
15. *Ibid.*, p. 292.

16. Treilhard, quoted in Foucault, *op.cit*, p. 217.
17. Sandeman to Ripon, 2 December 1882, *Ripon Papers* BM.ADD.MSS.43613, p. 201.
18. Quoted in R.I.Bruce, *History of the Mari Baluch Tribe*, p.27, *The Bruce Collection*, MSS.Eur.F.163/5.
19. *Ibid.*, p. 21.
20. *Foreign Department Note*, 29 April 1882, IFDP, Political A., July 1882, Nos. 249-260.
21. Sandeman, *Memorandum*, January 1888, *Curzon Collection*, MSS.Eur.F.111/54.
22. T.Hope, Member Foreign Department, *Note*, 19 January 1884, IFDP, A Political E, June 1884, Nos. 56-62.
23. Sandeman to Lyall, 16 January 1881, *Political and Secret Letters and Enclosures from India*, (hereafter PSLE),L/P&S/7/27.
24. Sandeman to Secretary Foreign Department, 20 September 1884, IFDP, External A, January 1885, Nos.153-155.
25. *Report of the Baluchistan Levy Committee*, 10 March 1884, IFDP, A Political E, June 1884, Nos. 56-62.
26. Notes of meeting of 4 January 1881, Appendix D, Enclosed in Government of India's letter of 23 February 1881, to the Secretary of State, PSLE, L/P&S/7/27.
27. *Report of the Baluchistan Levy Committee*, 10 March 1884, IFDP, A Political E, June 1884, Nos.56-62.
28. J.Ramsay, Agent to the Governor-General in Baluchistan, to A.H.Grant, Secretary Foreign and Political Department, 28 May 1915, Foreign and Political Department Proceedings, Frontier A, August 1915, Nos.11-19.
29. Viceroys' speech, Quetta Durbar, 20 November 1899, *The Englishman*, 22 November 1899.
30. H.Lefebvre, *op.cit.*, p. 143.
31. W.J.Cunningham, Secretary Foreign Department, *Note*, 23 February 1899, India Foreign and Political Department Proceedings, Frontier A, Nos.1-5.
32. E.F. Chapman, *Memorandum on the Condition of the Defences of the North West Frontier*, 23 June 1887, *Dufferin Collection*, MSS.Eur.F.130/88.
33. G.Deleuze, *op.cit.*, p. 213.
34. Sandeman to C.Grant, Secretary Foreign Department,15 August 1884, PSLE, L/P&S/27/43.
35. Sandeman, *Memorandum*, 5 October 1888, *The Bruce Collection*, MSS.Eur.F.163/7.
36. H.Lefebvre, *op.cit.*, p. 143.
37. G.Deleuze, *op.cit.*, p. 212.
38. *Ibid.*, pp. 212-213.
39. *Ibid.*, p. 271.
40. *Ibid.*, p. 213.
41. *Parliamentary Debates*, Commons 14 February 1898, Fourth Series, Vol. LIII, col. 602.
42. R.I.Bruce, *History of the Mari Baluch Tribe*, p. 61, p. 63, *The Bruce Collection*, MSS.Eur.F.163/5.
43. *Parliamentary Debates*, Lords, 8 February 1898, Fourth Series, Vol. LIII, col. 42.
44. Salisbury to Lytton, 28 December 1877, *Lytton Papers*, MSS. Eur.E.218/4B.
45. *Parliamentary Debates*, Commons, 14 February 1898, Fourth Series, Vol. LIII, col. 602.

46. James Browne, to Secretary Foreign Department, 24 January 1896, 24 January 1896, IFDP, External A, October 1896, Nos.84-96.
47. G.Spivak, *Post Colonial Studies Reader*, p. 38.
48. *Manual of Customary Law*, p. 189, *Political and Secret Department Library*, L/P&S/2/B.297.
49. Homi Bhabha, *The Location of Culture*, p. 45.
50. E.Gellner, 'Tribal Society and its Enemies', p. 439, in R.Tapper ed. *The Conflict of Tribe and State in Iran and Afghanistan*.
51. Oliver St.John to C.Grant, 14 November 1881, IFDP, A Political E, February 1883, Nos.62-65.
52. *Quetta-Pishin District Gazetteer*, pp. 72-73.
53. H.Wylie, Officiating Agent to the Governor-General in Baluchistan, to W.Cunningham, Secretary Foreign Department (demi-official), 26 May 1898, K.W.No.2, IFDP, External A, January 1899.
54. R.Guha, 'The Prose of Counter Insurgency', *Subaltern Studies*, Vol. II, p. 15.
55. G.Deleuze, *op.cit.*, p. 222.
56. *Ibid.*, p. 212.
57. Quoted in C.E. Bruce, *The Sandeman Policy as Applied to Tribal Problems Today*, The Bruce Collection, MSS. Eur.F. 163/80.
58. Nietzsche, quoted in H.Lefebvre, *op.cit.*, p. 139.
59. Quoted in Crary, *op.cit.*, p. 81.

5

In the Mirror of Meaning: Imperial Translations in Tribal Space, as Point and Margin, Time and Text, Place and Power, 1876-1905

The tribal sign entering the imagistic plane of imperial consciousness, as the negation of history, mirrored a petrified, primitive landscape, iconic of decaying time, pointing towards the void, and the extinction of the idea of the human. This imaging of man against man, signified an oppressive sense of fatal schism in the human scheme, as racial and spatial separation. Here representation occurred in the apprehension of divisions, disfiguring the philosophy of civilization. In this understanding, as Levi-Strauss points out,[1] the primitive tribe placed on the border of biology, could only be brought within the meaning of historical humanity, by its displacement in the internalizing process of colonialism, that conferred reason/purpose to an original humanity which was without it. Growth of reason had to be conceived to occur at the expense of the past itself, as it lingered in the present in the savage form. The point like purpose of imperial picturing, was to write history against the historical segment of primitivism. History as translation, displacement, dispossession, became possible in the structure of the colonial margin, the primitive other, of the self.

The reduction of the tribe to pure figure, like Carlyle's original 'Chaos of Being', allowed the imperialist to assume the posture of both observer and agent, to represent, translate and recompose. In the metaphoric construction of the tribal field as chaos, resided the ideological places of savagery and strangeness, against which civilization threw up society, to translate the horror, and capture the fear. The hard, cruel edges of tribal form, bruised and encrusted with blood, entered imperial mirroring as the plane of explanatory description, and point of redemptive appropriation. As one Member of Parliament put it in 1898:

> "It is a question of dealing with the tribes wisely ... so that these men, who have only one court of law, and that a court of assassination, and who spill each others blood at the slightest provocation, will see that there are higher interests and will be led ... to become our ... subjects".[2]

The threat of the savage and promise of the convert, that stalked imperial redescriptions of the tribal margin, made it the scene of translation, in the language of nineteenth century Naturalistic fiction, that the meaning of culture was "to make a tame and civilized animal, a domestic animal out of the human wild beast".[3] Since the unconscious after Lacan is structured as language, the paradoxical representation of the tribal image as "impression of the past" and as a "sign of the future",[4] may be read as the resolution of the meaningless within the meaningful, the purging of horror in hope, through the intermediacy of language, by which the verbal configuration mediates between the prefiguration of the malefic, and its refiguration as the beneficent.

The design for translation, was a Messianic dream of the empire's 'beautiful civilizing mission', that would trace a new moral topography in the savage space of the tribe. Behind the representational optics of the ethical and noble, that structured the view point of the mission, was a Promethean concept of human possibility, leaning on the Romantic imagery of an epic combat between the powers of reason and unreason, which would provide the drama of history, and prove the ultimate transcendence of the heroic and civilized over the fallen, the lost, the irrational. The poetics of the civilizing mission translated the romantic vision of Herder, while claiming the ideological territory of Hegelian 'state-spaces' to appropriate meaning, control, order. Herder's belief that "Reason and justice alone endure: madness and folly destroy the earth and themselves",[5] reached into imperialism as the voice and subject of its historic manifesto against the dark, distortions of unreason. The analogy between the time and space of empire as the history of rightful reason, colonizing an exterior ground of lapsed humanity, was explicit in the language and logic of imperial discourse. Following the contours of the romantic imagination, imperial time was symbolic of a heroic self-consciousness, abolishing the despair of the themes of the night, those images of primitive blindness, darkness and opacity, that needed to be dispelled to perfect the order of creation. The verbal model representing imperial time as oppositional, structured on the difference and distance between the conquering, victorious ego of English exceptionalism, and the subjugated body of the colonized Asiatic, may be inferred from Lytton's rhetoric on the understanding of conquest as construction, when the agency for such action belonged to the Western imperialist. Justifying the idea of aggression, in reclaiming the Indian frontier from its wild, tribal time, Lytton clarified:

> "What is conquest? ... It may mean such an operation as the conquest of Attilla, and massacres, confiscation ... the sale of the inhabitants into slavery ... it may mean such as an operation as the conquests of some Mahommedan princes: the imposition of a grinding tribute, ...degradation ...But when it means only that good government is to be substituted for anarchy, and that security for life and property is to supersede robbery and murder, and that a few English officials ... are to replace lawless *sirdars* – then I really cannot see that conquest is a terrible thing."[6]

Temporalities of East and West, verbalised in significations of right and wrong, suggested the violation of one present by another, as the moment when the abstraction of imperial time was born in the order of primacy, certainty, and translation. The sign of this time, would be mirrored in the ascendancy of the self, seeking to control meaning from the site of its European epistemological tendency, pushing up its ground of certainty to dispossess the doubt configured in the strangeness of the other, the mind of the thoughtless brute, no longer synonymous with reason, to justify its appropriation in an imperial temporality, as Augustine's immutable right of reason[7] to invade the contours of unreason.

If the point like present of imperial time, mirrored the historic moment of the European translation of Asia, the content of the script aspired to the search for extending boundaries of meaning, that would privilege the idea of Europe, in texting the place of the colonized. The symbolic mediations of imperial presence and purpose in conquered terrains, occurred in the idiom of evolutionary parable, and dialectical exchange between civilization and barbarism. In 1897 the *Times* pointed out:

> "The history of British power in India has been one of slow but irresistible expansion. In India as elsewhere, barbarism has receded before civilization, or been absorbed by it, and this expansion

must continue until it meets with a wave of civilization advancing to meet it from the opposite direction. We have tried ...to live at peace with our turbulent neighbours. Times without number, instead of the punishment of fire and sword which...some blood curdling atrocity would have amply justified, we have contended ourselves with pecuniary fines, temporary blockades ... and sometimes even paid them a subsidy, in the hope of encouraging their supposed peaceful tendencies. All in vain! instead of ... beating their swords into ploughshares...they became every year more formidable ... to ... escape the constant annoyance and inconvenience of frontier troubles...we should disarm the tribesmen, construct roads through their country, and bring the whole population under an efficient administration...[Such] pacification would be final".[8]

Both the point of view from which the writer observed the field of imperial-tribal history, and his tone of narration were grounded in approximations of difference and distance, to confirm the theme of a barbarian menace to civilization, whose negative consequence could be avoided only if an evolutionary analogy was preserved, between the time of savagery and civilization, predicated on the decline of the former and growth of the latter, as inevitable fate, predetermined and predicted. But the immediate disturbing proximity of the savage to the frontier of the civilized, produced the sombre mood, and metonymic language to redescribe the intimacy of a danger that was parasitic to the imperial idea, its premises and parameters of soul and body. The anticipatory image of the final submission of the savage to the civilized, allied to evolutionary axioms of racial retreat and advance, determined by genetic codings of high and low, translated history as hierarchy, to centre the notion of imperial movement as always transcending the limits of its present, as unstoppable impulse, destined to claim the future in the sign of victory, and certainty, over the gothic gloom and despair that inhabited the savage horizon. As A Member of Parliament, justifying the picture of aggressive imperial landscaping, in the wild recesses of tribal terrain put it:

"You can no more cry stop to the expansive tendencies of our race than Canute could cry 'stop' to the advancing waves".[9]

The metaphoric resemblance between the energy of imperial flows, and the recurring motion of waves, elevated the spirit of empire to the idea of the irresistible, signifying a totality of power assaulting surfaces of human consciousness, with the omnipotence of its eternal being and meaning. This sense of unfettered flows, carrying the empire towards the threshold of the absolute, signified the extreme spiritualization of state power, as the mark of a transcendent interiority, absorbing in its space, dimensions of difference, situated outside, exterior to itself.

In this unceasing flow of content and expression, imperialism figured as another dimension, "a cerebral ideality" as Deleuze described, "that is added to, superimposed on the material evolution of societies, a regulating idea or principle of reflection that organizes the parts and the flows into a whole".[10] The philosophic point of this ideality, was the invention of order to control and own the threat, configured in temporalities of discordance and dissemblance, that troubled the dream of permanence. Reversals imagined in the apocalyptic model of primitive scenes, prefiguring the terrors of the end of time, situated the locus of order as the nostalgic homeland of a Western imperial psychologism, confronted with the 'heart of darkness' in the savage shape. As a newspaper correspondent, observed from the North West Frontier in 1903, "The heart of the tribe is more unsearchable than the heart of kings...[a] tissue of inscrutable intrigues",[11] that lived by the gun, bought with British subsidies and was completely unworthy of trust. Alfred Lyall offered a more extended view of the tribal paradigm, that undermined from within the plane of order, that sustained the experience of imperial temporality. He pointed out:

> "We have to realize the fact that the conquest of these wild highlands is a new sort of undertaking, materially different from our previous conquests in India. Hitherto we have only had to contend, on the Indian plains, with ... disorganised rulerships, we have overturned them and taken their places with the passive acquiescence...of the people, most of whom welcomed the advent of peace and orderly government. ... But the highland tribes do not wish for orderly government; they desire above all things freedom, and it is most improbable that for many years to come they will be content to be ruled by foreigners... the establishment of regular administration will be most unpalatable to the tribes."[12]

The dysjunction mapped in Lyall's discourse, between imperial and tribal inscriptions as order and its lack, foregrounded the tribal problematic as the inner enemy of the empire's philosophy of rule, regulation, and ownership, that structured its core surfaces of political perception.

As the tribal identity came to imply an ever present margin of threat, signifying from its interior a time of primal freedoms, the repression of which was crucial for the genesis of imperial time, significations of the free and unfree were reversed in discourse, to represent the imperial pictorial as the battle of the high, moral self, seeking to impose restraint in the place of unrestraints, that was the wild space of the tribes, abandoned to primitive passions, savage gestures, animal anger, unable to transcend the evolutionary level of barbarism, as: "...their... one great commandment is blood for blood ... they are ...sensual... avaricious...predatory... excited by fanaticism. Such... is their character, replete, ... with that mixture of opposite vices and virtues, belonging to savages."[13] This picturing, where the freedom of the tribe was contracted to pure negativity, was the preface for establishing the 'unfreedom' of imperial time, its disciplines, immanent laws, and structural compulsions, within the province of truth and the dialectics of dominion, as prima philosophia, realizing the higher and conscious self-determination of mankind.

Imperialism as a map of meaning, the setting and mirror, for a dialectical exchange between the difference that separated the savage principle, from the civilized principle, historicized in a Hegelian vein on the paradigm of progress. Hegel, starting from the premises that: "The state of nature is predominantly that of injustice and violence, of untamed natural impulses and inhuman deeds"[14] grounded the idea of progress as rearrangements, leading to the increasing perfection of elements through the process of exchange, between the savage consciousness and civilized consciousness. Within the frame and compass of Hegelian picturing, imperial subjectivity could participate in the optical distortions of imagining a picture of the real, that it could only enter along the perspectival axes of order combating anarchy, of civilization rewriting the pathos of savagery. This absorption in what Nietzsche termed as imparting Apollonian form to Dionysian chaos,[15] structured the chorology of empire as explanation and description of its purposeful point and promise. As Lytton's apocalyptic end of empire imaging presumed:

> "The Empire must ... be maintained, because its fall would involve 200,000,000 people in anarchy and bloodshed, and relegate them to the barbarism from which they are slowly emerging."[16]

This imagining of imperial place as a relationship between propositions, where the ascendancy of Western meanings would translate the form and content of alien ground, to compose the poetics of another truth of the hierarchies of temporal experience, grounded the centricity of the European mind, as a kind of subliminal determinant, conferring dimensions of distance and danger on landscapes of otherness, existing in the gap between pre-history and history.

The violence of the imperial interpretive, pursued an aesthetics of order, that would translate intransigence through the insertion of state-spaces, that would mediate between the topoi of culture and anarchy, in the Hegelian sense of the moral state, and the state mechanism as the instrument of such mediation in concrete existence. 'Order' as the language of presupposition and transformation, would compose the moral atoms of a redemptive truth, that would situate tribal insignias of the past in the future of hope. The symmetry of expectation and description signified in the redemptive idea, followed the contours of a Christian moral topography of sin, suffering and expiation, within which the fearful imagined as the pityful, could be reduced from the plane of threat to salvable matter in the form of reformed spirit, allowing the primitive to migrate from the ground of the fallen to the sanctuary of the moral, the space of the soul, the confines of creation. Writing from the Frontier in 1854, John Jacob had proposed the premises of a critical moral gaze, that would empower "all good men, as a matter of course", to look on all predatory tribes, "as objects of pity, not of dread, with hatred perhaps, but never with fear... Violence, robbery, bloodshed held as equally disreputable...the abandonment of such practices ...as most honourable", to be encouraged in every way.[17] Subsequently, Robert Sandeman bringing this moral perpsectivism on the amoral, within the compass of religion and redemption, put it: "What are my views, but simply those which every Christian man or woman ought to feel towards their less fortunate neighbours."[18]

The enclosure of a Roman state model within the Christian view of ultimate liberation, connected the moral to the political, in mapping the desired terrain of the civilizing ideal. Rome offered an image of political space that deeply haunted the time and text of the English imperial imaginary. The sanction of violence, of war and the military machine in creating the place of empire, mirrored the Roman aesthetics of the totalitarian state space, signifying the aggressive confiscation of the time-place inscriptions of other histories and other subjects, to ground dominion in the coercion of the singular, the universal, and totalizing abstractions of the desiring state machinery. The mimesis of Roman spatial violations in the worlding of British imperial power, was explicit in the polemical defence of war, as the birthmark of empire and civilization. As Lytton insisted in Parliament:

> "...No one can denounce war ...in absolute unmeasured terms...without denying at the same time one of the most potent agents of civilization. The greater part of Europe consists of fragments of the Roman Empire, an empire created by wars which rendered possible the diffusion of Christianity and the development of law. The whole of America ...has been conquered from its original owners who were savages chiefly by Englishmen and Spaniards. The enormous Russian empire has been formed by a series of obscure wars waged against barbarians impenetrable to any other civilizing process, and the whole fabric of the British Empire in India is an additional illustration of the same thing".[19]

Lytton's polemical pointings occurred within the binaries, of what Hayden White has described as the Roman apprehension of the world in metonymic contiguities of form and chaos, and comprehension in a synecdochic system of relationship, of parts aligned to the whole. The imposition of form on chaos through language, i.e. the mediations of civilization and war, would bring into history, the signification of empire as the perfect sum of its parts, the point and parameter of the sublations of strangeness, and standardisations of the abnormal that were integral to its text and context.

The appearance of Roman space as the 'gendered place', where as Henri Lefebvre described, "masculine virtues and values, ... of the military man and the administrator were in command",[20] was reflected in the symmetries of the British imperial design, riefying the icons of army and authority, law and limits, of pacification and power. In 1893, the Chairman of the London Chamber of Commerce addressing the subject of the army and empire, in the course of a speech honouring Lord Roberts of Candahar as an emblem of high imperialism, proposed that Pax Britannica included and transcended the old Roman peace of siege and subjection; for it was at once the place of peace and war, the site of an apostolic translation of St.Paul's metaphor: "Let peace garrison your hearts". He continued, that when they thought of the two "great theatres of modern administration, Egypt and India – might they not recall with pride that India, for instance had seen railways, and canals, and irrigation works and codes of law greater than the Code Napolean – works which would be a monument to our services to that great dependency. At the same time they must not forget that the great source of our power has been war, and that our colonies had been chiefly acquired by conquest; nor must they forget that the time might come when the force of right should be asserted by the right of force, when the sword alone would keep the sword in the scabbard".[21] As this redescription suggests, the limit of the imperial idea and its representational space, was the limit of force and power, making its constitutive field less like the Pauline metaphor, and more like the Roman place of the conquering sign, implicated in the violations of displacement and translation, but seeking to escape the guilt of this implication, in the idea of a moral pacification, i.e. 'Pax Britannica'.

The language of pacification was disciplinary re-writing to alter the premises of chaos, to replace it "by an image, by an audible representation, by a word, and then by a concept",[22] to fabricate a coded construct, governed more by the expected meaning effects, rather than the material to be encoded. Primitivism recoded in signs of 'docility', and 'obedience', functioned at the intersection of text and reality, to bring the inhuman within the reach of the human, by virtue of its appropriation within the meaningful, standardising surface of imperial representational power, seeking to bring the ultimate contradiction of the chaotic and abnormal, within the boundaries of lasting possession. Sandemanised Baluchistan, that captured the picture of tribalism relocated from the site of savagery to subjection and duty, was the ideal view, within which the imperial eye could observe the translation and ownership of meaning, signified in the recomposition. By bringing contradictions of the tribal interior within the rule of the norm, to make it mimic gestures of capitulation and consent demanded by the imperial regulating machine, Sandemanism indulged in the emptying and conferring of identity, evacuating the space of autonomy in the tribal condition, and colonizing it in forms and fetters of subservience, to refigure tribal surfaces as translated spaces in the text of pacification. The immanence of constructed imagery and meaning within the orbit of ideology, may be inferred from Sandeman's stated object of creating a "peaceful province in place of a congeries of fighting tribes".[23] The reterritorializing implied in the description 'peaceful province,' denoted the act of political intervention across the spatial history of the tribe, burying its recalcitrance in the cartography of a silenced place, the predetermined outcome of imperial intentionality.

Sandemanism offered the perspective of bringing the incommensurable within the commensurable, by decentring the assertion of force, in favour of accentuating the intimacies immanent in the sovereign-subject pairing, to entice the savage impulse to enter the terrain of civility, bend to the rule of discipline, and place itself in the web of power. The power of proximity to displace the savage limit, and situate it in the righteous recesses of imperial ground, would function through the correctives of character and conduct, of example and excellence, of the English presence asserting itself in the place of disquiet. This presence acquired figural proportion, as "The English mind, to whose leading all these wild spirits will bow",[24] in John Jacobs's phrase; it was also the spectacle of "every day acts... of earnest, upright English gentlemen that lasting influence must be obtained",[25] in Lytton's polemic; and it was finally the spirit of English exceptionalism in Curzon's rhetoric, that claimed: "It is a question not of rifles, of cannons, but of character, and of all that character can do amid a community of ... men".[26]

In the imaginings of empire and English character, Sandemanism was the mythic text of the erasure of force, compulsion, constraint, in willing the savage to be what the civilized wanted him to be, from the depths of desire and demand. 'Order' would persuade the savage to become civil; his body would carry inscriptions of control, his gestural language would signify subservience; in effect, he would assume the form stamped on him by the structure of imperial power relationships. The invented form in which the savage appeared to renounce his 'jungle' existence, and move towards a grounding in English humanness, was the sign of the translation, of civilizing the barbarian, without the violence of force. Sandeman's bloodless victories in Baluchistan were seen to be part of this shaping, the conquest of peace, the romance of retrieving the human from chaos. But this text of translation evaded the ironies rippling on the smooth surface of imperial pacification; for geometries of tribal consent did not mirror a cultural odyssey, so much as a disciplinary war of surveillance and censure, the coercion of the norm, the rule of regulation, that made the tribe docile and useful simultaneously, to structure topographies of power and powerlessness in the place of usurpation and translation. This remaking may be configured in Adorno's meaning as a dimension of dominance, in which "Truth is abandoned to relativity and people to power".[27]

As the act of civilizing was also one of refiguring, in which the tribes alienated from their original meaning, served as veins and capillaries for circulating the life blood of the imperial system, the political signification overpowered the moral, by making the tribe not the equal of the civilized, but an object to be regulated, used and manipulated to defend the privileges of power. Pictures from Sandemanised Baluchistan, of tribesmen turned policemen guarding the interiority of order, of sedated tribal elites tranquilized by subsidies and status, disavowing dissent to protect the parameters of consent and conformity, captured the distortions of dominance, delegating the violence of its purpose to the dominated. The tribesmen disengaging from the anarchy of instinct, was redefining himself within the reality principle of imperial rule, by becoming the instrument of its power, enacting his own enslavement. This alienation of meaning, that produced the identification of the victim with victors,[28] was the cynicism of the ruler's code, its civilizing vocabulary a mask to mystify the reality of appropriation which existed within the representational signs of peace, harmony, progress, that were only the fables of power entombing the truth of the 'other' in the strength of its fiction.

The ambiguity in the sign of the translated tribe, situated within fabrications of the civil and servile, mirrored the schizophrenia of imperial culture, stemming from what Eric Cheyfitz has described, as "the conflict within the ideology of imperialism between what this ideology represses (that imperialism is always acting in the interests of its own power), and what it admits (that imperialism is acting in the interests of enlightening the other).[29] Language formulated on this Janus like surface of comprehension, would propose to cure when it implied control, falsifying the object of its description, dissolving subjectivity in suppression, to configure the reassurance of permanence in the consent of the captive.

Signatures of primacy and power, that informed and deformed the text of imperial translation, came from a perception of time and place imbricated in fears of loss and reversal. The Great Game was a metaphor for this precariousness of power, that generated the anguish and anger, in which boundaries and borders were seen as limits and lines of self ascendancy, against the enemy which menaced from a distance, but was firmly lodged inside the perception and apprehension of the tragic, a dread of the mortality of power. Imperial time, reflecting the desiring impulse to own the point and plane of temporal sequence, became the succession of moments combating the disempowering of desire, to acquire significations of pre-eminence, conviction, eternity. The metaphysics of defending desire against its denial, translated as the dialectics of the Great Game, where the time of the self was always confronted by the fear of its future ruin, within the negation implied in the desiring dimensions of the rival other.

The abstraction implied in the ownership of time, was realized in the concrete, within referents of prestige, honour, reputation, in order to invest the field of perception with lasting impressions of imperial primacy and invincibility, to expel doubt completely from its premises of permanence. Thus Tsarist Russia was figured in a visuality, that presented the danger in order to disarm it, framing it within significations of a future, in which British imperial history would be asserted or emptied. Within this predictive view of imperial history, time became inscribed in the perspective of logic, i.e., the expected reduction of the Asiatic in the horizon of European expansionism. The expected submission of Asia, functioned as the imagined time of imperial reachings, when British India would touch Tsarist Russia, based on the annihilation of separation, of the difference in the gap, that signified "another time",[30] as Fabian described, of the backward time of the Asiatic other. But this new imperial time, based on the confiscation of other times, was imbricated in the terrors of desire, of civilization cannibalizing itself on the mimetic terrain of imperial visions and vocabularies.

The Europeanizing of Asiatic time, in the expected end of civilization crushing the barbaric gap, brought the proximity of power within significations of anxiety, and the fear, that primacy would become the contested ground of play between England and Russia, acting as doubles of one another, seeking the same image of power, with nearness translating into paranoic hostility. This imperial future, became the predictive text, the truth of a visual logic, that led Lytton to claim: "The conclusion that England and Russia are destined sooner or later to be practically coterminus in Asia, must ... appear as certain as that water will run downhill when the way is free to it".[31] The moment of meeting, was then appropriated in apprehensions of difficulty and danger, of desire always betraying the limits of its verbal confinement, to pursue the satisfaction of "national interests ... tendencies and passions"[32] beyond definitions in the present, to acquire form in the infinity of future variants. This narcissistic time of the desiring self of Tsarist Russia, registered as the critical moment of meaning, burdening the British Empire with the final despairing implication of:

> "Holding India as tenants at will to Russia, and fortifying her Frontier behind the mountains, at a vast expense, upon a scale fitted for its protection, not merely against mountain tribes, but against the organized Military Power of a great European rival, supported by their cooperation, and encouraged by the shaken confidence of your own subjects in your ability and determination to resist its advance."[33]

This image of fear that translated imperial proximities as the ultimate danger of time, also allowed for the exploitation of the sign of fear, to rescue primacy and permanency from regressions into retreat and resignation.

In Dufferin's description, contiguity "with a great military power" was the perceptual point that decreed the drive, "to take the same precautions along our frontier in the way of military works etc., as ... Russia".[34] The military inscription of power to address the threat of reversal, became allied to a metaphoric reading of time within political significations of loss and gain, to privilege ideas of aggression and advance as the promise of the future, the prestige of ascendancy, the denial of which was the negation of past and present, the forfeit of power. As Curzon quoting Warren Hastings in 1898 put it: "To stand still in India is danger, to recede is ruin".[35] The freezing of purpose, as Curzon seemed to envisage, in an imperial temporality divorced from signs of expansive movement, would result in what he termed as losing the battle against the external enemy from within. It would mean the repudiation of signs of presence, that had empowered the idea of imperial subjugations inside and outside the borders of India, erase the signatures of past history and blacken English faces before "all Asia and India. The native princes of India whom we guarantee, the Sikhs and the Gurkhas ... the peaceful millions of India who... [rely] on the protection we assure them, would all turn from us, even if they did not turn upon us in contempt for our cowardice".[36] Here Curzon was dramatizing the scene of imminent loss to configure a poetics of power, that would draw the imperial image as conquering sign, to suppress significations of danger, to negate the pessimism of absent conviction, and repossess time in the totality of power. From the precipice of loss, the empowered figurative form of empire would be extricated, to confirm that British India "stands as the strong man armed, and looks out upon the troubled waters of Central Asian intrigues with the calmness which comes of conscious strength and full preparation for all emergencies."[37] The escape from fear in the magic of power, mirrored the hauntings of the self, seeking consolations of permanence in the illusions of imagined time.

The desired perenniality of the imperial translation, mirrored a threat to place, as much as time; this occurred in the perception of place as property and possession, and was therefore imbricated in the possibility of its loss. The territory of the threat acquired imaginative dimension, as the place of union, between the tragic overwhelming, feared in the imperiality of a rival desire, and the savage horror signifying the mutilation of civilized norms. Within this visuality, the frontier assumed significance as the place of critical concern, the site of impending crisis, deliberately summoned in the intentionality of linguistic representation, to configure a terrible terrain, where Tsars and tribes would gather to prey on the space of British imperial power. The anticipatory image of displacement, mirroring the tragic and the savage threat, was premised on the projection of a lowly intimacy between the Russian and Asiatic minds. "Starting from a lower level of civilization", the *Pioneer Mail* asserted that "Russian nature, the Russian way of dealing proves more congenial to Oriental people".[38] Unlike British rule, which rested on "higher qualities",[39] the Russians would appeal to the base instincts governing "the poor, greedy ambitious races" across northwest India, to view "the booty of India as a prey" on which to feed after invasion, and darken the reflection of British power with fear and doubt, that "men of different blood, of different...faith"[40] i.e. the natives, would easily accept, thereby threatening the place of empire as unchallenged dominion. The dialectics of danger that produced itself in frontier space, also produced that space as violence and excess, the junction point of war and friction, that demanded retrieval and refiguring, in the counter signs of equilibrium, stability, power defended.

Possession as the complement of power, sought to manifest itself in the exclusiveness of ownership. The ambiguity of the frontier as the place of doubt, the possible Russian road to India, the chaotic sign of the wild, brought it within the argumentative locus of British imperial thought, as the ground that needed to be conquered as sole possessor from all other combatants, to bring it within the inventory of property, certainty, identity. In this transformation, the space of the frontier, alienated from other meanings, would emerge as the inscriptional place of the univocal, singular, reality of imperial being. The desire to appropriate meaning through possession, bound imperial political inscription to the notion of the property relation to human beings, asserting the right to priority, of seeking to own the specific, to realize exclusive aspirations to totality. Curzon designing this architecture of ownership, traced its three essential properties; namely, to encompass the landscape of passes and roads such as the Gomal and Khyber in imperial framings; disempower the tribes, by ensuring they were not "at liberty to side with our enemies";[41] and finally, as a canonical maxim, the tribes "must be our men and the men of no other power".[42] In this encoding, tribal terrain was refigured to exist as the 'representational place' of imperial meaning, as its sign and surface, reflecting the image of the invented identity that would be manipulated to serve the history of empire.

The problem of this frontier architecture in Baluchistan, was comprehended within perceived angles of the chronic weakness of Persia and Afghanistan, that 'magnified the Russian danger to India',[43] both as spatial text by appropriating the rim to frame a view of Russia's military might, and as ideological message, to draw the west Baluch and north east Pathan tribes from the British side of the Perso-Baluch borderland to the place of Russian power, by the strength of spectacle, that would orchestrate a general tribal surrender across both sides of the border. The notion of a pan tribal surface spanning across the boundary line, to transport the sinister corpus of Russian aims to the interior of the Indian frontier, was the critical margin of concern, within which the British possession of Baluchistan, eluded final closure, to remain the property of doubt, that always demanded new visibility to dispel its own darkness. In this seeing, the seen was problematised as the negation of possession, that needed to be brought back within the optics of re-possession. Writing from the edge of the uncertain, A.H. McMahon, Agent to the Governor-General in Baluchistan, 1907, reflected darkly, that if Russia occupied Herat and North Afghanistan, "the ethnological affinity of Baluchistan with Southern Afghanistan would come into notice...cause despondency", while further unhindered Russian advances would even lead the tribes "to make terms with the conqueror."[44] The view from the west, along the Perso-Baluch frontier, was equally tied to a perspectival displacement of power. Here, McMahon mapped the critical margin within a mounting "obssession" of the people with Russian activities, and intrigues in Siestan, expecting to see "Russian troops ... on their way to Persian Baluchistan. Such rumours...were actually believed and exerted a disturbing influence on the minds of the people, and it was really considered advisable to remedy this state of affairs, by putting ourselves more in 'evidence' in this part of the Persian frontier".[45] As McMahon's observation suggests, the danger of the frontier, was in its indeterminate locus in the gap between belief and disbelief, from which surety had to be won.

To address the ambiguity of the gap in the meaning of presence as power and property, brought it within the interpretive of fence and boundary, track and terminus, roads and reachings. As Cheyfitz has suggested, the sign of place (as property), the sign that is of enclosure, was the fence".[46] The symbolic fencing implied in boundary making, represented the visible contours of an imperial landscape, nuanced to exclude the antagonistic and foreign from its essential space. The boundary was the mark on the map, that configured the political edge of power, where possession was haunted by proximity to the external, and had to be therefore defended in the aggression of battle, the fatality of war, the consolation of conquest. As Curzon, bringing the visuality of the space of the boundary, within significations of imperiality, and its imbrication in the territoriality of place, as identity, as locus of the self, stated:

> "If you agree upon a boundary with a great power, one party cannot run away from its side, both parties must occupy or ...exert their influence up to the limit of that boundary. Russia has done so... She has pushed her soldiers right up to the waters of the Oxus, and we are equally bound to do the same ... in these wild parts nature as elsewhere abhors a vacuum."[47]

In this conception, the idea of the border signified the usurpation of the limit, to write a history of power within the constructed meanings of imperial place, property, and permanence. To suppress the ambivalence of place and perception, that bound the border to the sign of the transient, required as McMahon put it, the conquest of "success", that would mirror "the success of ...arms in the field",[48] grounding the fencing of power in the desired premises of asserted ascendancy, declared dominion.

To keep the place of conquest safe within the enclosure of the boundary, the strangeness of its originary interior remote from any meaning, had to be brought within the intimacies of possession, by means of access to its wild parts through tracks and paths that would render the distant near, enabling power to reach its objects of concern, to form and transform their properties, to create the field of its perceptual truth, in the disempowering of danger that was the content of the unfamiliar. Implicated in this visuality, was the perception of roads and railways as metaphors of power, penetrating surfaces of tribal terrain, functioning as checkpoints of consciousness on the boundary between impulse and restraint. Locating the symbol of the road in the coercion of the mind, Henry Green mapped its disciplinary text:

> "These frontier roads ...exert a considerable moral influence on the robber tribes. Many a party of marauding horsemen has been stopped on coming across a made road; they knew that if they crossed this well marked line they are committing themselves, and once across they never knew when they may not meet with British troops, or whether their retreat may not be cut off".[49]

In this symbolism of the road, that allowed the sign of the civil to overpower the space of savage intention, was the underlying assumption of owning the obedience of the primitive, to secure imperial landscaping in the stillness of silenced dissent, to situate the place of power across the threat of the savage inscription itself.

The idea of the road and railway belonged to a military text as well, in the sense of bridging distances between fortifications, to heighten the power of surveillance, directing the invention of the disciplinary landscape of routes and regiments imprinting the drill of the army, the rigour of routine, in the place of the primal freedoms of the wilderness. Mastery of the scene of the primitive, was the preamble, for engaging with what lay beyond, the desert and mountain rim that overlooked Persia and Afghanistan, where as Curzon described, the "Russians were visibly nibbling at one, and biting hard at the other".[50] The Quetta-Nushki railway attempting to bridge the desert for a slice of Siestan, the Chaman railway pointing at Qandahar to hold it in the coercive gaze of British Indian imperiality, mirrored the military model of arming the edge of power, to journey beyond it, to grasp the forward point in the plea of saving the rear. As the terminus of power, at the end of the road, was where the threat to place had to be defended against the fear of loss, in the mark of the military, the sign of struggle, the coercion of command.

The refiguration of the Baluch frontier, in time and narrative, as the inscriptional place of imperial history, brought it within the play of the agonistic, the polysemy of meaning in which the self struggled to mirror its essence in the philosophy of right, the poetics of perfection. It became the translated place of the central metaphor of empire, the 'Great Game', the tropic locus of contested signs and symbols, of fear and fiction, where the dubiety of belief was the predicament of power. The text of the Great Game presupposed the space of the real and ideal, that could be explored and entered, to figure the utopic totality of the imperial sign in the dimensions of history, the curve of congruence, that recomposed human surfaces to mirror the geography of the same, based on the denial of distances of difference, that problematised the picture of bringing views of the 'other' within horizons of the self. The narcissism of the narrative, fetishized the desolation of the Baluch wilderness as desired object and dark danger, placing it in the spell of fantasy and fear, that was the ironic content of imperial form, driven by the ghostly presence of negation towards the limits of the new, those thresholds of power in which to wear masks of control, that would suppress the inner haunting, in the exterior calm of confidence, ease, harmony. Making the Baluchistan boundary within the optics of the Great Game, the mimesis of competing imperial desires, interned its meaning within the idea of a playing field of power, the passive surface of signs and signatures, that mirrored not its own truth, but that of another, the intruder, appropriating representational meaning as construction and correction of the actual, to claim the space of imperial narrative demands. Within this remaking, the disempowering of tribal text and time, allegorized the idea of empire, in the literalization of its moment of power, of vision attained. As in Kipling's *Kim*, this time of extravagant possession, was the epic adventure of the Great Game, the heroic hour of repossessing possession, by expelling the fear of the foreign adversary from the ground of empire, revisiting the exoticism of its place of power, to subdue its Indianness in the Englishness of vision; to compel the strange to submit to structures of the known, reducing the body of the possessed to the interpretive of conferred meaning, constructed image; to imbricate the migration of identity in imperial mirroring, within representational connotations of willing surrender, desired subjection; to idealize the view of imperial place, mythologizing its space in fictions of absent conflict.

Imagining the pacific empire, the fabled place of translated union from the contradictions of discordant difference, was the derangement of imperial reading, where the illusion of consent was mystified as the truth of the real, of presence desired, of the place in "which the other's freedom consents to lose itself",[51] in the imperial existent. In demanding this hallucinatory response from the interior of the colonized, imperialism was allowing the dream wish to invade its structures of being, of keeping the body of the disempowered colonial geography permanently locked inside a self affirming point of view, in a surreal spatiality in which the imaginary and real existed as perspectival reflections of the constituting consciousness. The odd, the paradoxical, and offensive, that inhabited regions of 'otherness', were submitted to retrial and re-examination under the scrutiny of the 'knowing vision', derived from the Platonic gaze, aspiring for Cartesian certainty, premised on the Hegelian schismatic of inner and outer planes of comprehension. Within this optics of truth, the act of vision inspected by the intellect, the inner eye of the mind, was the essence of mirroring the external as representations of the real, making knowledge congruent with looking, empowering the grip of the gaze as the place of privileged access to views of otherness, existing outside the limits of the self. As this picturing was the property of a perspectivism, that belonged to the knowing subject, its topography was depicted in the exoticism of the extraordinary, the spectacle of the strange, that was the province of Western imaginary inferences, rather than an empirical place. The mirror here, was not the clear glass of incorrigible knowledge, but more like an "enchanted glass, full of superstition and imposture".[52] Otherness was born from this visual transgression of its place, its displaced meaning being "the result of a violent act which is perception itself",[53] as Merleau Ponty has observed.

Inability to view the foreign, from a ground other than its own, was the aporia in which the knowing self bound itself to a state of antagonism and suspicion of alien presences, waging a sort of Hegelian war against the consciousness of the external, to negate it in the premises of the dominant self. The absence of language to read the other in the truth of its alterity, made it the heart of darkness that was the fiction of the observing mind. The making of the imperial frontier, the marking of the Baluchistan boundary, mirrored this perspectival intrusion of the self, across the space of the wild, contesting its alterity, apprehending it as obstruction and challenge, from the limits of a visual vocabulary, that configured the unreadable as strange and fearful, oppressing the reach of reason and meaning. This discursive icon of otherness, functioned as ground and impediment for the self seeking to transcend the non-points of culture, that disconcerted the anchorages of certainty and conviction in which it sheltered. It was ground in the sense of being the intended place for imperial translations, becoming the object of epistemic fixity, in the knowledge that was the dissolution of otherness, to make it the symbol of intentional domination in the historical process. And it was impediment, as latent resentment built into the space of confiscated otherness, that carried the threat of reversal, of the violated other striving to recover subjectivity from the depth of its surrender, apprehension of which, kept the self from seizing its imperial present with certainty, of always viewing ascendancy with a tentative look.

The Baluch frontier as the figural space of primal instruction, where the language game of making the 'savage' 'civil' prevailed, mirrored the deception of culture, seeking 'self-preservation' while seeming to dispense civilization. As power defended itself by strategies of disempowering, the tamed tribe became the totem of disfiguring dominion, of subjectivity torn out from the old frame of primitivity, to iconicize the disciplined body, as an accomplice to power, surrendering its surface as the inscriptional ground of imperial truth. This displacement of the wild, to centre the sign of the obedient, was the ultimate utilitarian reduction of the tribe, bringing its remaking within the maximizing, exploiting framework of imperial purpose, to form and transform primitivism, to make it bear the burden of civilizing its ground in the interests of the imperial intruder. In this forming, the savage condition was annexed to the demand for profit, productivity, and progress that signified the margin of imperial reality, the site of hope, history and evolution. Within these shifts of meaning and marks of making, the borderland of the tribes separating the condition of created beings from that of fallen beings, was tacitly crossed[54] to symbolize the universal being of imperial time and place.

Reversal, recognition, and redemption that appeased the myths of imperial transformation, empowered the ritual of actions in which significations could be bounded and defended. Playing the 'Great Game' was the act of addressing the possible reversal at the end, by dramatizing the place of the frontier, as 'space in motion'[55], of moving columns ready to strike, of fortified posts covering defence, of railways and roads tracked through deserts and mountains, to suggest a theatrics of power, calculated to overwhelm the adversary in natural and human form. The agonism of the game, the need to place the answering voice of the self across the perceptual plane of the other, was the struggle for recognition in the eyes of the other, as Hegel would put it. Addiction to image, prestige, honour in playing the game, was the desiring self, seeking to annex power by implication, suggestion, inference of its omnipotence. The boundary marked on the ground was the physical enclosure for the idea of dominion, nuanced to exclude other 'freedoms' from interrupting its manifest text of possession and pre-eminence. In this eclipse of the other's freedom, was the transcendence of the imperial freedom existing within the given of its time and place "by being its own prohibition against surpassing it".[56]

The eclipsing was encoded in the expected meaning, not of disappearance, but that of "apparent survival and real anticipation"[57], of the 'other' being liberated from primitivity, fallacy, ignorance, into the new time of an imperial renaissance, the place of culture and redemption, where the 'animal' in man would be lost through the discovery of the 'angel',[58] the moral spirit of man, as Tocqueville wrote. In this understanding, the enslaved, the uncivil were foils for the perception of power, and concept of culture. Like the slave mediating the master's power, imperial visuality needed to store the other in images of the unfree and servile, to map the topography of dependence, on which it could structure iconographies of power. Within this exploitation of the premises of the weak to figure the province of the strong, was the repudiation of the redemptive scrolling that ornamented the imperial text, the irony of the false liberation that bound the subjectivity of the other to the ego of the appropriating self, that objectified him as property, divested him of character in the contempt for instinct and impulse, subjugating his life to the production of power, mocking the truth of salvation in the narcissistic possession of the other's autonomy. This was the schizophrenia of an imperial temporality, that mirrored the reflective point of Adorno's description, of the deforming vision of total power, in which, "The will to live finds itself dependent on the denial of the will to live: self preservation annuls all life in subjectivity".[59]

The rigour of imperial worlding, was the shift to a consciousness, always positive and justifying, of the rationality of dominance as the desired superstructure of existence. This illusion of perception that penetrated deep into the subconscious of imperial truth, reduced reality to representational fictions of usurpation as union, coercion as cure, to dislocate meaning in the imaginary bounds of pictures and propositions, where mirror images and scheme content would correspond to the political uncontroversial, that was the homeland of imperial escapist philosophy. The empire of perfect order, of eternal promise was the utopic place, where the imperialist like Prospero in Shakespeare's *Tempest*, could "dream undisturbed the dream of imperial power, the dream of an eloquence that literalizes immediately in the world".[60] Dream as the alibi of conquest induced the trance like vision of reality, as the place of euphoria and elation, the time of uncontested power, of the self embracing its horizon of hope. The dream was defended by the fencing of language and action, to exclude shadows of the strange from disturbing the pleasure of power, the ardour of playing the game that was the spirit and substance of the imperial abstract. Reality as the mimetic place of the dreamscape, became the site for seeking universal commensuration in a final vocabulary, the definitive translation of that most radical of otherness, the primitive horror, Emersons' "not me"[61] that was now brought within the power of the self, to sacrifice its difference at the altar of sameness, that was the political religion of imperial consciousness. But the non-totalizable part of otherness, that escaped the net of totalizing vision, was the sign of nomadic intransigence that could be stabilized within the meaning of order, but never completely fixed. The recurring nightmare of the tribal scene, its haunting text of rebellious violence, its savage story of animal instinct, was the hidden danger beneath the surface calm of imperialised primitive space. As the "image of all human contradictions, and of the contradiction in principle"[62] the tribe tormented perception, from its buried state in the sepulchre of discipline, to its feared resurrection in time as historic chaos. As Lord George Hamilton put it, "From their past history", of paralysing the normal, of murdering governors, sacking towns, "omens may be gathered for the future."[63]

In its ghostly haunting of imperial order, as the return of the abnormal to trouble the province of the normal, the tropic fear of the tribe was the vision of despair, that impaired the hope of the dream. But the insolence of the dream, born from the usurpation of power and time, needed to escape the dread of vulnerability, the illegitimacy of its reign, in the pretence of intimate union, shared purpose, mutual interest. This was the hallucination of power, Nietschze's "marvellous illusion to cover...dissonance with a veil of beauty"[64], seeking to deny the sinister other at the edge perception, by imposing the structure of an order-form to tranquilize the dread, "drawing boundary lines"[65] in, through and around the threatening chaos, to shelter in the truth of appearance, turning the predicament of power, into an occasion for heroic affirmation. The final playing of the game in the bewitching twilight of imperial power at the close of the nineteenth century, mirrrored the dream and despair of its fabled place and time, the enchantment of reality in the radiance of perfection and promise, destined to pass as the romance of picturing, the reflection of a period in history.

NOTES

1. C.Levi-Strauss, *The Savage Mind*, p. 248.
2. *Parliamentary Debates*, Commons, 15 February 1898, Fourth Series, Vol. LIII, col. 707.
3. R.N. Stromberg, *Realism, Naturalism, Symbolism*, p. 141.
4. P. Ricouer, *Time and Narrative*, Vol.I, p. 12.
5. Quoted in H.White, *Metahistory*, p. 75.
6. *Parliamentary Debates*, Lords, 10 January 1881, *Hansard*, Third Series, Vol. CCLVII, col. 296.
7. R. Rorty, *Philosophy and the Mirror of Nature*, p. 53.
8. *The Times*, 28 December 1897.
9. *Parliamentary Debates*, Commons, 14 February 1898, Fourth Series, Vol. LIII, col. 609.
10. F.Deleuze and G.Guttari, *Anti-Oedipus: Capitalism and Schizophrenia*, p. 219.
11. *The Daily Telegraph*, 16 February 1903.
12. A.C.Lyall, *Minute on Frontier Affairs*, 8 October 1897, *Political and Secret Memoranda*, L/P&S/18/A 129.
13. Extract from R. Temple's *Report on the Independent Tribes of the North West Frontier*, quoted in T.H.Thornton's *Memorandum* of 18 November 1867, *Parliamentary Papers*, Afghanistan, 1878-1879, Vol. 88, p. 27.
14. Quoted in H. White, *op.cit.*, p. 111.
15. *Ibid.*, pp. 339-340.
16. *Parliamentary Debates*, Lords, 10 January 1881, *Hansard*, Third Series, Vol. CCLVII, col. 299.
17. J.Jacob, *Sind Frontier Proceedings since 1846*, 9 August 1854, quoted in *Frontier and Overseas Expeditions from India*, Vol. III, p. 49.
18. Quoted in C.E.Bruce, *The Sandeman Policy as Applied to Tribal Problems of Today*, 'Journal of the Royal Central Asian Society', Vol. xix, January 1932, p. 58.

19. *Parliamentary Debates*, Lords, 10 January 1881, *Hansard*, Third Series, Vol. CCLVII, col. 298.
20. H.Lefebvre, *The Production of Space*, p. 249.
21. *The Times*, 25 May 1893.
22. H.Lefebvre, *op.cit.*, p. 138.
23. R.G.Sandeman, *Memorandum*, January 1888, *Curzon Collection*, MSS. Eur.F.111/54.
24. J.Jacob, *Suggestions Towards the Permanent Defence of the North West Frontier of India*, 1856, *Parliamentary Papers*, Central Asia, 1878-1879, Vol.77, p. 118.
25. *Parliamentary Debates*, Commons, 14 February 1898, Fourth Series, Vol. LIII, col. 605.
26. *Ibid.*, 15 February 1898, col. 679.
27. T.Adorno, *Minima and Moralia*, p. 61.
28. *Ibid.*, p. 183.
29. E.Cheyfitz, *The Poetics of Imperialism*, pp. 160-161.
30. Quoted in T.Barnes and D.Gregory, ed., *Reading Human Geography*, p. 63.
31. *Parliamentary Debates*, Lords, 10 March 1884, *Hansard*, Third Series, Vol. CCLXXXV, col. 965.
32. *Ibid.*
33. *Parliamentary Debates*, Lords, 10 January 1881, *Hansard*, Third Series, Vol. CCLVII, col. 300.
34. Dufferin to Mazhar Pasha, 31 August 1887, *Dufferin Papers*, MSS.Eur.F.130/B&C.
35. *Parliamentary Debates*, Commons, 15 February 1898, Fourth Series, Vol. LIII, col. 675.
36. *Ibid.*
37. *The Pioneer Mail*, 14 January 1885.
38. *The Pioneer Mail*, 6 February 1884.
39. *Ibid.*
40. *The Times*, 5 January, 1898.
41. *Parliamentary Debates*, Commons, 15 February 1898, Fourth Series, Vol. LIII, col. 678.
42. Speech on *Indian Affairs*, *The Times*, 7 December 1897.
43. A.H.McMahon, Agent to the Governor-General in Baluchistan, *Memorandum on Quetta*, 15 September 1907, *Political and Secret Memoranda*, L/P&S/18/166, p. 22.
44. *Ibid.*, p. 25.
45. *Ibid.*, p. 24.
46. E.Cheyfitz, *op.cit.*, p. 56.
47. *Parliamentary Debates*, Commons, 15 February 1898, Fourth Series, Vol.LIII, cols. 668-669.
48. A.H.McMahon, *Memorandum on Quetta*, 15 September 1907, *Political and Secret Memoranda*, L/P&S/18/166, p. 30.
49. H.Green, *Memorandum on the Rectification of the North West Frontier of India*, 30 December 1878, *Parliamentary Papers*, Afghanistan, 1881, Vol.70, Part I, p.172.
50. Curzon to Salisbury,18 May 1899, *Salisbury Papers*, HH., Curzon Correspondence.
51. J.P.Sartre, *Being and Nothingness*, p. 367.

52. R. Rorty, *op.cit.*, p. 42.
53. M. Merleau Ponty, *Phenomenology of Perception*, p. 361.
54. P. Ricouer, *op.cit.*, p. 28.
55. *Ibid.*, p. 210.
56. J.P. Sartre, *op.cit.*, p. 368.
57. P. Ricouer, *op.cit.*, p. 221.
58. Quoted in H. White, *op.cit.*, p. 197.
59. T. Adorno, *op.cit.*, p. 229.
60. E. Cheyfitz, *op.cit.*, p. 169.
61. *Ibid.*, p. 151.
62. G. Deleuze and F. Guttari, *op.cit.*, p. 278.
63. *The Times*, 15 February 1898.
64. Quoted in H. White, *op.cit.*, p. 344.
65. *Ibid.*, p. 341.

Bibliography

Manuscripts in the British Library

Papers of Richard Isaac Bruce: MSS Eur.F.163.

Papers of George Nathaniel Curzon, Marquis of Kedlestone: MSS. Eur. F.111.

Papers of the first Marquis of Dufferin and Ava: MSS.Eur.F.130.

Papers of the ninth Earl of Elgin: MSS.Eur.F.84.

Papers of Lord George Francis Hamilton: MSS.Eur.D.510 and C.126.

Papers of the fith Marquis of Lansdowne: MSS.Eur.D.558.

Papers of Sir Alfred Comyn Lyall: MSS.Eur.F.132.

Papers of the first Earl of Lytton: MSS.Eur.E.218.

Papers of Sir A.H.McMahon: MSS.Eur.B.228.

Papers of the first Marquis of Ripon: ADD MSS 43574-43617.

Papers of the first Earl of Northbrook: MSS. Eur.C.144.

Papers of Sir Richard Temple: MSS.Eur.F.86.

Papers of Sir Charles Wood: MSS.Eur.F.78.

Manuscript in Cambridge University Library

Papers of Richard Southwell Bourke, the sixth Earl of Mayo: ADD 7490.

Manuscript in South Asia Centre, Cambridge.

Papers of H.L.Showers.

Manuscript in Hatfield House, Hertfordshire.

Papers of Robert Cecil Gascoygne, third Marquis of Salisbury.

Records in the British Library

Political and Secret Correspondence with India, 2 Vols., L/P&S/7/1.

Secret Letters from India, L/P&S/5/269, 296.

Political and Secret Letters and Enclosures Received from India, 1880-1905, L/P&S/7/26-177.

Political and Secret Despatches to India, 1885-1896, L/P&S/7/330-341.

Political and Secret Subject Files, L/P&S/10/79,80.

Political and Secret Memoranda, L/P&S/18/A4, A 8b, A 9, A 14, A 16b, A 17, A 19, A 43-45, A 110, A 120, A 128-129, A 130, A 140, A 145, A 169, C 124, C 128.

Records in the National Archives of India, New Delhi.

India Foreign Department Proceedings, Secret Supplement, 1880.

_____, Secret, 1881.

_____, Political A, 1880-1882.

_____, A Political E, 1883-1884.

_____, External A, 1885-1903.

_____, Secret Frontier, 1890-1908.

_____, Frontier A, 1902-1907

_____, Secret E, 1890, 1894, 1898.

Official Publications

Aitchison, C.U. *A Collection of Treaties, Engagements and Sanads Relating to India and Neighbouring Countries*, Vols. 12-13, Calcutta 1933.

Baluchistan Blue Books 1, 2 & 3, London 1877, 1878.

Baluchistan Census Report, 1901, vol.5, Bombay, 1902.

Baluchistan Census Report, 1911, 2 Vols., Calcutta 1913.

Hughes Buller, R., *Imperial Gazetteer of India : Baluchistan* Calcutta, 1908.

_____, *Quetta-Pishin District Gazetteer*, Ajmere, 1907.

McConaghey, A., *Sibi District Gazetteer*, Bombay 1907.

Minchin, C.F., *Zhob District Gazetteer*, Bombay, 1907.

Parliamentary Debates

Hansard 1880-1900

Parliamentary Papers

Central Asia and Quetta, 1878-1879, Vol.77.

Afghanistan, 1878-1879, Vol. 88.

Afghanistan, 1881, Vol. 70, Part I.

Bray, Denys, *Ethnographic Survey of Baluchistan*, 2 vols, 1908.

Bruce, C.E., *Notes on Sheranis*, NWFP. Government, 1925.

Duke, O.T., *Report on Thal Chotiali and Harnai*, Calcuttta 1983.

Intelligence Branch Simla compiled, *Frontier and Overseas Expeditions from India* Vol.111, Calcutta, 1910.

Rai, Jamiat, *Manual of Customary Law*, New Delhi, 1932.

Schlogintweint, E., *Kelat the Brahui Kingdom on the Southern Border of Iran*, Simla, 1876.

Southey R., *Gazetter of Baluchistan*, Calcutta, 1891.

Baluchistan Agency, Annual Administration Reports, 1880-1908

Newspapers

The Times, 1875-1906.

The Pioneer Mail, 1880-1900.

The Englishman, 1885-1900.

Blackwood's Edinburgh Magazine, July-December 1884.

Bibliography

Further Reading

Adorno, T., *Minima Moralia*, Verso, London 1999.

Ahmad, A. S.,'Faith and Fire in Baluchistan', *Newsletter of Baluchistan Studies*, ed. A.V. Rossi, No.5, Fall 1988, Oriental Institute, Naples.

_____, *Pakhtuns* Routledge, London,1977.

Arnold, M., *Culture and Anarchy*, Cambridge University Press, 1960.

Asad, T., ed. *Anthropology and the Colonial Encounter*, Ithaca,1973.

Ashcroft B., *et al.* eds, *The Post-Colonial Studies Reader*, Routledge, London, 1995.

Augustine, St., *City of God*, Penguin, London, 1984.

Baluch, I., *The Problem of Greater Baluchistan*, Heidleburg, Sudasien Institute, 1987

Barker,F., *et al.* eds., *Literature, Politics, and Theory*, Methuen, London,1986.

Barnes,T.& D.Gregory eds., *Reading Human Geography : The Poetics and Politics of Inquiry*, Arnold, London,1997.

Barth, F., *Political Leadership Among the Swat Pathans*, Athlone Press, London, 1965.

_____, *Nomads of South Persia*, Allen and Unwin, London 1964.

_____, 'Competition and Symbiosis in North East Baluchistan', *Folk*, Vol.6, 1964.

Barthes, R., *Mythologies*, Paladin, London, 1973.

_____, *Image, Music, Text*, Fontana, London, 1990.

Bayly, C.A., *Imperial Meridian*, Longmans, Essex, 1889.

Benjamin, W., *Illuminations*, Fontana, 1992.

Bennet, T., *Formalism and Marxism*, Routledge, London, 1989.

Bernal, M., *The Afro-Asiatic Roots of Classical Civilization*, Vintage, London, 1991.

Berthoud, J., *Joseph Conrad*, Cambridge University Press, 1993.

Bhabha, H., *The Location of Culture*, Routledge, New York, 1995.

Bhatnagar, R., 'Uses and Limits of Foucault : A Study of the Theme of Origin in Edward Said's Orientalism', *Social Scientist*, vol.16, No.7, July 1986.

Bishop, P., *The Myth of Shangri-la : The Creation of a Sacred Landscape*, Athlone Press, London, 1989.

Boehmer, E., *Colonial and Post-colonial Literature*, Oxford, 1995.

Boon, J., *Other Tribes, Other Scribes*, Cambridge University Press, 1990.

Black, C.D.,'Baluchistan and its Possibilities', *Asiatic Quarterly Review*, Vol.xx, 1905.

Black-Michaud, J., *Cohesive Force*, Blackwell, Oxford, 1975.

Bloch E.,Lukacs G., Brecht B., et al. *Aesthetics and Politics*, Translation R. Taylor, Verso, New York, 1977.

Bray, D., *The Brahui Language*, Parts I & II, Royal Asiatic Society, 1909, 1934..

_____, *Life history of a Brahui*, 1913.

Bruce, C.E.,'The Sandeman Policy as Applied to Tribal Problems Today', *Journal of the Royal Asiatic Society*, vol.xix, 1922.

Bruce, R.I., *The Forward Policy and its Results*, London, 1900.

Campbell, J., *The Masks of God : Primitive Mythology*, New York, 1959.

Camus, A., *The Outsider*, Penguin, Harmondsworth,1982.

Caroe, O., *The Pathans*, Karachi, 1996.

Carter, P., *The Road to Botany Bay*, Faber and Faber, London, 1987.

Cecil, G., *The Life of Robert, the Marquis of Salisbury*, Hodder and Stoughton, London, 1921-32.

Chatterjee, P., *The Nation and its Fragments*, Princeton, 1993

Chamberlain, M.E., *Britain and India*, Newton Abbot, Devon,1974.

Cheyfitz, E., *The Poetics of Imperialism*, Oxford, 1991.

Chomsky, N., *Rules and Representations*, Blackwell, Oxford, 1980.

Clifford, J., *The Predicament of Culture*, Harvard,1994.

_____and G.Marcus eds, *Writing Culture*, University of California Press, 1986.

Coen, T.C., *The Indian Political Service*, Chatto and Windus, London,1971.

Conrad, J., *Heart of Darkness*, Penguin, Harmondsworth, 1994.

Cooper, F., and A.C.Stoller, eds, *Tensions of Empire*, University of California Press, 1997.

Crary, J. *Techniques of the Observer*, MIT Press, 1992.

Crosby, A. *Ecological Imperialism*, Cambridge University Press, 1986.

Curtin, P.D., *Imperialism*, Macmillan, London, 1971.

Curzon, G.N., *Persia and the Persian Question*, Vol. 2, Longmans Green, 1892.

_____, *Frontiers*, Oxford, 1907.

_____, 'The Fluctuating Frontiers of Russia in Asia' *Nineteenth Century*, xxv, February 1889.

Dames, M.L., *Popular Poetry of the Baloches*, 2 vols, Royal Asiatic Society, London, 1907

_____, *The Baloch Race: A Historical and Ethnological Sketch*, Royal Asiatic Society, London, 1904.

Daniell, N., *Islam and the West : the Making of an Image*, One World, Oxford, 1960.

Darwin, C., *The Origin of the Species*, Penguin, Harmondsworth, London, 1991.

Davies, C.C., *Problem of the North West Frontier*, London, 1974.

Deleuze, G., *Proust and Signs*, London,1973.

_____ and F.Guttari, *Anti-Oedipus : Capitalism and Schizophrenie*, University of Minnesota Press, 1983.

Derrida, J., *Writing and Difference*, Routledge, London, 1990.

_____, *The Postcard from Socrates*, Chicago University Press, 1997

_____, *Margins of Philosophy*, Harvester Press, Hertfordshire, 1973.

Diamond, S. ed., *Primitive Views of the World*, Colombia, 1964.

Dilke, C.W., *Imperial Defence*, 1892.

Disraeli, B. *Sybil*, Wordsworth editions, Hertfordshire, 1995.

Douglas, M., *Natural Symbols*, Penguin, Harmondsworth, 1972.

Drake, J.,'The Naming Disease: How Jakobson's Essay on Aphasia initiated Post-modern Deceits', *Times Literary Supplement*, 4 September 1998.

Dupree, L., 'Tribal Warfare in Afghanistan and Pakistan', in A.S.Ahmed and D.H. Hart, eds., *Islam in Tribal Societies*, London, 1984.

Bibliography

Eagleton, T. *Literary Theory*, Blackwell, Oxford, 1994.

_____, *Against the Grain*, Verso, London, 1991.

_____, 'Nationalism: Irony and Commitment', *A Field Day Pamphlet*, Derry, 1988.

Edny, M.H., *Mapping an Empire*, University of Chicago, 1997.

Edwardes, M., *Playing the Great Game*, Hamilton, London, 1975.

_____, *The West in Asia*, 1850-1914, Batsford, 1967.

Eldridge, C.C., *England's Mission*, Chapel Hill, University of North Carolina Press, 1974.

Elphinstone, M., *An Account of the Kingdom of Cabul and its Dependencies*, Richard Bentley, London, 1839.

Embree, A.T., ed. *Pakistan's Western Borderlands*, Vikas, New Delhi, 1977.

Epstein, A.L., 'Sanctions', D.L.Sills ed., *International Encyclopaedia of the Social Sciences*, Vol.14, Macmillan, U.S.A. 1968.

Evans, G.D., *On the Designs of Russia*, 1828.

_____, *On The Practicability of an Invasion of British India*, Richardson & Cornhill, London, MDCC xxix.

Fanon, F., *Black Skins, White Masks*, Pluto, London, 1993.

Ferrier, J.P., *Caravan Journeys in Afghanistan, Turkistan and Beloochistan*, London, 1857.

Foucault, M., *Madness and Civilization*, Routledge, London, 1997.

_____, *The Order of Things*, Routledge, London, 1994.

_____, *Discipline and Punish*, Penguin, Harmondsworth, 1991.

_____, *Power / Knowledge, Selected Interviews and Other Writings*, 1972-1977, ed. C.Gordon, the Harvester Press, Brighton, 1980.

Fraser, J.G., *The Golden Bough*, Papermac, London, 1983.

Freud, S., *Totem and Taboo*, Routledge, London, 1950.

Frye, N., *Anatomy of Criticism*, Princeton, 1957.

Gilbertson, G.W., *The Baloch Language*, 1923.

Gillard, D., *The Struggle for Asia*, 1828-1914, Methuen, London, 1977.

Girard, R., *Deceit, Desire and the Novel : Self and Other in Literary Structure*, John Hopkins University Press, Maryland, Baltimore, 1965.

Gramsci, A. *Selections from Political Writings*, 1910-1920, Lawrence and Wishart, London, 1977.

Greaves, R.L., *Persia and the Defence of India*, 1884-1892, Athlone Press, London, 1959.

Greenberger, A.J., *The British Image of India*, London, 1969.

Greene, M., 'A Real Historical Fiction : Allegories of Discourse in Canadian Historiography', *Commonwealth*, vol. 21, No.1, Autumn 1998.

Guha, R., 'The Prose of Counter-insurgency', *Subaltern Studies*, Vol.II, New Delhi, 1983.

Hawbsbawm, E., *The Age of Empire*, Weidenfeld and Nicholson, London, 1987.

_____ and T. Ranger, eds., *The Invention of Tradition*, Cambridge University Press, 1983.

Hegel, G.W.F., *The Philosophy of History*, Dover Publications, New York, 1956.

_____, *Phenomenology of Spirit*, Selected Translations by H.P.Kaunz, Pennsylvania, 1994.

Hobson, J.A., *Imperialism*, reptd. Ann Arbor, University of Michigan, 1972.

Holdich, T.H., *The Indian Borderland*, London, 1901.

_____, *Political Frontiers and Boundary Making*, 1916.

Hopkirk, *The Great Game*, London, 1990.

Hunter. W.W., *The Indian Mussalmans*, reptd., Premier Book House, Lahore, 1964.

Hutcheon, L., *The Poetics of Postmodernism*, Routledge, New York, 1988.

Hutchin, F., *Illusions of Permanence*, Princeton, 1967.

Hughes, A.W., *The Country of Baluchistan*, London, 1877.

Hughes, E., 'Imperium of the Noble Eye', *Times Literary Supplement*, 20 May 1994.

Inden, R., 'Orientalist Constructions of India', *Modern Asian Studies*, 20, 3, 1986.

Ingram, E., *Two Views of British India*, Bath, 1970.

Innes, J.J.M. *The Life of Major-General Sir James Browne*, London, 1905.

Irons W., and Dyson-Hudson, eds, *Perspectives in Nomadism*, Leiden, Brill, 1972.

Jameson, F., *The Political Unconscious : Narrative as Socially Symbolic Act*, Routledge, London, 1996.

_____, *Fables of Aggression*, 1979.

_____, *Marxism and Form*, Princeton, 1974.

Jung, K. *The Spirit in Man, Art, and Literature*, Routledge, London, 1989.

Kaye, J.W., *Life and Correspondence of Major-General Sir John Malcolm*, Vol.II, 1856.

Kiernan, V.G., *Lords of Human Kind*, Penguin, Harmondsworth, 1972.

Kipling, R., *Kim*, Oxford, 1987.

Kristeva, J., *Desire in Language*, Blackwell, Oxford, 1986.

_____, *Language, the Unknown*, Colombia, 1989.

Kazemzada, F., *Russia and Britain in Persia*, Yale, 1968.

Lacan, J., *Ecrits*, Routledge, London, 1977.

_____, *The Language of the Self*, Trans. A.Wilden, London, 1968.

Laclau, E., and C.Mouffe, *Hegemony and Socialist Strategy*, Verso, London, 1993.

Lefebvre, H., *The Production of Space*, Blackwell, Oxford, 1998.

Levinas, E., *The Theory of Intuition*, 1973.

Levi-Strauss, C., *The Savage Mind*, Weidenfeld and Nicholson, London, 1989.

Lilla, M., *G.B. Vico*, Harvard, Mass., 1993.

Lyall, A., *The Rise of British Dominions in India*, London, 1893.

Lyotard, J.F., *Lessons on the Analytic of the Sublime*, Stanford, 1995.

Macdonald, R.H., *The Language of Empire*, Manchester, 1994.

Macneill, J., *The Progress and Present Position of Russia in the East*, Third Edition, London, 1854.

Malinowski, B., *Crime and Custom in Savage Society*, Harcourt-Brace, New York, 1926.

Mannoni, O., *Prospero and Caliban : The Psychology of Colonization*, Methuen, London, 1956.

Bibliography

Mason, P., *The Men who Ruled India*, Rupa, 1985.

Masson, C., *Narratives of Various Journeys in Beelochistan Afghanistan, the Punjab and Kalat*, reptd., Karachi, 1977.

Memmi, A., *The Colonizer and the Colonized*, Orion, London, 1974.

Merleau-Ponty, M., *Phenomenology of Perception*, Routledge, London, 1998.

Mill, J., *History of British India*, London, 1840.

Mill, J.S., and J. Bentham, *Utilitarianism and other Essays*, Penguin, Harmondsworth, 1987.

Miller, H., *Lord Dufferin's Speeches and Addresses*, London, 1882.

Mony-Penny W.F. and G.E. Buckle, *The Life of Benjamin Disraeli*, Vol. 2, London, 1929.

Montesquieu, *Persian Letters*, Penguin, London, 1993.

Moore-Gilbert, B.J., *Kipling and Orientalism*, Croom Helm, London, 1986.

Morris, J., *Heaven's Command*, London, 1973.

Nandy, A., *The Intimate Enemy : Loss and Recovery of the Self under Colonialism*, New Delhi, 1983.

Nietzsche, F. *On the Genealogy of Morals*, Oxford, 1996.

_____, *Thus Spake Zarathustra*, Wordsworth editions, Hertfordshire, 1997.

O'Hanlon, R., *Joseph Conrad and Charles Darwin*, The Salamander Press, Edinburgh, 1984.

O'Hanlon, Rosalind, 'Recovering the Subject : Subaltern Studies and Histories of Resistance in Colonial South Asia', *Modern Asian Studies*, 22, 1 (1988).

_____ and David Washbrook, 'After Orientalism : Culture, Criticism and Politics in the Third World', *Comparative Studies in Society and History*, Vol.34, No.1, January 1992

Oliver, E., *Across the Border of Pathan or Baluch*, Chapman and Hall, London, 1890.

Pehrson, R.N., *The Social Organization of the Marri Baluch*, compiled by F. Barth, Viking Fund Publications, 43, Chicago, 1966.

Perkin, H., 'Infants in Barbarism', *Times Literary Supplement*, 20 May 1994.

Prakash, G., 'Can the Subaltern Ride? A Reply to O'Hanlon and Washbrook', *Comparative Studies in Society and History*, Vol.34, No.1, January 1992.

Pottinger, H., *Travels in Beelochistan and Scinde*, London, 1916.

Posipal, 'Feud', D.L. Sills ed. *Encylopaedia of the Social Sciences*, Vol.14, Macmillan, U.S.A, 1968.

Pratt, M.L., *Imperial Eyes : Travel Writing and Transculturation*, Routledge, London, 1992.

Prescott, J.R.V., *Political Geography*, Methuen, London, 1972.

_____, *Boundaries and Frontiers*, Croom Helm, London, 1978.

Ram, H., *Biluchinama*, Lahore, 1898.

Rabinow, P., *The Foucault Reader*, Penguin, Harmondsworth, 1991.

Raverty, H.G., *Notes on Afghanistan and Baluchistan*, London, 1888.

Ricoeur, P., *Time and Narrative*, 3 Vols, Chicago University Press, 1983.

_____, *Oneself as Another*, Chicago University Press, 1984, 1985.

Roberts, F., *Forty-one Years in India*, London, 1900.

Robinson, R., et al. eds, *Africa and the Victorians*, Macmillan, London, 1981.

Rorty, R., *Philosophy and the Mirror of Nature*, Princeton, 1980.

Said, E., *Orientalism*, Penguin, Harmondsworth, 1978.

——————, *Beginnings*, Granta, London, 1997.

——————, *The World, the Text and the Critic*, Vintage, London, 1984.

——————, *Culture and Imperialism*, Chatto and Windus, London, 1993.

——————, 'Yeats and Decolonization', *Field Day Pamphlet*, Derry, 1988.

Sahlins, M., *Tribesmen*, Prentice-Hall, New Jersey, 1968.

Sandison, A., *The Wheel of Empire*, London, 1967.

Sartre, J.P., *Being and Nothingness*, Routledge, London, 1998.

Shakespeare, R., *The Tempest*, Signet, Chicago, 1987.

Scott, G.B., *Afghans and Pathans : A Sketch*, Mitre Press, London, 1929.

Sinclair, A., *The Savage, a History of Misunderstanding*, London, 1977.

Sinha, M., *The Manly Englishman and the Effiminate Bengali in the Late Nineteenth Century*, Manchester University Press, 1995.

Smith, N., *Uneven Development : Nature, Capital, and the Production of Space*, Blackwell, Oxford, 1984.

Spivak, G.C., *In Other Worlds*, Routledge, New York, 1988.

Spooner, B., ed. *Desertifcation and Development*, Academic Press, London, 1982.

Stephen, L., et al. eds, *The Dictionary of National Biography*, London, 1937.

Stocking, G., *Victorian Anthropology*, Free Press, Toronto, 1987.

Street, B.Z., *The Savage in Literature*, Routledge, London, 1975.

Stromberg, R.N., *Realism, Naturalism, and Symbolism*, Macmillan, London, 1968.

Suleri, S., *The Rhetoric of English India*, Chicago University Press, 1992.

Sweet, L., 'Camel Raiding of North Arabian Bedouin : A Mechanism of Ecological Adaptation', *American Anthropologist*, Vol.67, 1967.

Tapper, R. ed. *Conflict of Tribe and State in Iran and Afghanistan*, Croom Helm, London, 1983.

Tate, G.P., *Frontiers of Baluchistan*, London, 1909.

Taussig, M., *Mimesis and Alterity*, Routledge, New York, 1993.

Thorburn, S.S., *Asiatic Neighbours*, Blackwood and Sons, London, 1894.

Thornton, A.P., *The Imperial Idea and its Enemies*, London, 1959.

Thornton, T.H., *Robert Sandeman*, London, 1895.

Tidrick, K., *Empire and English Character*, Tauris, London, 1992.

Todorov, T., *Symbolism and Interpretation*, R.K.P., London, 1983.

——————, *The Conquest of America*, Harper Collins, New York, 1984.

Tucker, A.L.P., *Sir Robert Sandeman*, London, 1921.

Vambery, A., *Western Culture in Eastern Lands*, London, 1906.

——————, 'Will Russia Conquer India', *Nineteenth Century*, xvii, January, 1885.

Bibliography

West, R., 'The New Afghan Frontier', *Nineteenth Century*, xxii, October 1887.

White, H., *The Content of the Form*, John Hopkins University Press, Baltimore, 1987.

_____, *Metahistory*, John Hopkins University Press, Baltimore, 1973.

Wint, G., *The British in Asia*, London, 1947.

Wurgaft, L.D., *The Imperial Imagination : Magic and Myth in Kipling's India*, Weslyn, 1981.

Wylie, J.W.S. eds., *Essays on the External Policy of India*, London, 1875.

Yate, C.E. *Baluchistan*, London, 1906.

Yapp, M., *Strategies of British India*, Clarendon Press, Oxford, 1990.

Young, R., *White Mythologies*, Routledge, 1990.

Zinkin M., and Zinkin.T., *Britain and India : Requeim for an Empire*, Chatto and Windus, London, 1964.

Index

Abdul Karim Khan, 92, 93

Achakzai tribes, 50, 65, 84, 92-93

Adorno, T., 104

Afghan, 19, 22-23, 28, 30, 37-38, 40-41, 44-45, 47, 49, 51, 53, 64, 69, 72, 79, 87, 92

Afghanistan, 14-15, 21-23, 28, 30, 38-42, 44-46, 47, 49, 50, 52, 86, 107-08

Afridis, 84

Ahmad Shah Abdali, 72

Aitchison, C.U., 81

Aleppo, 63

Allyar Khan, 71-72

Alterity, 1, 2, 8, 13, 31, 110

Alsatia, 68

America, 60, 102

Amir of Afghanistan, 26, 46

Amir of Kabul, 30, 31, 37-40, 42-43, 50, 53

Anglo-Persian Treaty 1810, 14

Apollonian form, 101

Apostolic, 3, 103

Appozai, 47, 48, 50

Araxes, 14

Argyll, Duke of, 33, 41

Aristotle, 5, 59

Asia, 15, 21, 25, 51-52, 99, 105

Askabad, 51, 54

Aslam Khan Arzbegi, 92

Attilla, 99

Auckland, Lord, 22, 23

Augustine, 99

Badini tribes, 69

Badra, 67

Badshah, 72

Bagao, 67

Balkh, 52

Baluch, 1, 8-9, 16, 18-20, 22, 28, 36, 38, 52-54, 61-65, 69-70, 75, 84, 90, 94, 107, 109-10

Baluchistan, 1-3, 7-8, 13-16, 19, 21-27, 28, 30-32, 36-39, 42-43, 48-56, 61-62, 64-66, 68-69, 71, 74-75, 78-80, 82-86, 89-91, 93, 103-04, 107, 109-10

Baluchistan Railway, 43, 55

Bargha tribes, 48

Barnes, H., 53, 71

Battista della Porta, G., 81

Behistan inscription, 63

Belooches, 16

Bengal Civil Service, 22

Berlin, 52

Bhabha, H., 2, 4, 76, 92

Biddulph, J., 42, 80

Billamore, Major, 23

Birjind, 51

Biroea, 63

Black Sea, 23, 61

Blackwood's Edinburgh Magazine, 51

Bokhara, 26, 51

Bolan Pass, 15, 25, 28, 47, 62, 84

Bombay Army, 14, 23

Bombay Civil Service, 23

Bori, 43, 46

Brahuik Range, 15

Brahuis, 16, 18-19, 63-65, 70-71, 90

Bray, D., 16, 18, 62-64, 74
Bride-price, 73-74
Brown, Capt., 23
Browne, J., 50, 91
Bruce, R.I., 36, 65, 90
Bugti tribes, 18, 22-23, 25, 61, 66, 68, 79, 82-84, 90
Bukhara, 22
Burnes, A., 22
Calcutta, 24
Canute, 100
Carlyle, T., 98
Cartesian 56, 109
Caucasus, 21-22
Central Asia, 14, 20-21, 23, 26-30, 33, 37, 43, 47, 51, 106
Chagai, 20, 50, 53-54, 61, 69, 86
Chakravorty, G., 3
Chamalang, 67
Chaman, 50, 108
Chapman, E.F., 86
Chappar Pass, 84
Chesney, G., 51
Cheyfitz, E., 104, 107
Christian, 59, 65, 102
Civilizing mission, 61, 90, 92, 99
Code Napoleon, 103
Cogito, 78
Connemara, Lord, 46
Confederacy of Baluch/Brahui tribes, 18
Connolly, A., 22
Constantinople, 14
Cranbourne, Lord, 55
Crimea, 23
Curzon, G.N., 20, 51, 54-55, 104, 106-08
Czar, 51

Dak land, 69-70
Daly, H., 50
Damani Tribe, 61, 69
Dames, M.L., 61-63
Dardanelles, 23
Darwin, C., 36, 60
Darwinian evolution, 9, 60
Darwinian other, 76
Darwinian paradigm, 3, 60
Deconstructivist, 4
Deleuze, G., 5, 38, 72, 80, 87, 89, 100
Dera Ghazi Khan, 25, 38, 46, 83
Derajat, 48-49
Descartes, R., 80
Dickens, C., 25
Dionysian chaos, 101
Discourse, 4-7, 10, 36, 38, 41, 59, 75, 79, 94, 99
Disraeli, B., 26, 29
Domandi, 53
Dombki tribe, 68
Dost Mohammad, Amir, 22-23
Dost Muhammad, Jogezai, Pathan, 47, 72
Draconian, 89
Dravidian, 64
Duffadar, 83
Dufferin, Marquis of, 15, 46, 86, 106
Duke, O.T., 67
Durand Agreement, 50
East India Company, 14
Eastwick, J.B., 82
Edny, M., 81
Edwardes, S., 79
Egypt, 13, 103
Elgin, Marquis of, 52, 54

Index

Ellenborough, Lord, 22
Emerson, R., 111
England, 7, 15, 18, 23-24, 27, 29, 40, 45, 51
Englishman, 47
Enlightenment, 1, 24, 59-60
Epistemic violence, 4, 40
Epistemological, 99
Eurasia, 14, 20
Eurocentric, 2-3
Eurocentrism, 9, 36
Europe, 1, 3, 10, 14, 24, 42, 56, 59-61, 63-65, 99
European gaze, 74
European mind, 101
Evans, G.de Lacy, 21-22
Fabian, J., 105
Ferrier, J.P., 75
Feud, 65-72, 74-75, 83, 87, 91
Fitzgerald, S., 24
Fort Monroe, 46
Foucault, M., 2, 5, 78, 95
Foucauldian, 3, 78
French, 13, 14, 59
Freud, S., 6
Freudian, 38
Frontier Crimes Regulation, 87, 89, 91
Frye, N., 37
Fuegian, 60
Ganges, 14
Georgia, 14
Ghaznavids, 61
Ghazni, 43, 47
Ghazzan Khan, Marri chief, 83
Gilbertson, G.W., 63
Gilgit, 42

Gomal Pass, 47-50, 55, 107
Gomal River, 49, 53
Great Game, 2, 7-8, 15, 22, 27, 30, 33, 44-45, 51-52, 54, 105, 109-10
Greek drama, 31
Green, H., 108
Guha, Ranajit, 94
Gulf Littoral, 51
Gurkhas, 106
Haines, F., 39
Hamilton, G., 50, 54, 55, 64, 112
Hamsayas, 17
Hamun, 68-69
Harnai, 84
Hartington, Lord, 39-40
Hassanis, 67
Hastings, W., 106
Hegel, G.W.F., 36, 51, 110
Hegelian, 5-6, 10, 46, 50, 76, 99, 101-02, 109-10
Helmund, 15, 39, 69
Herat, 22-24, 27, 28, 41-43, 45, 47, 51-52, 107
Herder, J.G., 99
Hermeneutic, 5
Himalayas, 27, 49
Hindukush, 45, 50
Hindus, 18, 29
Hobbesian, 9, 61, 65
Holdich, T.H., 15, 69
Hope, T., 84
Hughes, A.W., 23
India Council, 27, 55
Indian Army, 39, 45, 86
Indian Political Service, 22
Indore, 50
Indus, 13, 22-23, 29, 39, 42

Iran, 54
Ishak Kahol, 72
Islam, 64
Iwazana, 91
Izzat, 73
Jacob, J., 23-24, 82, 102, 104
Jacobabad Settlement, 26
Jallalabad, 38
Jamaldanis, 69
Jamalis, 61
Jameson, F., 7
Janus, 104
Jaro, 62
Jemadar, 83
Jihad, 38, 43, 50, 72
Jirga, 87-89, 91
Jogezai Pathans, 72
Kabul, 22, 30-31, 37-40, 42-43, 47, 51
Kahan, 67
Kahol, 66, 72
Kai Khusroe, 61
Kajuri Kach, 49
Kakar tribes, 43-44, 46, 66, 72, 79, 84, 90
Kako, 65
Kakozai tribe, 65
Kalat, 18, 23-25, 31-32, 63, 68-69
Kambar, 18
Kant, E., 74
Karez, 70
Kazakhs, 26
Khan, G.H., 93
Khan of Kalat, 18-19, 23-26, 28, 53-54
Khel, 19
Khelat, 24, 30

Khelat-i-Ghilzai, 39, 43
Khetran Baluch, 46, 90
Khetran valley, 46
Khiva, 22, 26-27
Khokand, 26
Khorassan, 51-52
Khudadad Khan, 24
Khwajak Amran Range, 46, 84
Khwajak Pass, 45, 84
Khyber, 22, 47, 107
Kibzai tribe, 44
Kidderzai tribe, 48
Kim, 109
Kimberly, Lord, 44
Kingsley, C., 25
Kinnear, J.M., 14
Kipling, R., 109
Kirman, 61
Koh-i-Malik Siah, 53-54, 68
Kundar Domandi, 49
Kurram, 38
Lacanian, 6
Lacan, J., 3, 6, 98
Lamarckian, 68
Lansdowne, Marquis of, 47-49, 51-52
Largha Sheranis, 48
Lascalles, F., 52
Lashari tribe, 62
Lefebvre, H., 8, 56, 86, 103
Levies, 25, 82, 85, 86-87
Levi-Strauss, C., 37, 98
London, 24, 40, 67
London Chamber of Commerce, 103
Luch-bahadur, 63

Index

Luni tribe, 66-67, 90-91
Lyall, A., 38, 40, 79, 101
Lyall, J., 48, 49
Lytton, Earl of, 29-32, 37-39, 99, 101-02, 104
Macnaghten, W.H., 22-23
Macneill, J., 21
Mahommedans, 29, 65, 99
Mahsud Waziris, 50
Malakand, 50
Malthusian, 60
Malcolm, J., 14
Mandai, 69
Mandai Baluch, 69
Mandokhel tribe, 47, 49
Marri tribe, 18, 22-23, 25, 28, 38-39, 61, 66-68, 70-71, 79, 83-84, 90-91, 93, 94
Marxist, 4
Mashkel Lake, 68
Masson, C., 16, 18-19, 74
Master-slave, 6, 31
Masterly inactivity, 29
Mayo, Lord, 25-26
McMahon, A.H., 53, 107-08
Meherulla Khan, Marri Chief, 70-71, 83
Mehrab Khan of Kalat, 18, 23
Merleau Ponty, M., 110
Merv, 27, 41-44, 51-52
Meshed, 51-52
Messianic, 99
Metaphor, 9, 37, 46, 79-80, 95, 98, 100, 103
Metonymic, 5, 80, 95
Mingal tribe, 53, 63, 69-70
Mins, 63
Mir Abdullah, Khan of Kalat, 18
Mir Ahmed I, Khan of Kalat, 18

Mir Chakar Baluch, 62
Mir Gwaharam, 62
Mir Hamza, 63
Mir Hazar Khan Marri, sub-sectional head, 71
Mockler, Col., 63
Mohenjo-daro, 64
Montesquieu, 59
Mughals, 19
Mukuddams, 83
Mulla Pass, 62
Musakhels, 44
Nadir Shah, 14
Napoleon, 13-14
Napoleonic, 81
Narcissism, 4, 109
Narcissistic, 1, 6, 67
Nari River, 15
Nasirabad, 61
Nasir Khan I, Khan of Kalat, 18
Nasir Khan II, Khan of Kalat, 23
Naturalistic fiction, 98
Nausherwan, 61
Nawab Kahol, 72
New Chaman, 46
Nharooes, 16
Nietzschean, 3, 60, 74-75
Nietzsche, F., 74, 101, 112
Nissau, 67
Norm-power of, 70, 85
Normative vision, 85
Northbrook, Lord, 28, 50
North West Frontier, 15, 37, 86, 100
Nushki, 53-55, 69
Nushki-Siestan route, 53
Onslow, Earl of, 37

Ontology, 2, 10
Ontological, 47
Orient, 1, 4, 28, 36, 41-42
Oriental, 25, 40, 106
Orientalism, 4
Oriental mind, 41
Ottoman Power, 23
Outram, J., 23
Oxus River, 27, 108
Panjdeh, 44-45
Panoptic, 4
Panoptic machine, 81
Panopticon, 83
Panopticon, geographic, 46
Panoptic surveillance, 10
Paris, 28
Paro, tribal segment, 16, 66
Pathans, 16, 19-20, 43, 47, 51, 64-67, 70-72, 92-93, 107
Patriliny, 16
Patrilocality, 16
Paul, St., 103
Pauline, 103
Pax Britannica, 85, 95, 103
Peshawar, 82, 84
Persia, 13-14, 21, 23, 51-55, 68-69, 86, 107-08
Perso-Baluch borderland, 15, 51, 54, 69, 87, 107
Peter I, Tsar, 21
Phalli, Tribal segment, 16
Phayre, R.B., 25
Phenomenological, 1
Philawar, 67
Phish, 63
Pioneer Mail, 43, 44, 106
Pira, tribal segment, 16, 66

Pishin, 15, 38-40, 43, 46-47, 80, 84, 92-93
Pishin Lora River, 15
Plato, 59
Platonic, 109
Post-colonial, 4
Pottinger, H., 14-18
Proclamation of August 1876, 31
Promethean, 99
Prospero, 111
Prussians, 28
Punjab, 25-26, 28, 46, 48-49, 61, 68, 81-83
Qandahar (Or Candahar or Kandahar), 22, 24, 38-40, 42-43, 45-47, 50, 84, 103, 108
Qandahar Railway, 43
Quat Mandai, 67, 80
Quetta, 15, 18-20, 22, 24, 26, 28, 37-38, 43, 45-46, 52-55, 71, 79-80, 86, 88, 91, 93
Quetta-Nushki Railway, 108
Quetta-Pishin, 84
Quetta Railway, 43
Race, 1, 5, 25, 60, 64
Raisani Brahuis, 71-72
Rakshanis, 53, 61, 69
Ramsay, J., 86
Rawlinson, H., 27-28, 39-40
Registan, 53
Reki tribes, 61, 69
Ressaldar, 83
Ricouer, P., 78
Rind tribes, 62-63
Ripon, Marquis of, 39-40
Roberts, F., 45-46, 50, 103
Roman space, 102-03
Roman State, 102-03
Rome, 102

Index

Rousseau, J.J., 60

Russia, 2, 7-9, 14-15, 20-23, 25-33, 37-38, 41-47, 51-52, 54-55, 102, 105-08

Russophobia, 21, 27

Rustomzai Brahuis, 71-72

Said, E., 4

Saidian, 4

Saint, John, O., 92

Salisbury, Marquis of, 28-32, 41-42, 45-46, 52, 90

Sandeman, R.G., 25, 28-29, 31-32, 39, 43-44, 46-50, 52, 68, 72, 79-84, 87-90, 92-93, 95, 102, 104

Sandemanism, 50-51, 103-04

Sanzar Khel Kakars, 72

Saraparae, 63

Sartre, J.P., 10

Savage, 2, 5, 6, 8-9, 13, 15-17, 22-23, 32, 36, 38-40, 50, 59-63, 71-72, 74-76, 78-80

Sayyids, 69, 88

Self and other, 1, 10, 17, 53, 66-67, 90

Seljuk Turks, 61

Semantics, 8

Semiotics, 4

Shadozais tribe, 66, 68, 79, 90

Shahbaz Khan, 44, 47, 72

Shahi Jirga, 88, 91

Shah Jahan, 43-44, 72

Shahnama, 61

Shah of Persia, 52

Shah Shuja, Amir, 22

Shakespeare, W., 111

Shalwar, tribal section, 16

Sharm, 73

Sharmana, 91

Sheranis, 48-49

Shorawak, 69

Sibi, 15, 38-40, 43, 61, 80, 84, 88

Siestan, 51-52, 55, 61, 108

Sikhs, 106

Sikh wars, 82

Sind, 18, 22-23, 25, 26, 46, 68, 82

Sind-Pishin Railway, 46

Sinjeranis, tribe, 61, 69

Sir Darya, 26

Sirdar khel, 17, 72, 93

Social Darwinism, 9, 61

Social Darwinists, 9, 60

Space, fugural, 1

Space, of language, 3

Space, of order, 78

Spencer, H., 60

Spencerian, 64

Spivak, G.C., 4-5, 91

Stein, A., 64

Strabo, 63

Subaltern, 5

Subject effects, 4

Subject-object, 5-7, 59, 84

Subject positions, 4-5, 10, 61, 78

Subject-predicate, 5

Suleiman Mountains, 47, 61

Sutlej, 22

Synecdochic, 102

Syntagm, 6

Syrian, 63

Tabas, 51

Takht-i-Suleiman, 48

Takkar, tribal section, 16

Tarins, 79, 90

Tartary, 16

Tate, G.P., 75

Teheran, 21, 52, 54
Tempest, 111
Temple, R., 19
Thal Chotiali, 68, 80, 84
Thermopylae, 28
Thorburn, S.S., 22
Thracian, 63
The Times, 42, 47, 99
Toba, 50
Toba Levies, 93
Tochi Pass, 47, 50, 55
Tocqueville, A., 111
Todorov, T., 5
Tokatu, 15
Topoi, 8, 47
Trans Caspia, 26
Trans Caspian Railway, 51
Trans Caspian Review, 54
Treaty of 1841, 23
Treaty of 1854, 24
Treaty of Gandamak, 1879, 38
Tribal Responsibility, 85-86
Tropes, 1, 6-8, 40, 95
Tropic, 4, 7, 59, 109
Tsarist, 2, 21, 26, 105
Tuman, Baluch tribe, 62

Turkey, 14, 21
Tylor, E.B., 60
Vambery, A., 22
Victorian, 9, 28, 40, 44, 61, 67, 75, 89
The Voix, 33
Wade, C.M., 22
Wano, 50
Waziris, 47, 49-50, 87
Waziristan, 50
Webb Ware, F., 53-54, 69-70
Westlake, J., 40
White, G.S., 48
White, H., 102
Wolff, D., 52
Wood, C., 23
Wylie, H., 94
Xerxes, 28
Yakub Khan, 38
Young, R., 4
Zaggar Mingal Brahuis, 69
Zarkhun Pathans, 67
Zhob, 15, 19, 43-44, 47-48, 50, 65, 71-72, 86
Zhob-Gomal route, 50
Zhob River, 15
Zulfikar, 45

Plate 1: The Quetta Fort (miri) 1875-1880.

Plate 2: View of a Camel Caravan in Quetta, 1889.

Plate 3: The Quetta Residency, 1890's.

Plate 4: Quetta Decorations for the Duke and Duchess of Connaught.

Plate 5: View near Bolan Pass.

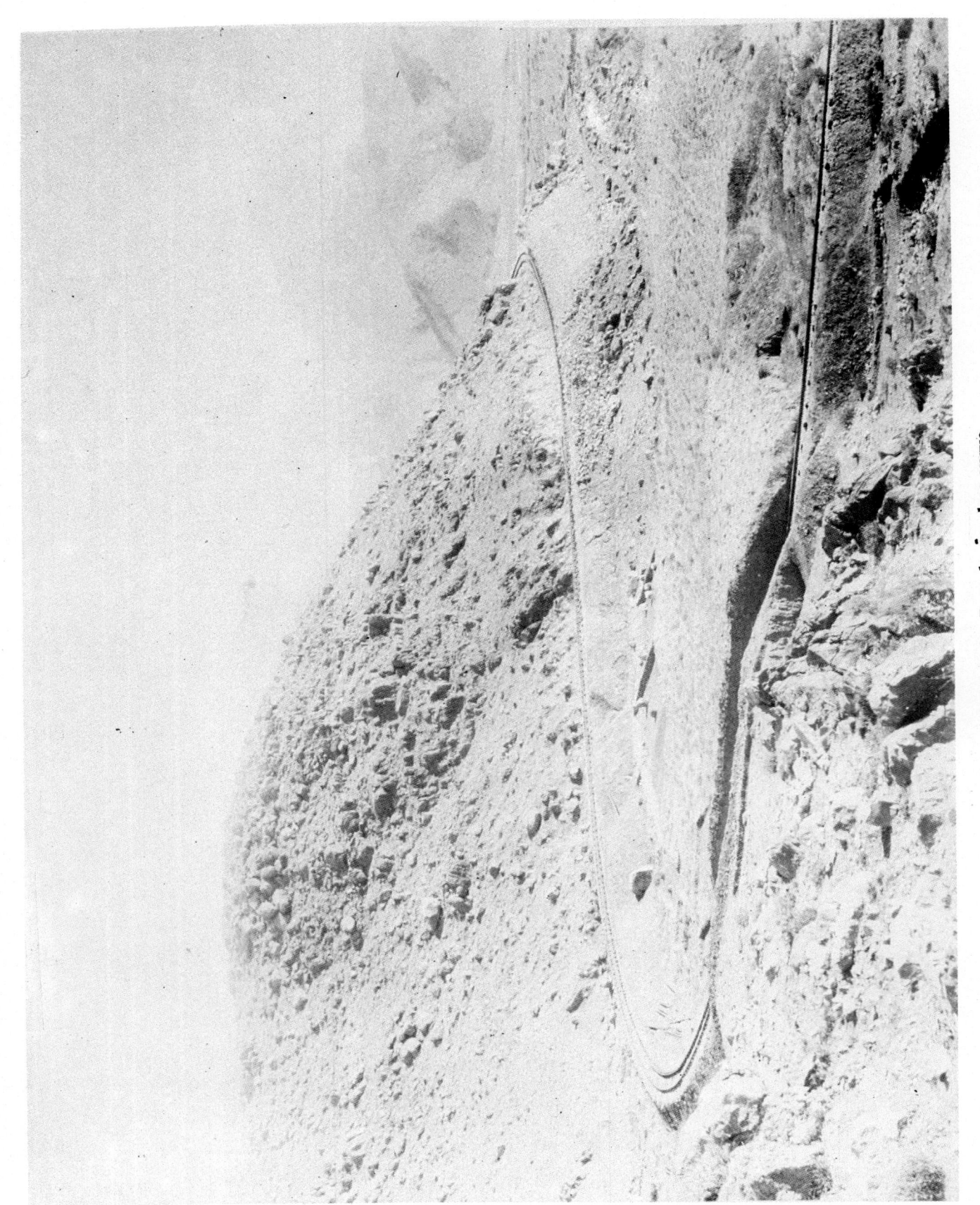

Plate 6: Bolan Pass; horse shoe curve.

Plate 7: Chappar Rift: Sind-Pishin Railway

Plate 8: The East Khwajak Valley.

Plate 9: Chaman Frontier Post: West Khwajak Valley, at the Qandahar Border.

Plate 10: Group at the Agency. Robert Sandeman and Khan of Kalat, 1889.

Plate 11: Baluch Chiefs in Ceremonial Dress.